The Wrightsman Lectures III

The Wrightsman Lectures

Rembrandt and the Italian Renaissance
by Kenneth Clark

Problems in Titian, Mostly Iconographic
by Erwin Panofsky

Byzantine Art and The West
by Otto Demus

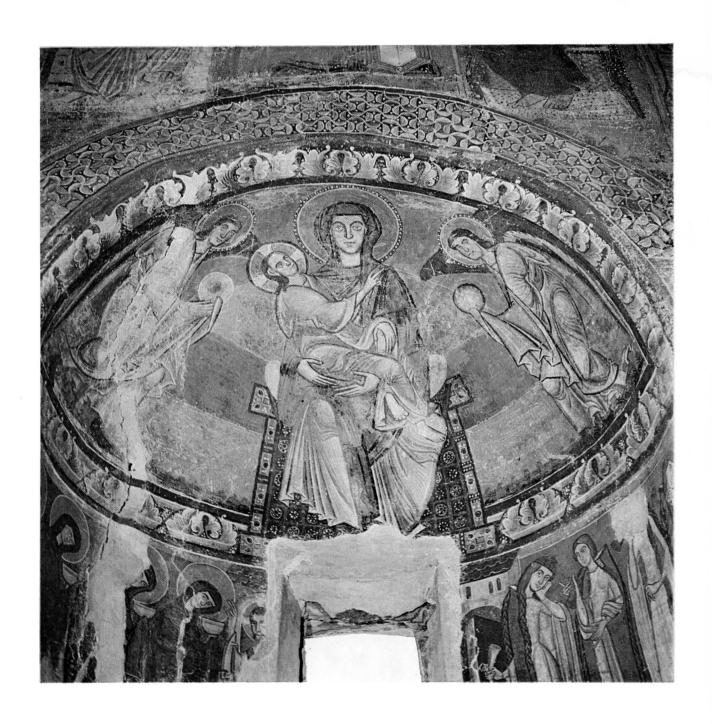

I *Hocheppan* (Castel Appiano), Italy, Wall Painting. Enthroned Virgin.

OTTO DEMUS

BYZANTINE ART
AND
THE WEST

The Wrightsman Lectures

Institute of Fine Arts, New York University

Delivered at The Metropolitan Museum of Art, New York, N.Y.

New York University Press

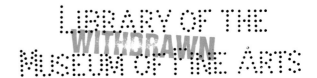

*This is the third volume
of The Wrightsman Lectures,
which are delivered annually
under the auspices of the
New York University Institute of Fine Arts*

Library of Congress Catalog Card No. 78-88132
SBN 8147-0116-7
Published in England by George Weidenfeld and Nicolson Ltd, London
Composed and printed by J. J. Augustin, Glückstadt, West Germany
First Impression

Foreword

It would be incorrect to say that this book has grown out of the Wrights-man Lectures given in 1966—it *is* these lectures. In preparing them for publication the author was faced with the alternatives of giving the text as it was when read to an audience in the auditorium of the Metropolitan Museum or writing a new book. Any intermediate course seemed to me to promise something hybrid and unsatisfactory, neither fish nor fowl. In deciding to publish the lectures as they were given I did not simply follow the path of least resistance (although considerations of this kind must play their part in the life of a university professor with work piling up on his desk). I believed that it would be wrong to call an entirely new book "The Wrights-man Lectures 1966." Also, it might have been somewhat unfair to pretend to have had certain insights in 1966 which came to me in 1969. Hence the only alterations I have made are the addition of notes and bibliography—to make the book useful for students—and the elimination of passages referring to illustrations that could not be printed in the book. As it is, the number of illustrations, although only about half the original number of slides, is very large indeed, and I am deeply grateful for the opportunity to include so many. Without a fairly large number of illustrations the author could not have made his point, which rests on cumulative evidence, and the book would have failed its purpose.

This purpose was, and is, to show the role played by the art of Byzantium in the development of Western art. The stress is not on "influences," which lead as often as not to deviations, but on the function of Byzantine artists as teachers and pacemakers and on the object lessons provided by Byzantine models in the West. It was my endeavour to concentrate on essentials and to exclude superficial effects leading to "half-baked" imitations. It will be for the reader to decide whether I have succeeded in presenting my case adequately without overstating it.

Much of what is contained in the following pages, though fairly new in 1966, is almost common property today. The problems were "in the air," and the progress of scholarship has been extremely rapid in this field, thanks to the work of a number of scholars, most of whom the author is privileged to call his friends. To many of these friends and colleagues I owe a great debt of gratitude, the greatest perhaps to those who took part, with me, in a symposium held in Dumbarton Oaks in the spring of 1965 under the direction of Ernst Kitzinger. Any one of the participants of the Symposium could have given the following lectures. It was my very good fortune to have been selected, and I am deeply grateful to Mr. and Mrs. Charles Wrightsman and to the faculty of the Institute of Fine Arts, New York University, for the opportunity to put my ideas to the test of a select audience and to publish them as a book.

I should also like to thank Professor H. W. Janson of New York University for his kind advice and help in the production of this book and to New York University Press for producing it in this form. I am indebted to Burr Wallen and Michael Jacoff for reading my text to eliminate mistakes in English. In addition, I am grateful to my assistants at the Institute of Art History at the University of Vienna, especially to W. Grape, and to the Institute's Photographic Department for help in assembling the illustrations. Finally I want to thank Professor Hugo and Mrs. Buchthal, whose friendship made my stay in New York in 1966 a series of happy days.

Vienna

Contents

List of Figures

20. *London*, Brit. Mus., Cotton Bible; Water-color copy. Third Day of Creation. *After Weitzmann. Courtesy of the Trustees of the British Museum.*

21. *Venice*, San Marco, Mosaic. Creation, Detail. *Phot. Böhm, 3008.*

22. *Venice*, San Marco, Mosaic. Creation, Detail. *Phot. Demus.*

23. *Santa Maria di Castelseprio*, Lombardy, Wall Painting. Angel appearing to St. Joseph, Detail. *Phot. Fabris.*

24. *Garde*, Gotland (Sweden), Wall Painting, Saint. *Phot. Statens Histor. Museet.*

25. *Monte Cassino*, Abbey, Cod. 98 H. Death of the Virgin. *After Ladner.*

26. *Monte Cassino*, Abbey, Cod. 98 H. Presentation of Christ. *After Ladner.*

27. *Monte Cassino*, Abbey, Cod. 99 H. Annunciation and Dream of St. Joseph. *After Ladner.*

28. *Mt. Athos*, Vatopedi, Mosaic. Angel of Annunciation. *Phot. Hautes Etudes (Millet) C 246.*

29. *Rome*, Bibl. Vat., Cod. lat. 1202. Dedication of the Book to St. Benedict. *Phot. Bibl. Vat.*

30. *Baltimore*, Walters Art Gallery, Conradin Bible. *Phot. Walters Art Gallery.*

31. *Friesach*, Austria, Wall Painting. Feeding of the 5,000, Detail. *Phot. Bundesdenkmalamt, Vienna.*

32. *Pürgg*, Austria, Wall Painting. Feeding of the 5,000, Detail. *Phot. Bundesdenkmalamt, Vienna.*

33. *Venice*, San Marco, Mosaic. Feeding of the 5,000. *Phot. Alinari.*

34. *Rome*, Bibl. Vat., Pattern Book, Cod. lat. 1976. Prophets. *Phot. Bibl. Vat.*

35. *Torcello*, Cathedral, Mosaic. Paradise. *Phot. Alinari.*

36. *Freiburg*, Germany, Augustinermuseum, Leaf from a Pattern Book. Christ and Zachaeus, Two Saints on Horseback.

37. *Monreale*, Cathedral, Mosaic. Christ Healing. *Phot. Alinari.*

38. *Mt. Sinai*, Icon. Two Saints on Horseback. *After Weitzmann.*

39. *Wolfenbüttel*, Germany, Herzog August Bibliothek, Pattern Book. Seated and Standing Figures. *Phot. Herzog August Bibliothek.*

40. *Athens*, Nat. Library, Cod. gr. 118. St. Matthew. *Phot. Öst. Nat. Bibl., Vienna.*

41. *Wolfenbüttel*, Germany, Herzog August Bibliothek, Pattern Book. Figures from Transfiguration of Christ. *Phot. Herzog August Bibliothek.*

42. *Mt. Athos*, Iviron Monastery, Cod. No. 1. Transfiguration of Christ. *Phot. Hautes Etudes (Millet) B 63.*

43. *Wolfenbüttel*, Germany, Herzog August Bibliothek, Pattern Book, Figures from Harrowing of Hell. *Phot. Herzog August Bibliothek.*

44. *Formerly Strasbourg*, Library, Hortus Deliciarum of Herrade of Landsberg. Agony in the Garden. *After Straub and Keller.*

219. *Stuttgart*, Landesbibliothek. Psalter of Hermann von Thüringen. Harrowing of Hell. *After Löffler.*

220. *Göss*, Austria, Former Episcopal Chapel, Wall Painting. *Phot. Bundesdenkmalamt, Vienna.*

221. *Rome*, Bibl. Vat., Cod. gr. 756. St. John. *Phot. Öst. Nat. Bibl., Vienna.*

222. *Venice*, San Marco, Mosaic. Christ Emmanuel. *Phot. Istituto di Storia dell'Arte della Fondazione Giorgio Cini, Venice.*

223. *Stuttgart*, Landesbibliothek, Psalter of Hermann von Thüringen. Calender Page. *After Löffler.*

224. *Goslar*, Germany, City Hall, Gospel Book. Adoration of the Magi and Evangelist. *After Goldschmidt.*

225. *Wolfenbüttel*, Germany, Herzog August Bibliothek, Pattern Book. Evangelists. *After Weitzmann.*

226. *Hildesheim*, St. Michael, Ceiling Painting. St. Luke. *After Sommer.*

227. *Wolfenbüttel*, Germany, Herzog August Bibliothek, Pattern Book. Evangelists. *After Weitzmann.*

228. *Hamersleben*, Germany, Relief. St. Peter. *After Fründt.*

229. *Donaueschingen*, Germany, Library, Psalter. The Virgin. *After Boeckler.*

230. *Assisi*, San Francesco, Upper Church, Fresco by Cimbabue. St. Luke. *After Salvini.*

231. *Paris*, Bibl. Nat., Cod. gr. 54. St. Luke. *After Lazarev.*

232. *Venice*, San Marco, Relief. St. Leonard. *Phot. Naya.*

233. *Pescia*, Italy, San Francesco, Panel Painting. St. Francis and Scenes from his Life. *After Sirén.*

234. *Sinai*, Monastery of St. Catherine, Icon. St. George and Scenes from his Life. *After Sotiriou.*

235. *Orvieto*, Church of the Servi, Panel Painting. The Virgin. *After Bologna.*

236. *Mileševo*, Yugoslavia, Wall Painting. Virgin from Annunciation. *Phot. Radojčić.*

237. *Washington*, D.C., National Gallery of Art, Icon. Enthroned Madonna and Child. (Gift of Mrs. Otto H. Kahn). *Phot. National Gallery.*

238. *Washington*, D.C., National Gallery of Art, Icon. Enthroned Madonna and Child. (Andrew Mellon Collection). *Phot. National Gallery.*

239. *Washington*, D.C., National Gallery of Art, Icon. Enthroned Madonna and Child. (Andrew Mellon Collection), Detail. *Phot. National Gallery.*

240. *Istanbul*, Hagia Sophia, Mosaic. Head of Virgin from Deesis. *After Whittemore.*

241. *London*, National Gallery. The Virgin, Detail of Triptych, No. 566, by Duccio di Buoninsegna. *Phot. National Gallery, London.*

242. *Rome*, Santa Cecilia in Trastevere, Wall Painting by Cavallini. Last Judgment, Head of St. Andrew. *After Toesca.*

List of Plates

I

Subtilitas Graecorum

About half a century ago, when the so-called Byzantine question began to be most heatedly debated, papers and lectures on Byzantine art and its importance for European art used to open with an expression of regret about the neglect in which inquiries of this kind were held by art historians in general. The right thing to do for speakers or writers on the subject was then to become somewhat bitter and even aggressive in pointing out that, although the Byzantine factor was beginning to be recognized as an important element in the arts of the Middle Ages, it was, by and large, forgotten as soon as it was mentioned, or it was treated as an exotic ingredient which was better left to specialists, and so forth. This was surely a very tiresome attitude on the part of Byzantine scholars, a typical attitude of people who take the scant attention paid to their pet problems as a personal offense.

In the meantime, things have not changed much. Our problems are still neglected by historians of Western art and by the public in general; we still would like to begin our lectures with the invectives of 50 or 60 years ago, topping our philippics with the statement that this neglect is even less pardonable today than it was at the turn of the century. We believe, moreover, that we have made some progress since that time and that we are trying not to present the hoary Byzantine question in terms of a cultural chauvinism that sees Byzantine influence everywhere. The leading scholars in the field are now rather apt to be very critical and, if anything, to play down the effect of Byzantine influence on Western art.[1]

The most important change since 1900 in our attitude toward the question of Byzantine influence in the West is a shifting of emphasis from iconographic schemes and types and decorative motifs—those superficial evidences of superficial contacts—to the more purely artistic values. What interests us today is not the amount of copying and borrowing that went on from the seventh to the thirteenth centuries but the role which Byzantium played in the formation of Western art; not so much the question of influence but that of teaching and guidance, of help in evolving the West's own artistic language. The great achievement of Western art can be understood and properly evaluated only if the conditions of its formation are known, including all those elements which came from outside. These lectures will not deal with all the Byzantine elements that can be found in Western art but only with those which have something to do with art in the proper sense of the term and especially with the creation and the evolution of the artistic language in the figurative arts. From this point of view, it is of little importance to know exactly what Byzantine motifs Western artists adopted to give themselves a cosmopolitan air; or to count the lions and textile patterns of Eastern origin—most of them Oriental rather than Byzantine—in Western medieval art. The wearing of Byzantine imperial costumes by Western emperors and kings is a matter of the greatest interest to historians; to art historians it is only a symptom from which certain tendencies may be deduced. The same is, of course, true of the adoption of Western fashions in Byzantine lands. For this same reason the question of the role of ornament will also be excluded from the present study.

Iconography is, of course, a good deal nearer to the heart of the matter. Especially in the formative period of Western representational art, iconographic models were of the utmost importance not only for the transmission of subject matter but also for questions of format, composition and mode—hieratic, narrative or otherwise. In addition, iconographic models were often the carriers of stylistic influence, and a proper diagnosis of these models, that is, of their date and provenance, may also help the art historian in his search for the sources of stylistic inspiration. Of course, to be useful in this context, iconographic analysis has to go beyond generalities: given the wide diffusion and the persistence of certain iconographic schemes, similarities have to be very specific indeed if they are to be interpreted as proofs of direct connections.

Scholars have only just begun to differentiate between the various sources of Byzantine influence. A great deal of work remains to be done before it can be said with any degree of certainty whether an impulse came from Constantinople itself, from one of the provinces or from one of the colonial centers of Byzantine art outside the territory of the Greek empire, and before it can be

2

determined whether it was the art of contemporary Byzantium or that of an earlier phase that produced the observed effect. Nevertheless, it is not enough even today to speak of Byzantine influence pure and simple. Byzantine art was not a stationary and homogeneous phenomenon, it was a live, constantly evolving tradition, divided into many branches and subject, at times, to profound changes. One of the great difficulties in trying to find out which branch and which phase of this evolution furnished the models for certain Byzantinizing currents at work in the West, is the fact that the development of Byzantine art did not proceed in a straight line from abstract to naturalistic principles, or vice versa, or from Hellenistic to medieval methods of representation. It moved, so to speak, in spirals—and not in regular spirals at that—deviating from the ideals of classical art and forever returning to them in a series of renascences which, at times, followed each other so quickly that scholars speak of a perpetual renaissance or of perennial Hellenism. Works produced in parallel phases may look so much alike that they are apt to be mistaken for one another, although their dates may be up to three hundred years apart. Examples are numerous and easy to find: what with the longevity of iconographic formulae and the cyclic recurrence of stylistic attitudes, almost every book on Byzantine art contains one or more mistakes of this kind.

Another of the difficulties which beset the scholar who would inquire more closely into the relationship of Byzantine and Western art is the fact that so much of the evidence is lacking. A vast amount has been destroyed in the West—especially in the field of monumental painting; but in Byzantium the situation is even worse: the ravages perpetrated by Arabs, Slavs, Seljuks and Mongols, the sacking of Constantinople by the Crusaders in 1204, and the fall of the empire to the Ottoman Turks obliterated whole branches of the art of Byzantium, leaving us with a very few works, the number of which surely does not amount to more than one percent—and probably less—of the total production. The extent of these losses becomes apparent whenever groups of works are brought to light in something approaching their original density, such as the frescoes of Cappadocia, the church decorations of Kastoria or the icons of Mount Sinai. Of course, these and other discoveries can be of great assistance in establishing a balanced overall picture of the Byzantine development, especially if the works are conscientiously cleaned, published and seen in their proper perspective. Thus, the frescoes of Cappadocia fill a large gap in our knowledge as long as they are recognized for what they are, namely provincial, very often lowly works which only in part mirror the great contemporary art of Constantinople while others are the outcome of long-lived

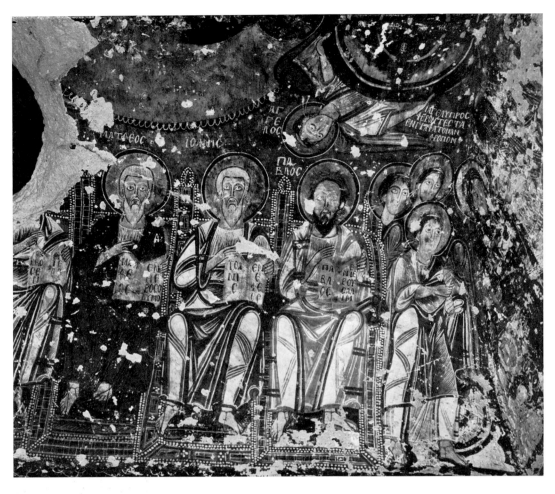

Fig. 1 *Ayvali Kilise*, Cappadocia, Wall Painting. Detail from Mission of the Apostles.

local or oriental traditions. It was pardonable in the first flush of discovery but, nevertheless, quite mistaken to regard this art as the fountainhead of important influences which penetrated to Italy, France (Figs. 1, 2), England or Spain. The sometimes astonishing similarities in form and technical treatment must be explained in other ways—namely, as parallel echoes of a tradition that issued from the really important centers of Byzantine art. Seen in this light, the frescoes painted by Cappadocian monks can help us in reconstructing with all due caution, the style of the lost wall paintings of the ninth and tenth centuries in Constantinople itself.[2] In other cases, works preserved in outlying regions can be regarded without qualification as creations of metropolitan art: this is, for instance, the case with regard to some of the frescoes of Yu-

4

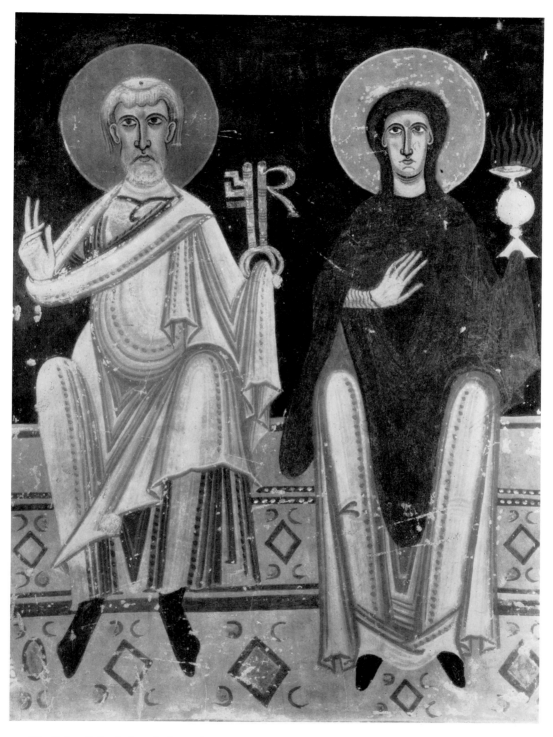

Fig. 2 *San Pedro de Burgal*, Catalonia (Barcelona, Museo de Arte de Catalunya), Wall Painting.
The Virgin and St. Peter.

goslavia (Fig. 3), works of Greek painters in exile, which have given us entirely new insights into the development of painting in Byzantium during the thirteenth century.[3]

In the West, too, some gaps have been filled by new discoveries.[4] Wall paintings have come to light in southern Italy which demonstrate the strength and continuity of the Greek element in these regions (Fig. 4),[5] and a cycle of frescoes discovered in Lambach (Pl. III),[6] near Salzburg (Austria)—the only work of monumental painting of the eleventh century in a region otherwise very productive in the field of book illumination—bears witness to the force of the Byzantine current in the North. Other works have been rehabilitated, as it were, by "de-restoring," that is, by undoing the sinister work of nineteenth century restorers, as in Pürgg in the Austrian Alps (Fig. 5), of the second half of the twelfth century.[7] These and other finds have certainly done something to fill the gaps; but some gaps which are especially embarassing in our quest continue to exist: there is, for instance, the almost entire lack of Byzantine

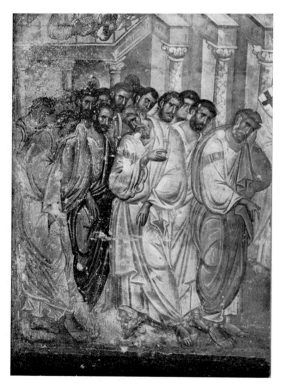

Fig. 3. *Sopočani*, Yugoslavia, Wall Painting. Death of the Virgin, Apostles.

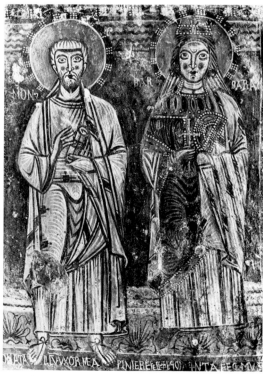

Fig. 4. *Calvi*, Grotta dei Santi, Campania, Wall Painting. Two Saints.

6

paintings of the iconoclastic period, the eighth and ninth centuries, one of the most important formative periods of Western painting, and conversely, the dearth of paintings in the West of the tenth century, which saw one of the most productive renaissance movements in the East.

Thus, it is hardly possible today to give more than a bird's-eye view of some of the questions raised by our theme and to suggest answers to a few of them. Perhaps the most fundamental question in this field is why Western art took Byzantine art for its model even after the initial period, after the establishment of iconographic cycles that covered all demands of Church and State. The answer to this question is, apparently, that Byzantine art possessed qualities which Western art lacked and which were as essential to its evolution as catalysts are for initiating certain chemical processes.[8]

There is no doubt that this life-giving, activating force of Byzantine art is closely connected with its Greek heritage. Byzantium was the greatest storehouse of classical art not only in the material, antiquarian sense of owning and

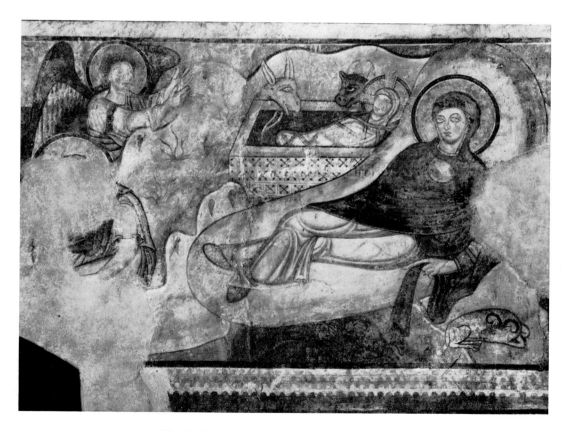

Fig. 5. *Pürgg*, Austria, Wall Painting. Nativity.

7

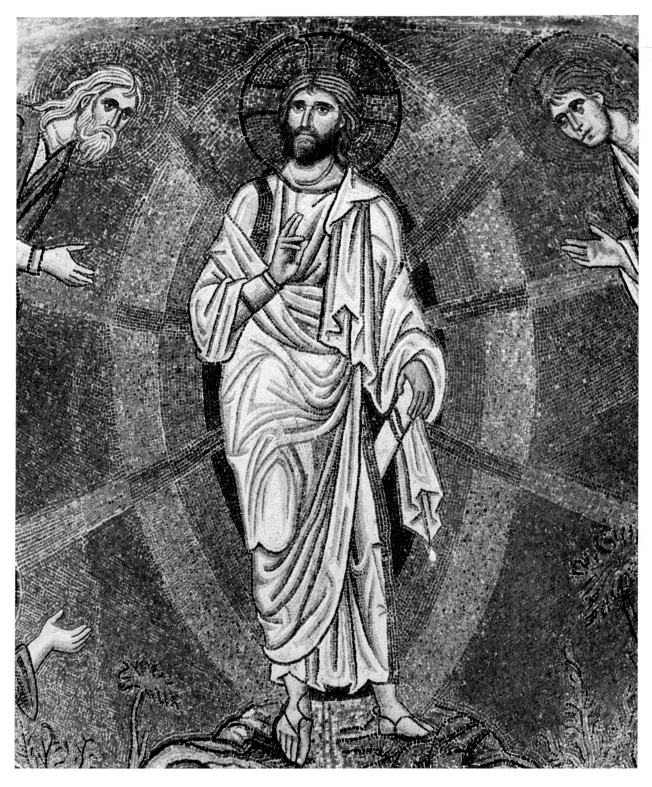

Fig. 6. *Daphni*, Greece, Mosaic. Transfiguration, Detail.

8

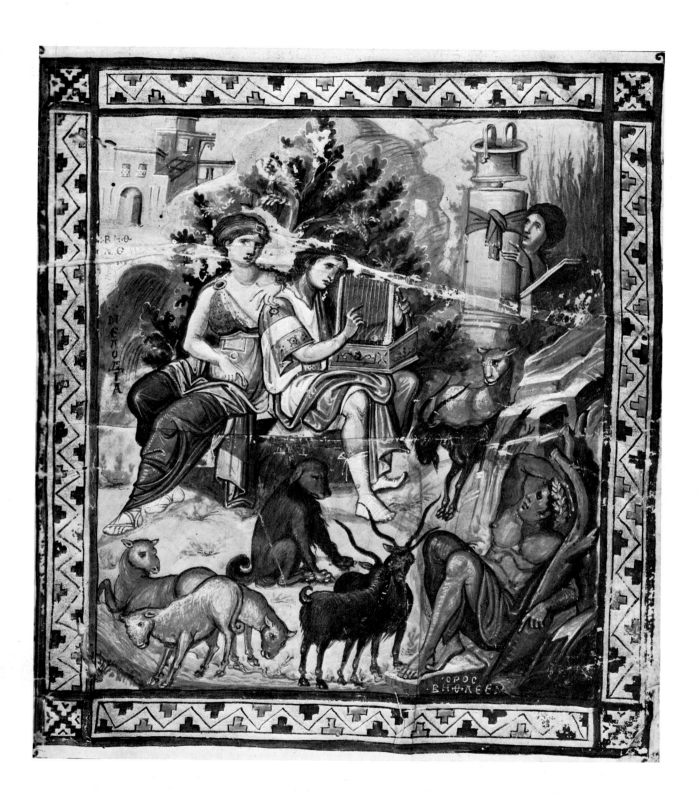

Fig. 7. *Paris*, Bibl. Nat., Psalter, MS. gr. 139. David as Shepherd.

displaying one of the greatest collections of Greek statuary ever brought together, but also foremost in the sense of a living tradition. Greek statues
and reliefs seem to have come to life in mosaic figures—in Daphni, for instance, soon after 1100 (Fig. 6). Holy figures are conceived as character
portraits; Hellenistic allegories appear in Old Testament representations (Fig.
7). The movements and attitudes of draped figures expressing sentiments or
taking part in events are conceived in the Greek spirit, and architectural and
landscape backgrounds perpetuate or recall Hellenistic scenery. Extreme practices of late antique illusionism (Fig. 8) were revived in the tenth century and

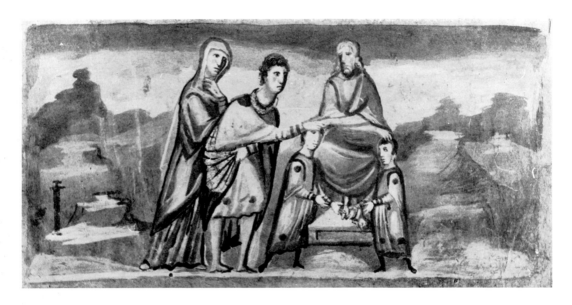

Fig. 8. *Vienna*, Nat. Bibl., Genesis, Cod. Theol. gr. 31. Jacob blessing the Children of Joseph.

lived side by side with neoclassical forms of meticulous neatness and precision.
All these various parts of the classical heritage were accessible at more or
less the same time so that artists could take their choice. That it was alive
was one of the great advantages which the classical heritage in Byzantium had
over that which lay dormant in Rome and the West in general, where artifical
revivals did not really succeed in making this heritage an integral part of the
artistic and cultural life, at least not before 1200.[9]

As a living art, the classically inspired art of medieval Byzantium was, of
course, in various degrees medievalized, an assimilation which made it much

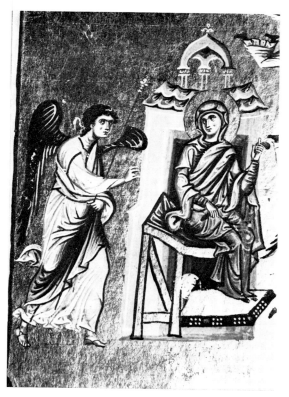

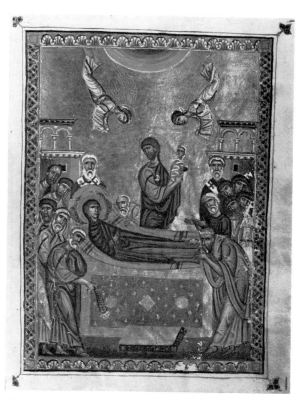

Fig. 9. *Rome*, Bibl. Vat., Homilies of James of Kok-kinobaphos, Cod. gr. 1162. Annunciation.

Fig. 10. *London*, Brit. Mus., Psalter of Queen Melisande, MS Egerton 1139. Death of the Virgin.

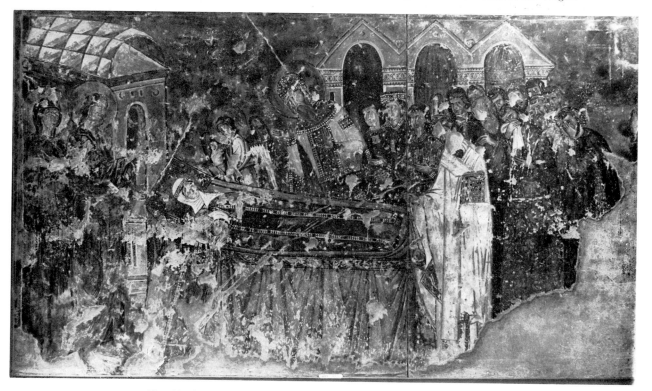

Fig. 11. *Sopočani*, Yugoslavia, Wall Painting. Death of Queen Anne.

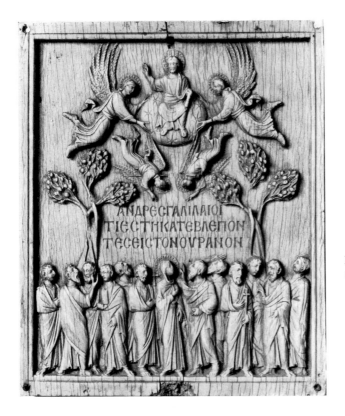

Fig. 12. *Florence*, Museo Nazionale (Bargello), Ivory plaque. Ascension.

easier for the West to understand and copy works of this kind. It was to the great advantage of Western artists in search of models that they found in these works some of the bewildering wealth of Hellenistic art boiled down, so to speak, some of the highly complicated forms broken down into their constituent parts. In Byzantine art, forms have become divisible and this divisibility is perhaps one of their most characteristic and, from the Western medieval point of view, one of their most useful attributes. This feature emerged first in technique and modeling, when the continuous gradation or the illusionistic color patch technique of Hellenistic painting was supplanted by a three- or four-tone system in which a medium tone is modified by one or two darker and one or two lighter shades, all quite distinct and not merging into each other (Pl. II); a similar principle dominated the representation of the human figure, which was divided into its component parts, parceled out, as it were, and put together like model figures, with the joints clearly articulated and the movements somewhat mechanized and overstressed (Figs. 9, 90). The same spirit of division and articulation ruled Byzantine composition: the arrangement is simple, legible, paratactic and quasi-geometrical; compositions can easily be taken to pieces, and every one of their parts may be substituted

12

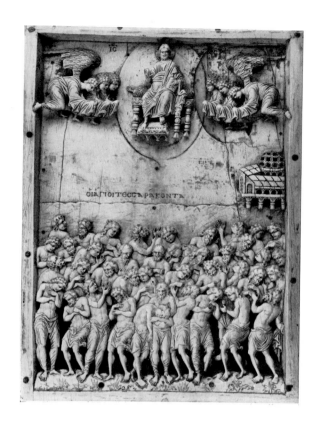

Fig. 13. *Berlin-Dahlem*, formerly Staatl. Museen, Ivory Plaque. Forty Martyrs of Sebaste.

by another. This enabled artists to express a new content by applying minor adjustments to ready-made, traditional forms. The time-honored scheme of the Death of the Virgin, the Koimesis, for instance (Fig. 10), could easily be made to do for the death of a saint or of a member of a princely family—in Sopočani that of Anna Dandolo, the consort of Stephen I of Serbia (Fig. 11); and only a few changes were necessary to transform the iconographic pattern of the Ascension of Christ, with the agitated group of standing figures in the lower and the apparition of Christ borne up by angels in the upper half (Fig. 12), into a plausible representation of the ordeal of the Forty Martyrs of Sebaste, with the contorted figures of the saints in their death throes taking the place of the apostles (Fig. 13). The fact that the compositional scheme was derived from an older and more sacred representation added to its authenticity.

To pursue this strain a little further, only some very small changes were needed to transform a group of the Martyrs of Sebaste, dying of cold for their faith (Fig. 14), into a group of damned souls, freezing in hell for their sins (Fig. 15); and another change of costume made them into penitent monks, torturing themselves by hunger and cold according to the penitential canon of John Klimakos (Fig. 16). As a matter of fact, most Byzantine compositions

13

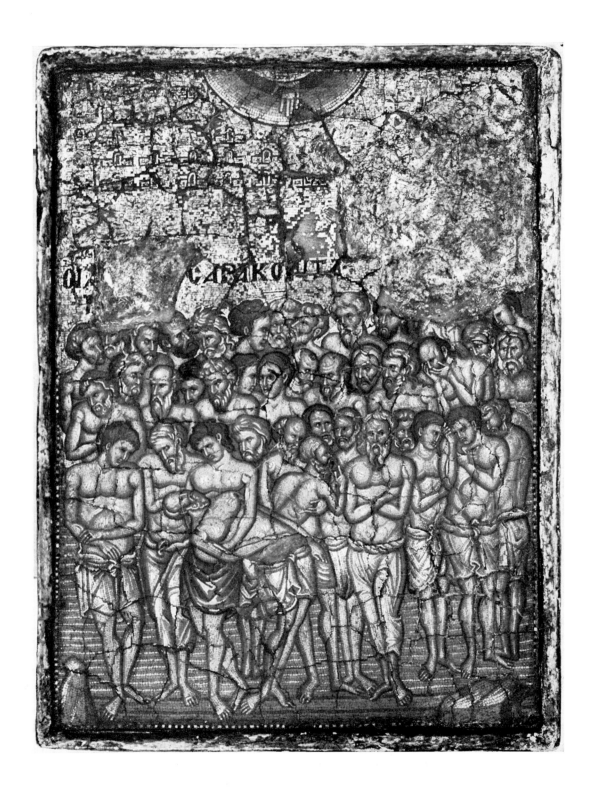

Fig. 14. *Washington*, *D.C.*, Dumbarton Oaks Collection, Mosaic Icon. Forty Martyrs of Sebaste.

14

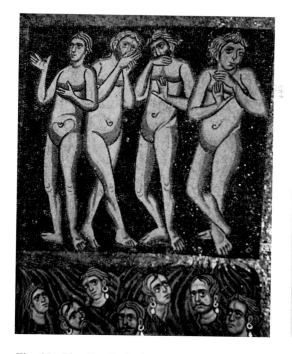 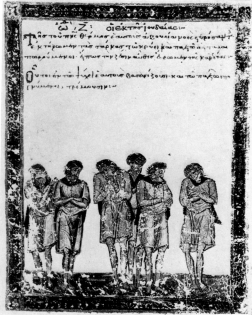

Fig. 15. *Torcello*, Cathedral, Mosaic. Last Judgment, Detail.

Fig. 16. *Rome*, Bibl. Vat., Penitential Canon Cod. gr. 1754. Penitent Monks.

or parts of compositions lent themselves to transformations of this kind by substitution. There is something general about them, something unspecific which, however, does not impair their clarity and their comprehensibility: they are like those useful words which, by the addition of small prefixes, can be made to mean almost anything, and to mean it with absolute distinctness.[10] This absolute distinctness of meaning is another of the attributes which enabled Byzantine art to become the *magistra Europae*. Every representation, from the simplest to the most complicated, compound image, had its specific message that remained unchanged through centuries; and every image had a solemn grandeur which made it a fit representation of the Holy.

The apprenticeship of Western artists with respect to Byzantine models began, of course, in the technical field. Western treatises from the *Schedula diversarum artium* of the so-called Theophilus to the *Trattato* of Cennino Cennini are full of recipes derived from Byzantine sources.[11] Some techniques, such as mosaic or cloisonné enamel, it is true, remained for a long time virtual monopolies of Byzantium; but even these opened up new possibilities in the West: Italian wall painting profited from the way in which mosaic decorations were articulated, divided by frames and enriched by ornament, and certain modeling practices evolved in mosaic were eagerly copied by fresco painters.

15

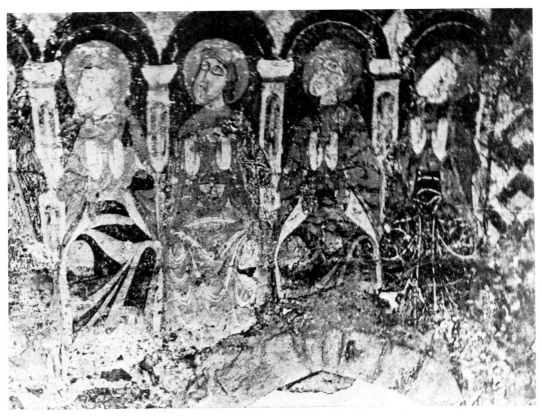

Fig. 17. *Kempley*, England, Wall Painting. Apostles.

Moreover, the monopoly was broken in some places, especially Rome and Venice, where mosaic became one of the most important fields for Western artists to come to grips with Byzantine methods and forms, since they worked side by side with Greek specialists. The technique of cloisonné enamel was rarely used in its pure form by Western artists. Parts executed in this technique—single heads or ornaments—are sometimes employed as insets, in works realized in the technique of champlevé. But the development of champlevé enamel itself was indebted, in the early stages of Limoges, for instance, to Byzantine cloisonné models. Some of the finest early pieces of Limousin enamel follow the lead of cloisonné linearism to such an extent that they could almost be called adaptations of Byzantine models. Certain coloristic and modeling effects of Byzantine cloisonné enamel inspired Western artists even outside the technical sphere of enamel itself. The arrangement of contrasting colors in form-defining stripes in English wall paintings (e.g. Kempley) is doubtless derived from tenth century cloisonné enamels like those of the Limburg reliquary; it will be shown later that even Western sculpture received certain stimuli from this source (Figs. 17, 18).[12]

16

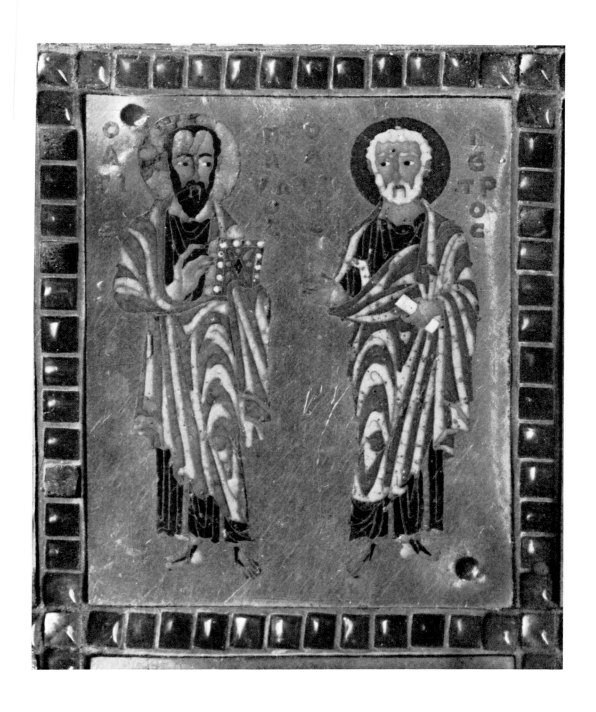

Fig. 18. *Limburg* (Lahn), Cathedral, Staurotheque. Two Apostles.

17

The most important techniques which the West derived from Byzantium were, of course, those of panel and wall painting, the one in tempera, the other in a combination of fresco and tempera. Between them, these two media carried the development of European painting. Byzantium had evolved these two techniques to the highest pitch of prefection by the application of transparent or semitransparent glazes which gave depth and luster to the picture surface. The complicated technique which makes the Cluniac frescoes of Berzé-la-Ville so different in effect from those of Tavant or Saint-Savin that French scholars have made it the chief criterion for dividing Romanesque wall painting in France into two "schools," owes much to Byzantium.[13] More important, however, than the technical procedure is the sense of monumentality in panel painting and especially in wall painting. Nowhere but in Byzantium, not even in classical Roman art, could the West have found this sense of monumentality which Byzantine art instilled into all its products, from book illumination to mosaic decoration, the most monumental of all the figurative arts. Western painting or sculpture would never have developed it by themselves: the Western approach to content was much too intellectual for this, even at a time when Byzantine influences had already begun to transform Western art. Thus in Ottonian art the written word, in the form of inscriptions, was allowed to dominate an illuminated page to the extent of destroying it as an image[14], whereas in Byzantium even the smallest images were imbued with monumental grandeur. The most impressive and the most novel kind of monumental art was, of course, that applied to the decoration of interiors, in which every element had its ideal place from which to produce the grandest effect. The great art of Romanesque apse decoration would never have come into existence without these Byzantine models to follow (Pl. I).

Thus Byzantine art was eminently suited to serve as a model to Western artists in search of guidance—eminently suited in spite of (perhaps, in certain cases, even because of) its shortcomings, its rhetorical dryness, its lack of empathy and humor and despite the inclination of the Byzantine artist to work by rote and, finally, despite the fact that Byzantine works of art could be imitated but not really duplicated. They possessed refinements, especially as regards the relation, in a complex decoration, of the parts to one another and to the whole, refinements of lighting, of placement and of a certain kind of perspective, which escaped imitation and thereby contributed to the enormous esteem in which this art was held.[15]

This high regard accorded to Byzantine art by Western artists was paralleled, on the part of the patrons, by its great political prestige as the art of the

18

Christian Empire of the East. It was felt that Byzantine art, and especially certain techniques of this art conferred on patrons a semblance of rank which no other art was able to bestow. Mosaic, especially, was seen as the imperial art par excellence and was therefore used by secular potentates, such as the kings of Sicily or the doges of Venice, and ecclesiastical ones such as the popes, who wanted to compete in some way with the Byzantine emperors.[16]

The problem for patrons and artists alike was how to acquire this art, how to imitate its qualities and how to learn from its methods. The most interesting aspect of this problem for the art historian is that of transmission. What were the actual means of transmission, the vehicles or carriers of the contagion? Did this contagion spread along certain lines, did it keep within the boundaries of the species or techniques of the models or did it spread from one field to another, from painting to sculpture, from miniature to fresco, from mosaic to book illumination? What was the part played by wandering artists, Byzantine artists in the West or Western artists in the East? What was the rôle of the great historical processes and events? These are questions which will have to be asked and answered individually. There are, however, some general aspects which can be dealt with before we enter into the historical details.

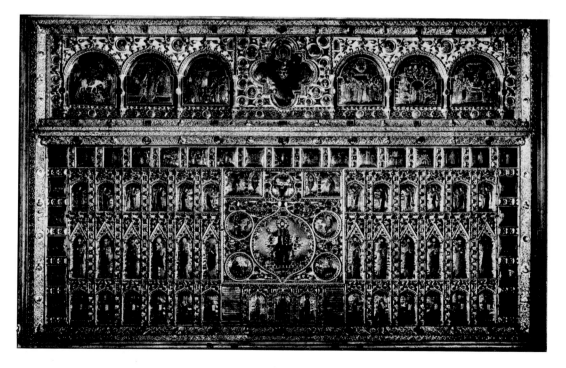

Fig. 19. *Venice*, San Marco, Pala d'Oro.

19

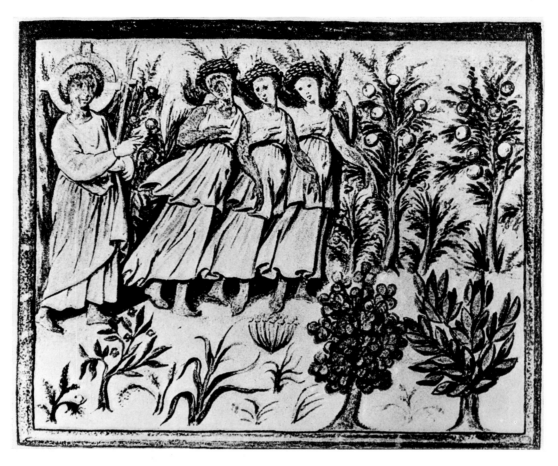

Fig. 20. *London*, Brit. Mus., Cotton Bible; Water-color copy. Third Day of Creation.

It is not necessary to dwell at length on the opportunities which existed for cultural exchanges between the East and the West. Embassies from either side, pilgrimages to Constantinople and the Holy Land, journeys of Greek monks to the West in order to collect alms, the cult and the acquisition of relics, the Crusades with the foundation of Frankish states in the Levant and in Greece, culminating in the establishment of the ill-begotten Latin Empire of Constantinople, the Venetian domination over Greek islands, trade—all these contacts provided countless opportunities for the West to become acquainted with Byzantine art.[17] More important, however, seems to be an inquiry into the actual ways and means of transmission of models and influences. One of these means was, of course, the bodily acquisition of Byzantine works of art by gift, purchase, commission or plunder. Western church treasures still contain a fair number of such objects and many more must have perished. Some

20

of these must have been rather important for Western art. Thus we know that the bronze doors commissioned by the Pantaleoni in Apulia, Campania and Rome led to the establishment of very active workshops for the production of such doors in the south, that of Barisanus being only one of several.[18] It will be seen that the commissioning of the Pala d'oro (Fig. 19) and especially its conversion into an altar retable at the beginning of the thirteenth century had important repercussions on the genesis of the Venetian polyptych; and an illuminated Bible, a twin of the Cotton Bible of the British Museum or that manuscript itself, which came to Venice as part of the spoils of Constantinople after the sack of 1204, had, perhaps, the most far-reaching effects and the greatest impact that a book of miniatures ever had at any time: it not only provided the detailed iconographic model for the entire mosaic decoration of the atrium of San Marco, but also helped to shape the style of Venetian painting in the thirteenth century (Figs. 20, 21). The copying of the lively Hellenistic details of the Old Testament story from the sixth century manuscript or, rather, the translation of these picturesque details into mosaic—which is more than just copying—must have had a profound effect on the painters and mosaicists themselves (Fig. 22).[19]

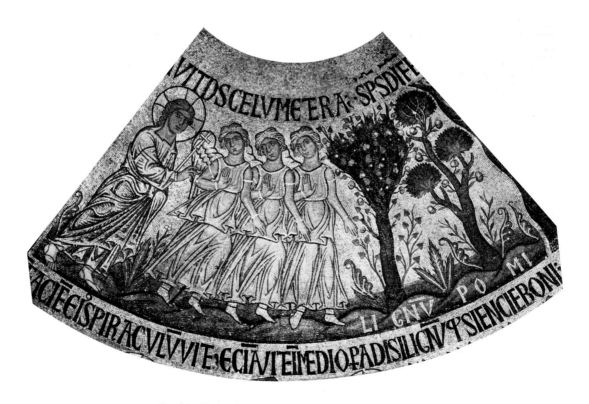

Fig. 21. *Venice*, San Marco, Mosaic. Creation, Detail.

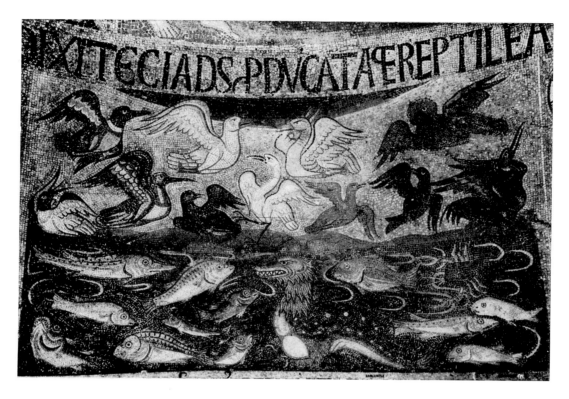

Fig. 22. *Venice*, San Marco, Mosaic, Creation, Detail.

In other cases we see only the effects, the Byzantine works which caused them having disappeared in the meantime. But the effects speak, in certain cases, so clearly that it is possible to say with a fair amount of certainty exactly what kinds of Byzantine illuminated books it must have been that, as treasured possessions of the scriptoria of Reichenau or Cologne, helped to shape the style of their miniature paintings.

Of course, we must not expect every Byzantine work of art that came to the West to have made an impression on Western art. We should be very hard put if we had to show that any effect was produced by the little Psalter (Vindob. Theol. Gr. 336) written and illuminated in Constantinople for Saint Pantaleon in Cologne in 1077 or by those rich objects in enamel which filled the treasury of San Marco after 1204; it is even unlikely from the very nature of the case that such objects, which were private possessions or were kept in cathedral treasures to be shown to the public perhaps once a year, should have exerted any influence on art or artists. For objects to be copied or used as sources of inspiration, they had, first of all, to be accessible.

A much more effective means than that provided by single objects for the transmission of Byzantine forms and principles of artistic creation was personal

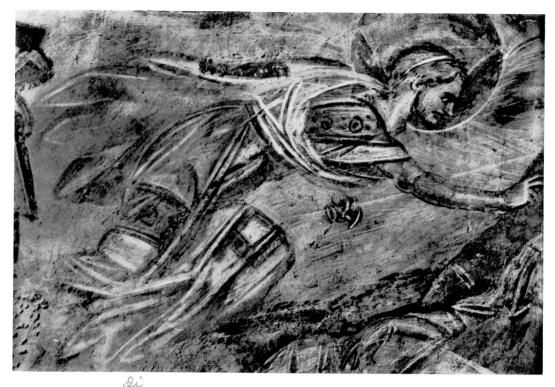

Fig. 23. *Santa Maria de Castelseprio*, Lombardy, Wall Painting. Angel appearing to St. Joseph, Detail.

contact with Byzantine artists working in Western countries. Some of these artists may have come to the West as members of embassies or trade expeditions. But it was surely more often the case that they were called to the West or sent there for the express purpose of executing certain works.[20] As a rule, these commissions concerned work in techniques foreign to the West: mosaicists were, therefore, most frequently invited, perhaps also metal workers and icon painters; wall painters least of all, because the technique of wall painting was by no means a Greek monopoly. Only in outlying countries would Greek fresco painters have been in demand. It depended on the circumstances whether works created by Byzantine artists in the West remained isolated and were forgotten or became the fountain heads of Byzantine influence. The more barbarian (in the Greek sense of the word) the surroundings were, the less was the likelihood of their exerting any lasting influence. This seems to have been the fate of the work of the really great painter who, at the instance of a Lombard princeling, painted—as we believe, in the later seventh or the early eighth century—the frescoes of Castelseprio (Fig. 23); they may help us to reconstruct in our minds the great art of Constantinople of that time but, as far as we know, they had no effect on subsequent develop-

23

ments in Lombardy.[21] The cultural and artistic distance between the painter and his patrons or the beholders, was too great for this isolated work to have had any significant effect. The same may be said of the Greek or Byzantine-trained, possibly Russian, painter who in the twelfth century executed the frescoes of Garde in Gotland: he, too, was a voice in the wilderness, and it took another two generations for Byzantine influences to establish themselves for good in Scandinavia (Fig. 24).[22]

The activity of Byzantine artists in Western countries had, of course, a much more lasting effect when they worked on soil that was already prepared to receive the seeds of Byzantine art and when they were not hopelessly isolated. The most famous case of a successful fertilization is that of Monte Cassino. Historians and art historians have looked (and are still looking) at Monte Cassino with a kind of fascination that is to be explained partly by the exalted position of the abbey and its great influence on religious movements and ecclesiastic politics, and partly by the fact that there exist a number of contemporary sources which describe the artistic activities inaugurated by its most notable abbot, Desiderius, in rebuilding and decorating the monastery in the sixties of the eleventh century. Here the historian has something to go by; and rarely have the claims of a self-styled rejuvenator of the arts been believed more readily than in the case of Desiderius. Of course, there is some truth in these claims, if they are cut down to their proper size, that is, to claims regarding the revival of certain techniques—mosaic, *opus sectile* and others—in Monte Cassino itself. It is also legitimate to assume that a great building and decorating campaign like that of Monte Cassino must have had considerable effect on the stylistic development of the region. It would be wrong, however, to make the entire future of Campanian and even Roman art dependent on the policy of Desiderius.[23]

In the field of Cassinese illumination, the effects of the Desiderian revival (if this is the proper term) are certainly quite conspicuous.[24] But then the Monte Cassino scriptorium seems to have been especially incompetent in the first two thirds of the eleventh century, much less capable of producing good, sensitive illuminations than any other southern Italian scriptorium—a fact which may be connected with the very unhappy history of the abbey down to the middle of the eleventh century. Here reform was really necessary and the only misrepresentation of which the eulogists of Desiderius—Leo, Alfanus and Aimé—were guilty was that they applied to the whole of southern Italy, even to the entire West, a judgment which fitted Monte Cassino alone. "Quoniam artium istarum ingenium a quingentis et ultra jam annis magistra Latinitas intermiserat" "Since the Latin West had neglected the exercise of these arts

24

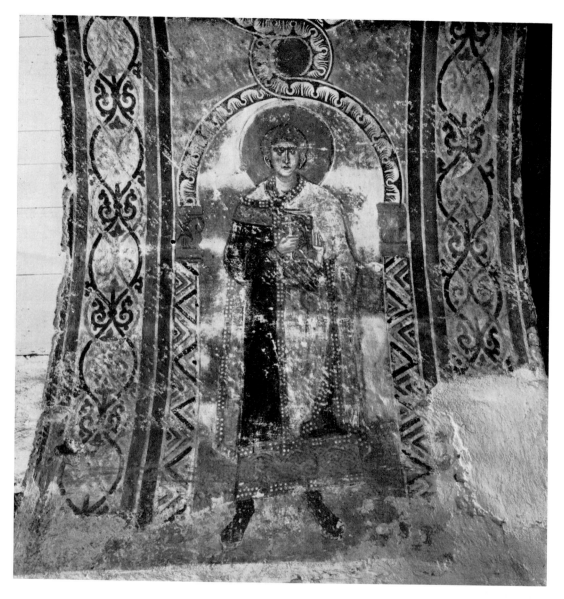

Fig. 24. *Garde*, Gotland (Sweden), Wall Painting. Saint.

for five hundred years and more"—this is how Leo of Ostia begins his *laudatio* of Desiderius, and he continues by saying that the abbot called artists from Byzantium and Alexandria in order to have the main basilica of the monastery adorned with figural mosaics and a splendid pavement. This famous opening statement, which has become one of the most overworked quotations relating to the history of the arts in the Middle Ages, is of course a gross

25

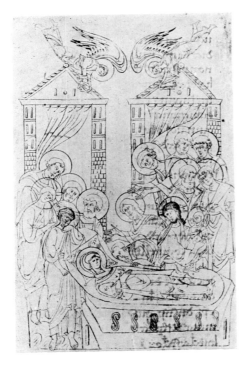

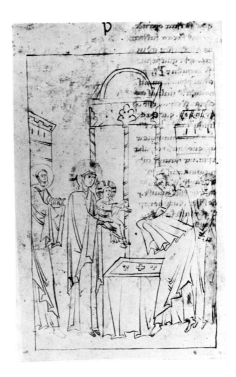

Fig. 25. *Monte Cassino*, Abbey, Cod. 98 H.
Death of the Virgin.

Fig. 26. *Monte Cassino*, Abbey, Cod. 98, H.
Presentation of Christ.

exaggeration: there was, for instance, a splendid burst of mosaic art in Rome at the beginning of the ninth century, that is, only 250 and not 500 years before Desiderius.[25] Besides, art historians have foisted on Leo things which he never said. What he, Amatus, and Alfanus did say was that Desiderius had mosaic specialists from Byzantium and Egypt brought to Monte Cassino, that he commissioned certain works of art in Constantinople, among them icons for the iconostasis, and that he sent young artists there to be instructed in the more difficult techniques. The exaggeration of the authors lies more in the tenor of the whole than in their factual statements, and the rest is due to the interpretation of art historians who made Monte Cassino a kind of Vasarian Florence, the magic fountain of youth of all the arts, a view that is made easy by the extreme dearth of monuments. We have not a single work referred to in the sources or executed in one of the techniques which are said to have been revived by the Greek artists of Desiderius. What we do have are frescoes and book illuminations, and, although these techniques are not mentioned by any of the authors concerned, it is by analyzing these works only that an idea can be formed of the effect which the philhellenic art policy of Desiderius may have had on the development of style in Monte Cassino, in Campania and

26

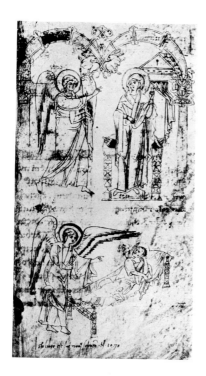

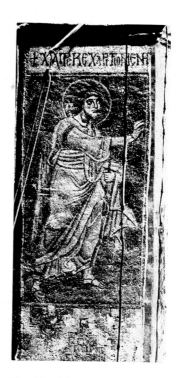

Fig. 27. *Monte Cassino*, Abbey,
Cod. 99 H. Annunciation and Dream
of St. Joseph.

Fig. 28. *Mt. Athos*, Vatopedi,
Mosaic. Angel of Annunciation.

beyond. The pen drawings of two Cassinese manuscripts, Codices 98 and 99,
exemplify various stages of Byzantine training, from simple and not too successful copying—with a complete mismanagement of figure distribution as in
a drawing of the Death of the Virgin copied after a contemporary Byzantine
original (Figs. 10, 174) with all the conscientious timidity of the learner (Fig. 25)
to drawings which are bold, superficially calligraphic and facile imitations of
Byzantine designs with a mannerist turn of lineament (Fig. 26). There are
in addition, drawings which show a highly correct Byzantine figure style—its
correctness can be seen from a comparison of the Angel of the Annunciation
in Codex 99 H (Fig. 27) with a mosaic Angel in Vatopedi, of approximately
the same period (Fig. 28). At the same time, this style is completely amal-
gamated with Campanian elements, the latter visible most clearly, but not
solely, in the ornamental framing. Such Campanian elements appeared as
early as in the first half of the eleventh century but are also conspicuous in
the fully developed style of Cassinese illumination, as it appears, in the Vatican Life of St. Benedict or the Paris Breviary of Abbot Oderisius, the successor of Desiderius.(Fig. 29). Thus the new art of Monte Cassino was not
just a creation of the Byzantine artists called in by Desiderius or an imitation

27

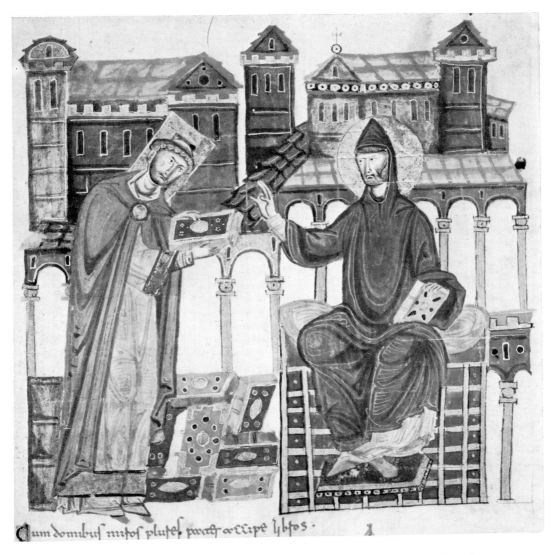

Fig. 29. *Rome*, Bibl. Vat., Cod. lat. 1202. Dedication of the Book to St. Benedict.

of their art. It was a very complicated product in which the Greek factor was represented not only by the newly imported styles but also by those Greek elements that had long been indigenous in south Italian art. There can be no doubt, however, that the recent Byzantine contacts acted as a catalyst.

The effect of Greek artists working in the West was, of course, the stronger the greater their number and the longer the time of their activity. At times they formed colonies and produced what has justly been called colonial art—which means Byzantine art transplanted to foreign soil where it had to meet foreign demands. How long Byzantine painters were able to retain their artistic (one

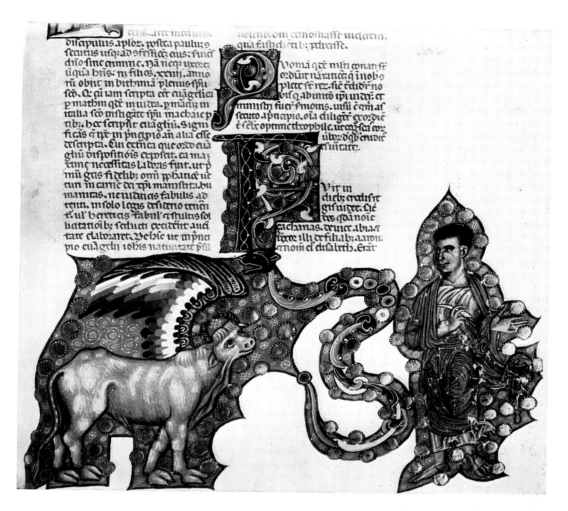

Fig. 30. *Baltimore*, Walters Art Gallery, Conradin Bible.

might even say their national) identity, depended on all kinds of factors. They did so to an astonishing degree in Sicily—owing to the fact that they appeared there as members of large specialist groups or workshops.[26] In Venice, where they worked in isolation, the opposite was the case, despite the fact that we meet there a number of Greek names, even with the added designation of "Greco," such as the mosaic master, Marco Greco Indriomeni, who is mentioned in a document of the middle of the twelfth century.[27]

A special problem is presented by the diaspora of Byzantine artists in the thirteenth century. Although we must assume with Professor Weitzmann that all artistic production did not cease in Byzantine in the period of Latin domination,[28] a substantial number of artists—and at that time we must reckon with lay artists as well as clerics—must have gone elsewhere to seek their

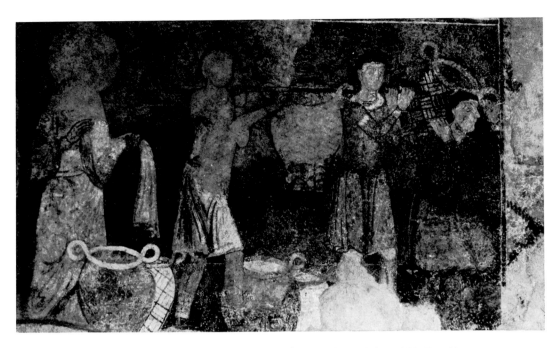

Fig. 31. *Friesach*, Austria, Wall Painting. Feeding of the 5,000, Detail.

livelihood. Some of them, mostly from Salonica, are recorded as having entered the service of Serbian princes, while others went to Italy where they plied their trade in the *maniera greca* which became one of the formative influences in the development of Italian panel painting. The role of these masters was certainly more important than that of the last group of Greek refugees, that is, those who fled to the West after the final fall of the Empire to the Turks in the middle of the fifteenth century and who suffered the fate of so many late-comers—they disappeared in the lowest stratum of the hierarchy of art, that of popular imagery.

Compared with the activity of Greek artists in the West, the travels of Western artists in Byzantine lands seem to have been less important for the transmission of Greek influences. However, recent research in the art of the Crusader States, Jerusalem, Acre and Cyprus, by Professor Buchthal and Professor Weitzmann suggests that the hybrid art which grew up in these regions from the symbiosis of Byzantine Armenian and Western artists may have had much more important repercussions on Western art, and especially on Italian art, than we were led to believe until now.[29] Venetian, Tuscan and central Italian painting seem to have received valuable impulses from these sources, and it is not unlikely that enigmatic works like the so-called Conradin

30

Bible in the Walters Art Gallery (Fig. 30), the origin of which has lately been sought in Umbria by Professor Longhi, will one of these days be seen as products of this backwash from the Levant.[30] However, Sicily, Rome and Venice were much closer and provided richer quarries for Western painters.

It is there that Western artists must have made their most intensive studies of the principles, the iconography and the style of Byzantine monumental art; and it is there that they filled the pattern books in which they carried home their harvest of observations, notes and copies. As these pattern books were subjected to the most grueling treatment, being used in the workshops and on the scaffoldings and handed down from father to son, it is only to be expected that hardly anything of the kind has come down to us, and little in anything like good condition. In most cases the use of pattern books can only be inferred, as, for instance, in the case of the wall paintings of Friesach (Fig. 31) and Pürgg (Fig. 32) in Austria, both of which show the identical composition of the Feeding of the Five Thousand, an elaboration of a Byzantine original that was also used as a model in San Marco (Fig. 33). There are numerous other cases.

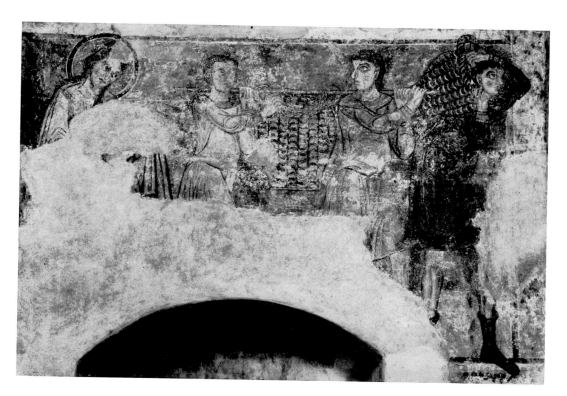

Fig. 32. *Pürgg*, Austria, Wall Painting. Feeding of the 5,000, Detail.

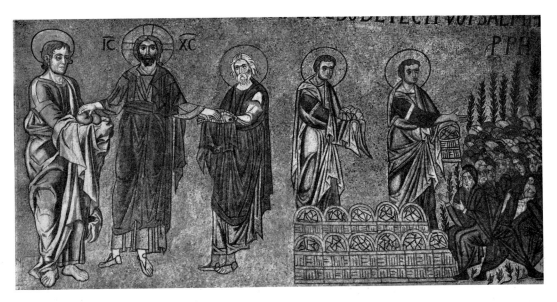

Fig. 33. *Venice*, San Marco, Mosaic. Feeding of the 5,000.

The most complete and most interesting book of this kind—more of a note-book than a patternbook, that of Villard d'Honnecourt, is too late a production to be of great assistance in our quest. Of other collections only fragments are left, none of them older than the late twelfth century, all of them disfigured by secondary use, pasted into book bindings or written over at a later period. Altogether, it is a rather meager harvest which has been collected in a recent survey of medieval model books.[31] The few fragments we do have show the multiplicity of sources upon which the artists drew. A sheet in the Vatican (Fig. 34), by a rather incompetent German draftsman of the late twelfth century, contains two Old Testament scenes, apparently copied from a Byzantine Bible, four seated Church Fathers and, as the most interesting part of its contents, twelve figures of standing prophets which are ultimately derived from a pre-iconoclastic source, the nearest parallel being the Syriac Codex No. 341 in the Bibliothèque Nationale, Paris, of the late sixth or early seventh century. Whether the model of the copyist was really such an early book or a later Byzantine copy, can hardly be made out owing to his weak draftsmanship. On a much higher level is the single leaf in the Augustiner-Museum Freiburg; by an extraordinary stroke of luck, it contains in addition to two drawings a good part of a table of contents in which the figures and scenes are enumerated in the order (or rather disorder) in which they appeared in the book, with additional remarks concerning the way in which they were represented: for instance, *dimidiae figurae Stephani et Laurentii*, or

32

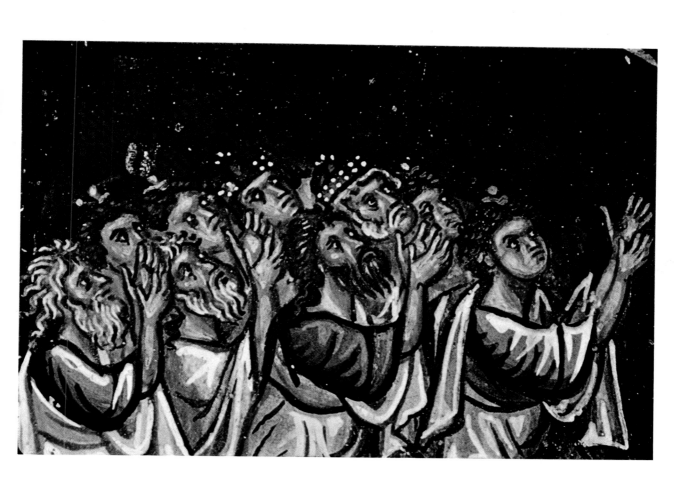

II *Rome*, Bibl. Vatic., Cod. gr. 1162, Miniature. Group of Figures.

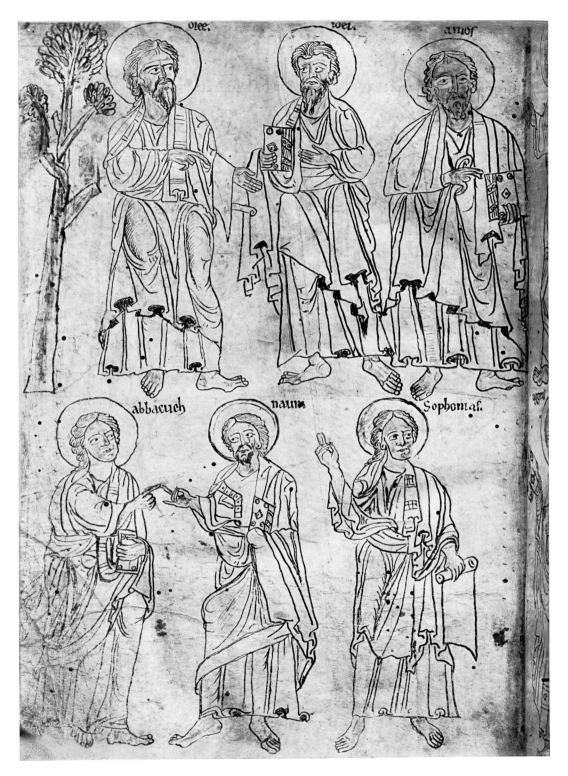

Fig. 34. *Rome*, Bibl. Vat., Pattern Book, Cod. lat. 1976. Prophets.

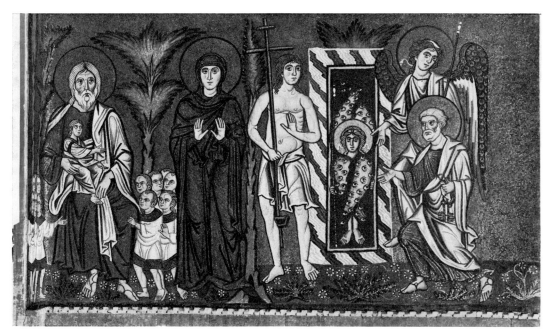

Fig. 35. *Torcello*, Cathedral, Mosaic. Paradise.

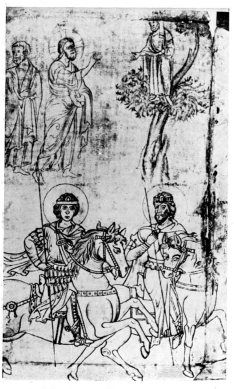

Fig. 36. *Freiburg*, Germany, Augustiner-
museum, Leaf from a Pattern Book. Christ
and Zacheus, Two Saints on Horseback.

Zachaeus

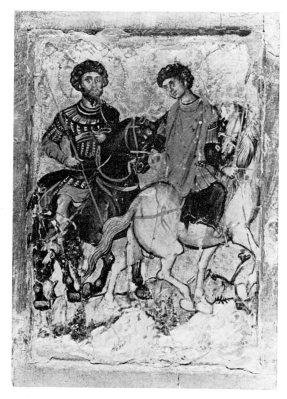

Fig. 38. *Mt. Sinai*, Icon. Two Saints on Horseback.

34

majestas, or *Maria sine filio*. The 78 titles show that some representations occurred two or three times, such as the Crucifixion, and that of others only parts were represented: the figures of the *crucifer latro iuxta cherubin angelusque et Petrus* were clearly taken from a representation of the Last Judgment similar to that of Torcello, perhaps from Torcello itself (Fig. 35). The two drawings on the verso of the leaf, referred to in the table of contents by the words *ubi Zachaeus in arbore* and *Theodorus equitans cum alio* (Fig. 36) are derived from two different sources and executed in two different techniques. The Zachaeus story must have been copied from a Byzantine mosaic or fresco very similar in composition, types and style to the mosaics of Monreale (Fig. 37). The actual scene is missing in Monreale, but the group of Christ and St. Peter is one of the stock motifs of the mosaics, down to the minutest detail. The two holy warriors on horseback, on the other hand, are most probably derived from a Crusader icon, similar to those preserved on Mount Sinai, where the warrior saints are also represented on horseback, while in purely Byzantine representations they are depicted as standing figures (Fig. 38).[32]

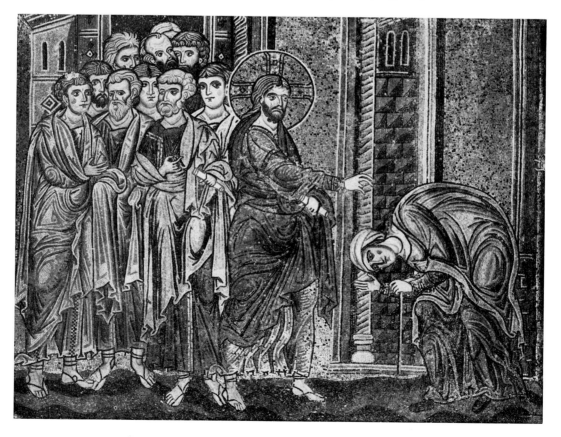

Fig. 37. *Monreale*, Cathedral, Mosaic. Christ Healing.

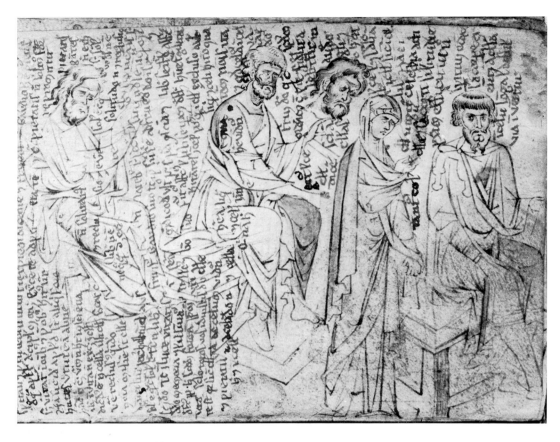

Fig. 39. *Wolfenbüttel*, Germany, Herzog August Bibliothek, Pattern Book.
Seated and Standing Figures.

Thus the Freiburg leaf, the work of a German painter of about 1200, shows the variety of sources from which model books were drawn. This should, perhaps, be kept in mind in dealing with the most interesting document of this kind that has come down to us, the so-called Wolfenbüttel pattern book (Fig. 39). Professor Weitzmann has shown convincingly that the chief source of this collection of drawings which a Saxon painter made in the early second quarter of the thirteenth century, was an almost contemporary Byzantine lectionary, which belonged to a group of works represented by Codex 118 of Athens (Fig. 40), and Iviron 5 of Mount Athos, these being themselves copies of tenth century originals. Two of the drawings of Evangelists in the pattern book correspond closely to the Athens Gospels, and a good many other figures and groups such as the Transfiguration (Fig. 44) can be paralleled in Iviron No. 5 or in earlier works belonging to the same pictorial tradition, such as, for instance, Iviron No. 1 (Fig. 42). However, there must have been

36

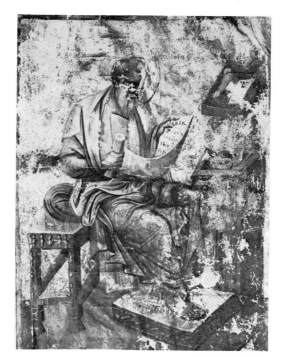

Fig. 40. *Athens*, Nat. Library, Cod.
gr. 118. St. Matthew.

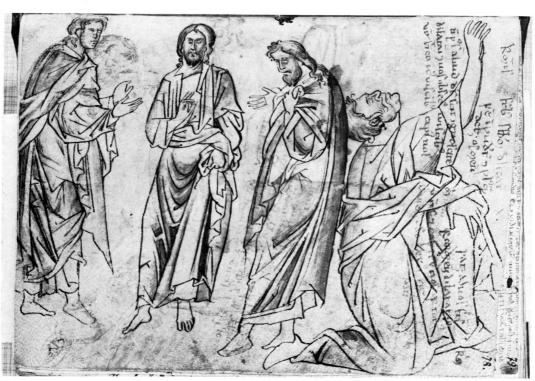

Fig. 41. *Wolfenbüttel*, Germany, Herzog August Bibliothek, Pattern Book.
Figures from Transfiguration of Christ.

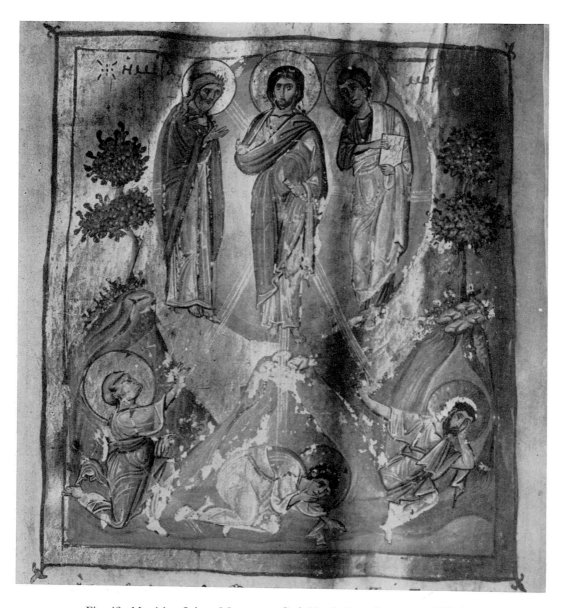

Fig. 42. *Mt. Athos*, Iviron Monastery, Cod. No. 1. Transfiguration of Christ.

other sources as well: some of the figures, such as the angel pointing to the empty sepulchre of Christ or the elaborate composition of the Harrowing of Hell (Fig. 43), can hardly be imagined as deriving from book illuminations—they must go back to monumental paintings, probably frescoes. We must not expect all these drawings to be traceable to a single class of model: pattern books were collections of excerpts made by artists from various sources over long stretches of time.[33]

38

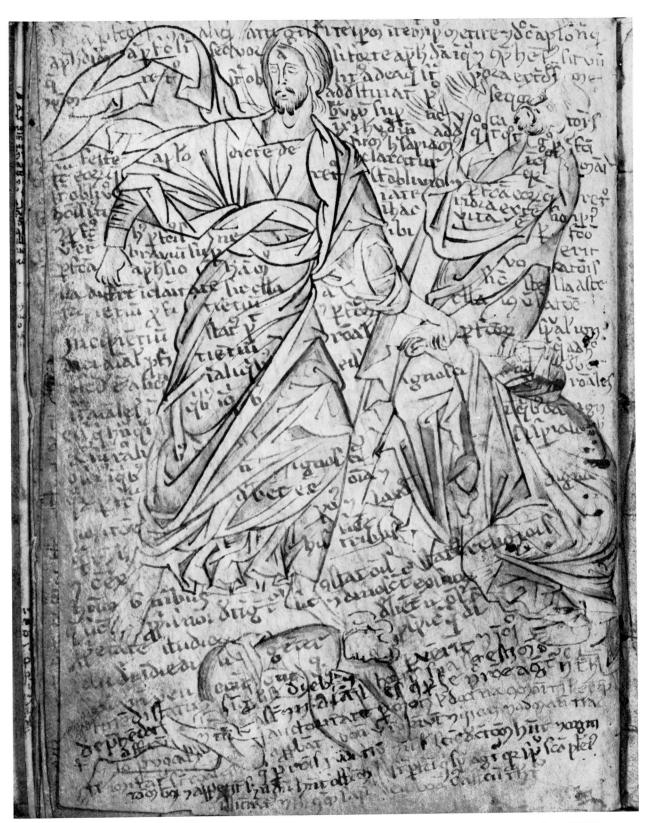

Fig. 43. *Wolfenbüttel*, Germany, Herzog August Bibliothek, Pattern Book. Figures from Harrowing of Hell.

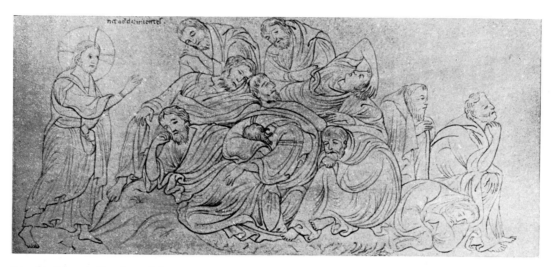

Fig. 44. *Formerly Strasbourg*, Library, Hortus Deliciarum of Herrade of Landsberg. Agony in the Garden.

A few examples will show how complicated the problems connected with the use of pattern books can be. One of them concerns the relationship between the mosaics of Monreale and the drawings of the so-called *Hortus deliciarum*, an odd kind of picture book compiled by the abbess of Hohenberg in Alsace, Herrade of Landsberg, for the edification of her nuns. This relationship is very close in some of the compositions, for example, that of the Agony in the Garden (Figs. 44, 45), where the greater part of the apostles' figures are represented in rather complicated attitudes which, nevertheless, are identical. This and other close resemblances, together with the fact that Sibylla, the widow of Tancred of Sicily, was confined in the nunnery of Hohenburg by Henry VI, led to the conclusion that some of the *Hortus* drawings (which are similar in style to those of the Freiburg Leaf) were copied from some kind of Sicilian picture book possibly brought to Hohenburg by Sibylla; this would have had to be a pattern book, as can be inferred from the fact that the figure of Christ, who ought to be represented as admonishing St. Peter, is standing on the wrong side, to the left instead of the right of the group, so that St. Peter is looking at nothing in particular whereas Christ is shown adressing the wrong man. This kind of mistake is typical of an unintelligent use of a pattern book, where, as a rule, only the variables of a cycle were represented and not ever-recurring figures such as that of Christ. This hypothesis seemed very convincing until a much closer parallel for the Agony drawing of the *Hortus* was found—namely, a fresco painting in the Protaton of Karyäs on Mount Athos, dating from the beginning of the fourteenth century (Fig. 46), but mirroring a much older prototype. There we find two of the figures of the

40

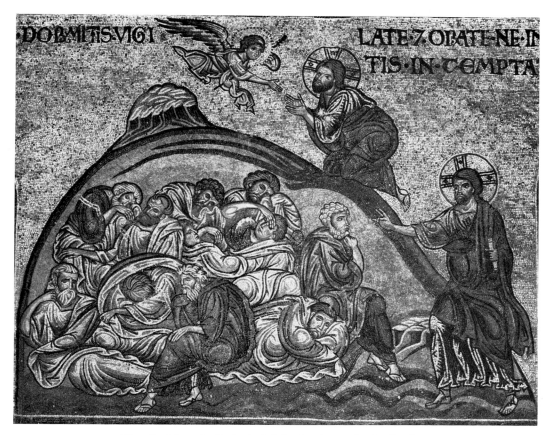

Fig. 45. *Monreale*, Cathedral, Mosaic. Agony in the Garden.

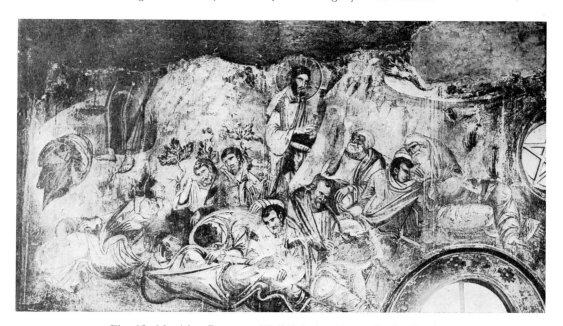

Fig. 46. *Mt. Athos*, Protaton, Wall Painting. Agony in the Garden.

41

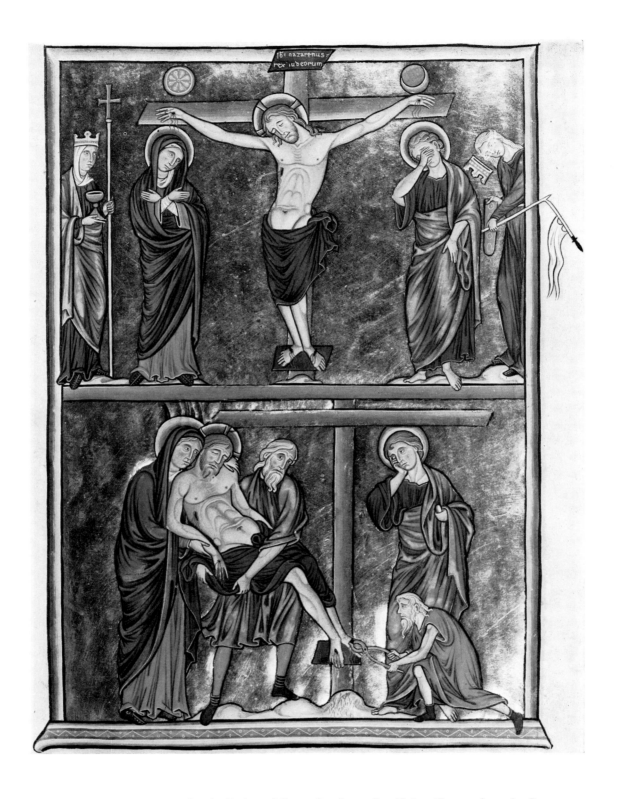

Fig. 47. *Chantilly*, Musée Condé, Psalter of Queen Ingeborg. Crucifixion, Descent from the Cross.

42

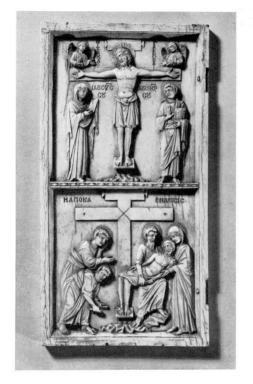
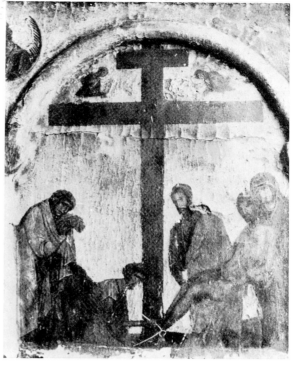

Fig. 48. *Hannover*, Kestner Museum, Ivory. Crucifixion and Descent from the Cross.

Fig. 49. *Mt. Athos*, Vatopedi, Icon. Descent from the Cross.

Hortus (the two apostles looking toward the left topping the group) which are not included in the Monreale mosaics. Thus the *Hortus* drawing cannot depend on the Monreale mosaics or on a pattern book connected with them; it is copied from a pattern book that was compiled from sources other than the Sicilian mosaics, and there is no need to conjure up the ghost of the unfortunate Sibylla.[34]

Another case which should make us aware of the many problems connected with the use of pattern books is that of the parallelism between a page of the Ingeborg Psalter (Fig. 47), an outstanding manuscript written and illuminated in northern France about 1200, and a Byzantine ivory in Hanover, of the tenth century (Fig. 48). The combination of the Crucifixion and the Descent from the Cross one above the other and the close resemblance (despite certain differences) of the two compositions of the Descent seem to suggest that the miniature was copied directly from the ivory. But in this instance too, a closer parallel can be found in a Byzantine icon (at Vatopedi) (Fig. 49), and it is very likely that paintings and not ivories were the chief sources of the pattern book used by the painter of the psalter.[35]

It is the omnivorous attitude of Western artists with respect to Byzantine models that makes it so difficult to decide exactly which kind of model was used in a given case. Perhaps this decision is, after all, not so very essential. It is surely more important to ask how Western artists used their models and what they made of them, what inspirations they drew from them and how, step by step, they grew out of their apprenticeship. To characterize the successive phases of this process will be the task of the following chapters.

2

Early Lessons and Revivals

About the middle of the eighth century, the chances for the survival of Christian figural art must have looked very poor indeed. Byzantium which, only a short time before, had been the main source of religious imagery this side of India was in the throes of iconoclasm.[36] Islam with its unqualified rejection of religious representation had spread over the entire Middle East, all North Africa and almost the whole of Spain. The indigenous art of the North and the Northwest was aniconic by preference; since the later sixth century it had also invaded large parts of Italy and in 751 even Ravenna fell to the Longobards. This does not mean, of course, that all figurative art was rejected by these peoples and creeds: secular representation continued to exist and even to flower at the courts of Byzantium, Damascus and Baghdad. We know something of the latter, but next to nothing has come down to us of the figurative art of iconoclastic Byzantium. This is one of the great gaps in our knowledge of the development of art in the early Middle Ages.

There were, it is true, a few islands of religious imagery in this sea of non-representational decoration, some of them in the outlying provinces of the Empire and the Caliphate, in Armenia, in Mesopotamia, in Coptic Egypt and perhaps even in Asia Minor; but the arts of these regions, isolated and provincial, had little importance for the survival and the subsequent revival of the figural religious tradition. There was, however, one part of the Mediterranean world where religious representation continued to exist and which became a kind of refuge for unrepentant Greek icon and wall painters: the Italian peninsula, with centers in Rome, Milan, and the Greek-dominated South. Our knowledge of this art has to be based on the comparatively well-documented development of wall painting in Rome.[37] The monument with the help of which this development can be studied under optimal conditions is the ruined church of S. Maria Antiqua, erected on the slope of the Palatine

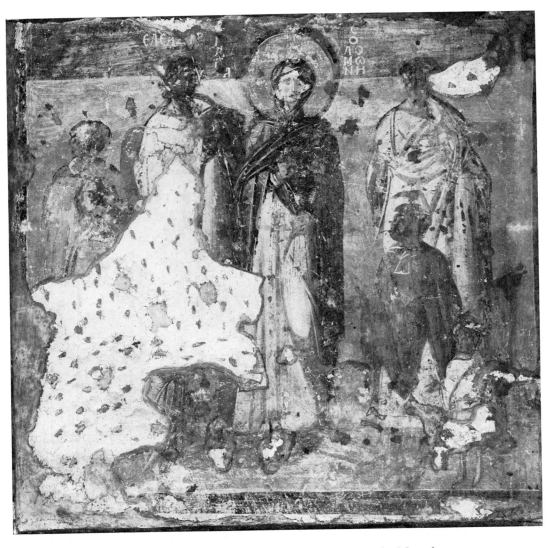

Fig. 50. *Rome*, Santa Maria Antiqua, Wall Painting. The Maccabees.

hill in the sixth century, as part of a monastery of Greek monks (Fig. 50). Enough is left of its original decoration to enable us to recognize in it a purely Byzantine style. A hotly debated question, however, is whether the accretions, which accumulated layer by layer on the walls of the church, were the work of Greek or of local painters. The problem is not easy to resolve because we have next to nothing in Byzantium itself which could help us to decide whether the stylistic changes visible in the successive layers correspond to an immanent development of Byzantine painting or whether they are, at least in part, due to the increasing influence of local, Roman factors. The process is not entirely continuous. The first half and the middle years of the seventh century show a

46

style which is not only decidedly Greek, but downright Hellenistic, and so sudden seems the appearance of this painterly style with its wealth of tonal gradations that a rather romantic explanation has been adduced to explain it: it has been connected with the great catastrophe which overtook one of the presumed centers of pictorial Hellenism when Alexandria fell to the Arabs in 642 and its Christian painters were forced to seek their livelihood elsewhere. It appears, however, that the art of Alexandria was not really as "Hellenistic" as all that; moreover, similar waves of a painterly, illusionistic style reached Rome and Italy in later periods as well, when there was no Alexandria left to fall to the Arabs and to pour out its painters. Nor do we need explanations of this kind to account for the appearance of wave upon wave of Greek styles in Rome, where a succession of Greek and Syrian popes ruled in the seventh and eighth centuries and where great Greek monasteries existed in Santa Maria Antiqua, San Saba, San Giorgio in Velabro and Santa Maria in Cosmedin, to name only the most important.

Rome was not the only recipient of these waves of painterly Byzantine styles. Special circumstances seem to have brought Greek artists to northern Italy as well. Whatever the exact date of the frescoes of Santa Maria di Castelseprio (Fig. 23)[38] and whatever the exact nature of the circumstances that brought them into existence, it can hardly be doubted that they are the work of Byzantine artists; the nearest parallels seem to be Roman frescoes of the period between 650 and 710. The beginning of the eighth century was actually one of the most fertile periods of Greek art in Rome. It was the time of the learned Greek Pope John VII (705–707), who gave Santa Maria Antiqua a new coat of frescoes, in a style that must have been newly imported direct from Constantinople (Fig. 51). Compared with the frescoes of the middle of the seventh century, still imbued with the freshness of the Hellenistic revival of the time of Heraclius, those of the early eighth are somewhat less painterly; the patches of color lengthen into brush strokes which assume an increasingly calligraphic quality. Every one of these flourishes is, however, still readable as highlight or shade, quite dramatically contrasted at times. Nowhere do they as yet form a coherent linear pattern that defines the contours of the figures and subdivides them into their component parts. This, however, was the direction taken by the subsequent development. What had been calligraphic flourishes now become continuous contours, illusion turns into ornament, texture gives way to structure. A head of about the middle of the eighth century—the period of Pope Zachariah (741–752), the last of the continuous line of Greek popes—is already quite different in style from one barely fifty years earlier. And still the process continued: it reached its climax in the iconic

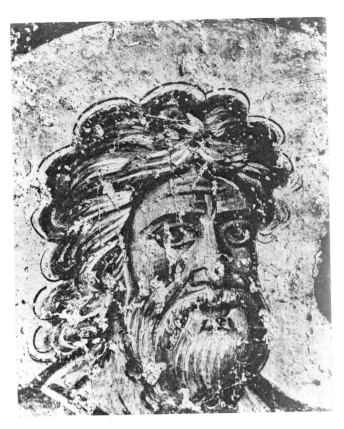

Fig. 51. *Rome*, Santa Maria Antiqua, Wall Painting. Head of Saint.

sternness and spartan linearism of the saints in the left aisle of Santa Maria Antiqua, which date from the end of the eighth or the beginning of the ninth century (Fig. 52).

Although it is not unlikely that the painters of these grim figures were just as Greek as those who produced the lively forms of the mid-seventh century, we can hardly say with certainty whether the development which took place between these two poles is a faithful echo of what happened in Byzantium. As regards Constantinople itself, there certainly existed no coherent development of religious painting in the center of iconoclasm; some of its secular art may have developed along lines similar to those we have seen in Rome, but it is very unlikely that the trend toward the abstract had any great importance in an art which seems to have taken its cue from either classical scenic art or Islamic decoration. There were, however, the provinces.

That provincial art in Byzantium did indeed develop toward increasing abstraction much as Greek art in Italy did, can be gauged from various groups of manuscripts and, in addition, from post-iconoclastic works of the late ninth century, such as some of the Cappadocian frescoes or the mosaics in the dome of Hagia Sophia in Salonica, whose abstract sternness is as yet hardly

48

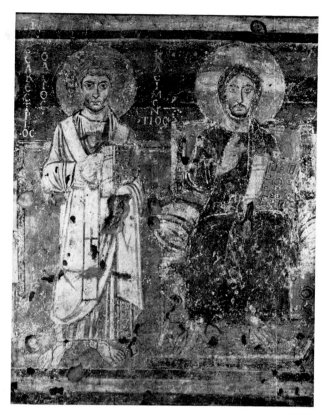

Fig. 52. *Rome*, Santa Maria Antiqua, Wall Painting. Seated Christ and Saint.

tempered by the classic revival that by then had already begun to color the new religious art of the capital.[39]

However, not all religious painting in Italy was inspired by Byzantine art, metropolitan or provincial. There existed several other currents, the most important of which seems to have been a survival, however attenuated, of an indigenous Italian version of early Christian art. This current seems to have been especially strong in book illumination; and since books were easily exported, it exerted an influence in the West and the North that was, perhaps, greater than the slender artistic value of its products warranted. Even earlier illuminations of this current were avidly copied in Northern scriptoria. It would, however, be wrong to ascribe the so-called Anglo-Saxon renaissance exclusively to the influence of western Roman models: Byzantine Italy and, in all likelihood, Byzantium itself also had their share in sparking this movement. It is very likely that Northern artists did not see any difference between western and eastern Roman art, nor cared, if they did see it. Their attitude, as reflected in their use of Ravenna ivories, sarcophagi and mosaics as models in the reliefs of the Ruthwell Cross, and of Coptic or Armenian motifs in Insular book illumination, can only be described as promiscuously eclectic.[40]

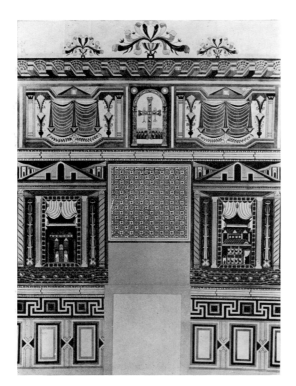

Fig. 53. *Oviedo*, Spain, San Julián de los Prados, Wall Painting. (Copy).

Nothing could be more different from this magpie attitude than that which Charlemagne and his "Board of Education" adopted toward foreign art in the framework of what must be called a planned *Kunstpolitik*—or rather, as is bound to happen in the political sphere, a succession of changing policies. Charlemagne's personal and political relations with Byzantium were not very happy. A matrimonial project which ought to have established close ties between Byzantium and the Frankish kingdom—the son of Empress Irene was supposed to marry Charlemagne's daughter Hruotrut—proved abortive, leading to a complete break and, ultimately, to warlike actions in 787. This happened to be the year of the second Nicean Council, which re-established icon worship in Byzantium. The temperamental Charlemagne, now intent on fighting Irene in every possible way, had the findings of the council declared invalid by a synod in Frankfurt and even asked the Pope to anathematize Irene and her son.[41]

This is the background against which the literary statement of Carolingian art policy, the *Libri Carolini*, has to be seen. They are—not exclusively but in the main—an anti-Greek political pamphlet, directed even more against image worship than against iconoclasm. Genuine religious feeling and political enmity, good sense and stubborness, combined here to produce one of the most fascinating documents of the eternal misunderstanding that prevails between

50

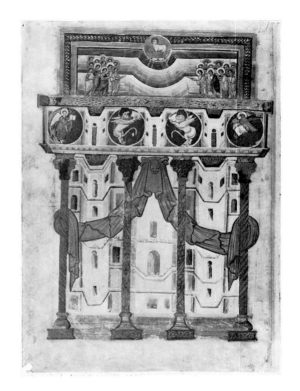

Fig. 54. *Paris*, Bibl. Nat. ᴍꜱ lat. 8850, Soissons Gospels. Adoration of the Lamb.

West and East. The author, who seems to have been Theodulph, Bishop of Orléans, concedes, it is true, a certain usefulness to religious images and condemns their destruction; but he is much harder on their worshippers than on their detractors.[42] The primary purpose of the pamphlet was, after all, to score against Irene, the champion of icon worship; and an additional edge may have crept into the text because Theodulph was a Spaniard and as such had a traditional revulsion against images. This viewpoint had found expression as early as 310 when the local synod of Elvira declared *picturas in ecclesia esse non debere, ne quod colitur et adoratur in parietibus depingatur.* As if to illustrate these words, San Julian de los Prados near Oviedo (Fig. 53) shows a décor from which not only religious representation but every figural element is rigorously excluded.[43] It is even possible that we have here an echo of Byzantine iconoclastic art, transmitted to Spain either directly or through connecting links in Frankish territory. In any event, we find similar motifs in Carolingian book illumination (Fig. 54) such as the Soissons Gospels.

The most interesting document of iconoclastic tendencies in Carolingian art proper is the apse mosaic (Fig. 55)[44] of Theodulph's oratory at Germigny-des-Prés; here the quincunx plan points to Spain and beyond Spain to Eastern prototypes, rather than to Aachen as an early source would have it. The mosaic represents the Ark of the Covenant (with two Cherubs on its roof)

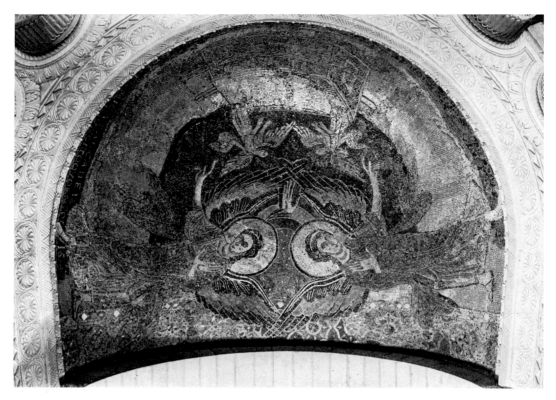

Fig. 55. *Germigny-des-Prés*, France, Mosaic. Ark of the Covenant.

flanked by two tall Angels with outspread wings. Now, the Ark of the Covenant, with its human-headed Cherubim, played an important part in the iconoclastic controversy: references to it were bandied about by iconodules and iconoclasts alike, and the *Libri Carolini* deal in four chapters with this problem of a figurative representation ordered by the Lord himself; the authors stress the uniqueness of the case and say expressly that it would be a great error to compare it with works fashioned by men (*manufactae imagines*). Thus the picture of the Ark attained the dignity of the sole permissible representation of the Deity, and as such it was programmatically placed in the apse of Theodulph's own church which thus became a second temple of Solomon, as it were.

There is no other representation of this kind preserved in the West; a badly damaged example is, however, to be found in Armenia (Tekor), and it is not altogether impossible that the theme existed in Byzantine art. As a matter of fact, the very odd movement of all four Angels at Germigny, the large as well as the small ones, is typically Hellenistic and is often to be found in Byzantium: the "lunge" with the upper body turned away and the hands stretched backward was one of the "fashionable" attitudes in metropolitan art, derived, of course, from late Hellenism and revived in all Byzantine renaissances, especially the Macedonian revival (Fig. 91). It would be strange

52

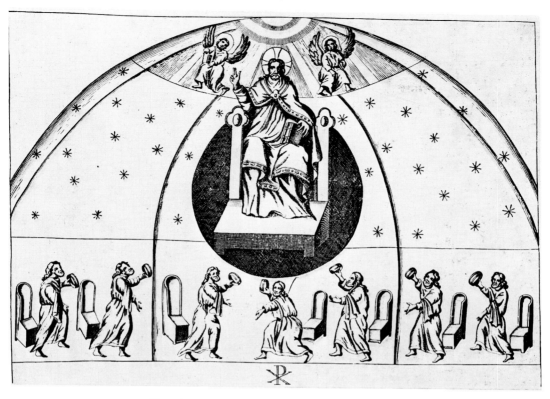

Fig. 56. *Aachen*, Cathedral, Mosaic (Engraving).

indeed if a work of art that was meant to convey a protest against Byzantium should have used Byzantine formulae.

The iconoclastic message of Theodulph's mosaic has recently served as the starting point for a new and somewhat radical investigation of the entire problem of Carolingian iconophobia. Its author, Professor Schnitzler of Cologne, came to the conclusion that, at a certain period, there existed in Carolingian art something like an embargo on representations of Christ in Majesty.[45] According to Professor Schnitzler, the enthroned Christ in the apse mosaic of Aachen, where he is shown receiving the homage of the twenty-four Elders of the Apocalypse, was inserted in the twelfth or thirteenth century. The present mosaic is a modern restoration, but the figure of Christ was included in its medieval predecessor, recorded in an engraving by Ciampini (Fig. 54). This hypothesis receives a certain corroboration in the late Romanesque form of the throne as shown by Ciampini and in the oddly eccentric placing of the enthroned figure. The Carolingian original, ascribed by Schnitzler to the years between 790 and 800, is said to have shown in its center only the Lamb—a composition that agrees with the text of the Apocalypse and with a good many other representations in early Christian, Carolingian and Romanesque art. It is further pointed out that the image of the Pantocrator occurs only in the earliest and the latest of the great Gospel manuscript of Charlemagne's

53

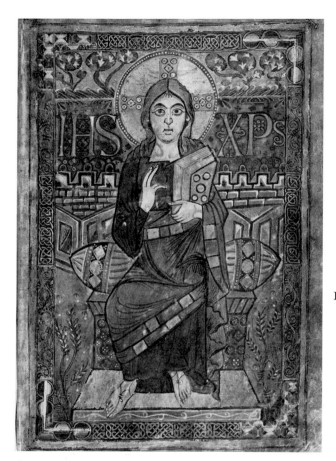

Fig. 57. *Paris*, Bibl. Nat., MS nouv. acq. lat. 1203, Godescalc Gospels. Christ.

palace scriptorium, i.e., the Godescalc Gospels of 781/783 and the Lorsch Gospels (divided between Paris, Alba Julia and the Vatican) of about 810, while it is missing in those which originated in the intervening years, a period, whose anti-iconic attitude is mirrored in the *Libri Carolini*. I must confess that I am greatly impressed by Professor Schnitzler's learned and ingenious arguments without however, being entirely convinced. The reasoning is a little too logical to fit a man like Charlemagne, who was not always guided by logic and consistency. One thing, however, is certain, namely, that anti-iconic tendencies, if not downright iconoclastic ones, did in fact exist during a certain period of Carolingian art and that these tendencies were connected with Charles's anti-Byzantine feelings.

Granted these facts, we must now ask whether anti-Byzantine trends played any part in the choice of prototypes to be used in Carolingian art and in the creation of an artistic language into which these prototypes were to be translated. Since such a language did not yet exist for religious representation, it had to be purposely invented.

54

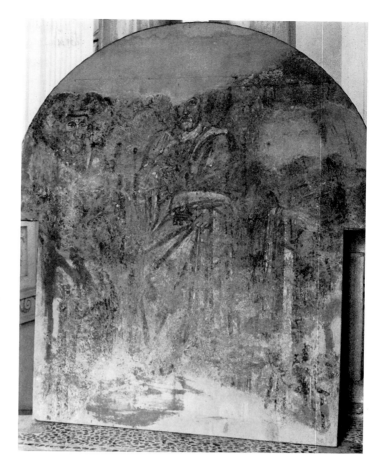

Fig. 58. *Ravenna*, San Vitale,
Wall Painting. Saints.

The earliest product of the court scriptorium, the Godescalc Gospels, commissioned in 781 and completed before 783, antedates the conflict with Byzantium by four years (Fig. 57). However, it also antedates the lifting of the iconoclastic embargo on religious representation in Byzantium itself. Hence there existed no contemporary Byzantine prototype which this first Carolingian Gospel Book with images of Christ and the Evangelists might have followed. The models for the figures thus had to be chosen from contemporary Italian art, from earlier Western books, or from earlier Greek manuscripts. It has been shown by the ingenious and painstaking work of a number of scholars, especially the late Professor Boeckler, Miss Rosenbaum and Professor Buchthal, that, in fact, all three of these sources were tapped. A recent study by Dr. Belting makes it very likely that a first synthesis of these elements was achieved in Ravenna, where the closest parallels to the Evangelists of the Godescalc Gospels were found in eighth century frescoes at San Vitale (Fig. 58).[46] The strongly formalized outlines, the abstract schematism of the figure and its features, the absence of any modeling other than by dark lines—these are in

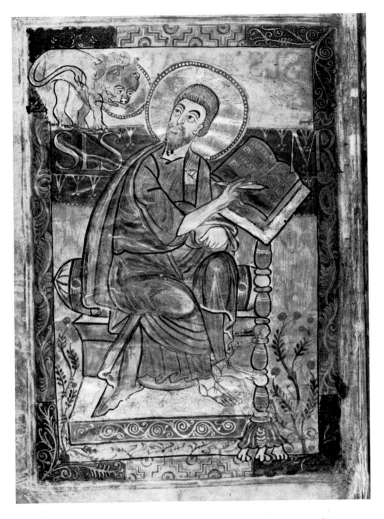

Fig. 59. *Paris*, Bibl. Nat. MS nouv. acq. lat. 1203, Godescalc Gospels.
St. Mark.

fact the main principles of early Carolingian, of Ravennate, and of Roman art as we find it in Santa Maria Antiqua (Fig. 52) and elsewhere. Since this style is a local variant of a provincial Greek style, Charlemagne's Court School started with a certain amount of Byzantine ingredients in its iconographic and stylistic raw material. For one of the four Evangelists however, a profile figure which, while bending forward, turns the head backward and upward (Fig. 59), Professor Buchthal has proved an even closer relationship to Byzantium: the attitude of this St. Mark, which is copied in the Mark of the Soissons Gospels and the Matthew of the Trier Gospels, two somewhat later works of the same scriptorium, must have been derived directly from an early Byzantine source, an ancestor of the eleventh century manuscript No. 1156

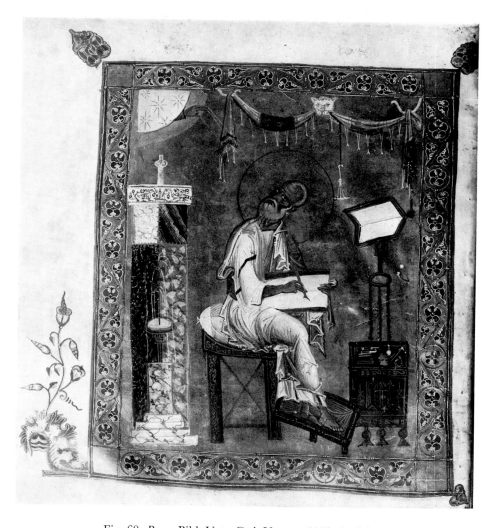

Fig. 60. *Rome*, Bibl. Vat., Cod. Vat. gr. 1156. St. John.

in the Vatican (Fig. 60). Since the iconoclastic controversy began in the 720's, the Byzantine model of the odd Evangelist must have dated from the first quarter of the eighth century at the latest.

In the subsequent and truly magnificent Gospel Books of the Palace School, the London (Harley), the Abbeville, the Trier, the Soissons and the Lorsch Gospels, contemporary Byzantine elements appear for the first time (Fig. 61). The distinguishing mark of the contemporary Byzantine style is the so-called crumpled silk effect, which is clearly visible in the drapery of the St. Mark in the Soissons Gospels, especially on the right thigh, and which is produced by the juxtaposition of oddly shaped, jagged highlights and darker, more or less linear, elements on a ground of medium tonality. A technically much superior

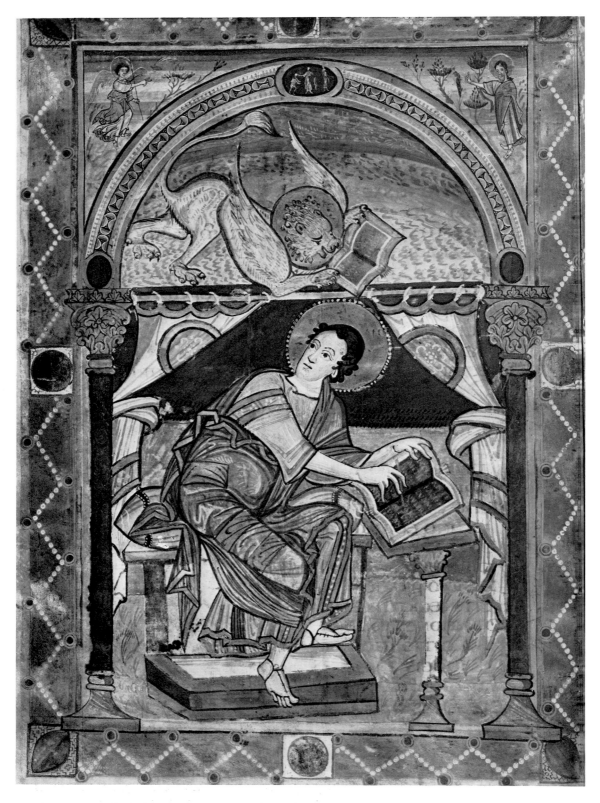

Fig. 61. *Paris*, Bibl. Nat., ms lat. 8850, Soissons Gospels. St. Mark.

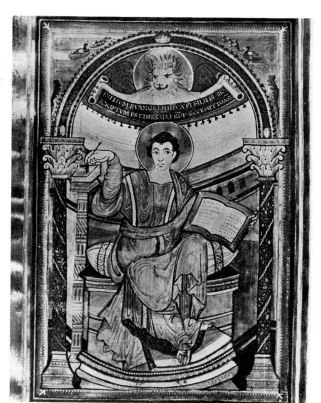

Fig. 62. *Trier*, City Library, Ada Gospels. St. Mark.

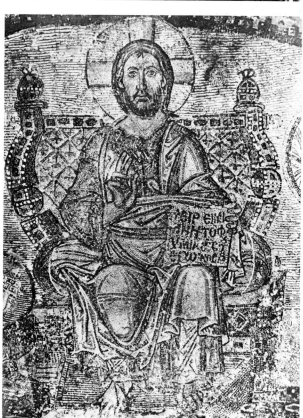

Fig. 63. *Istanbul*, Hagia Sophia, Narthex, Mosaic. The Pantocrator.

version of this style was used in Constantinopolitan manuscripts of the so-called Macedonian Renaissance of the late ninth and the first half of the tenth centuries, such as the Paris Psalter (Fig. 7), but it must be much older.[47]

Several other features of the Court School Evangelists also point to Constantinople. There are details such as the shape of the large hands and the ampleness of the drapery, with sheaves of hanging ends and undulating seams and zigzag hems (Fig. 62). They are seen in Byzantine late ninth century works, e.g., mosaics in Constantinople and Salonica and the miniatures of the Paris Gregory. To be sure, the enthroned Pantocrator of the Haghia Sophia in Constantinople (Fig. 63) is almost a century later than the Mark of the Trier Gospels, and we have to reconstruct the contemporary Byzantine counterpart of the Carolingian Evangelists by interpolation; but there can be no doubt that the new "gorgeous" style of the Court School is derived from one of the styles of contemporary Constantinopolitan art. The lavish use of gold, the rich color scheme with its whites, blues, greens and purples, laid on in bold juxtapositions and contrasts, the technique of jagged shadows and highlights on a medium ground—all this the Carolingian illuminators must have learned from Byzantine models. Of course, they did not copy them. They applied these practices and techniques to the established figure schemes that had been derived from early Italo-Greek prototypes, and they even overdid the effects—as pupils are apt to overdo the mannerisms of their teachers. This crude eclecticism in Carolingian illumination, the mixing of motifs from different realms, the mingling of various styles and modes, brings home the fact that this art was an artificial creation which had not yet had time to mature.

It was not very firmly established either, at least not firmly enough to ward off the intrusion of an entirely different kind of painting which turned up at the court of Charlemagne in the last years of the eighth century (Fig. 64)[48]. The sudden appearance of this new style is one of the most enigmatic facts in the history of early medieval painting. Even the late Professor Koehler, the great historian of Carolingian illumination and one of the soberest scholars in the field, waxes a little mysterious when he writes, in hushed tones as it were, of the sudden arrival of a small group of strangers, two or three artists who had apparently been called to the court by some august personage and been given the commission to write and illustrate a most precious Gospel Book, the one which, according to tradition, was found on the knees of Charlemagne when Otto III opened his tomb in Aachen. Since a long series of German emperors took the oath of office on it, the Gospel Book, now in the Imperial Treasury of Vienna, is one of the great relics of European history.

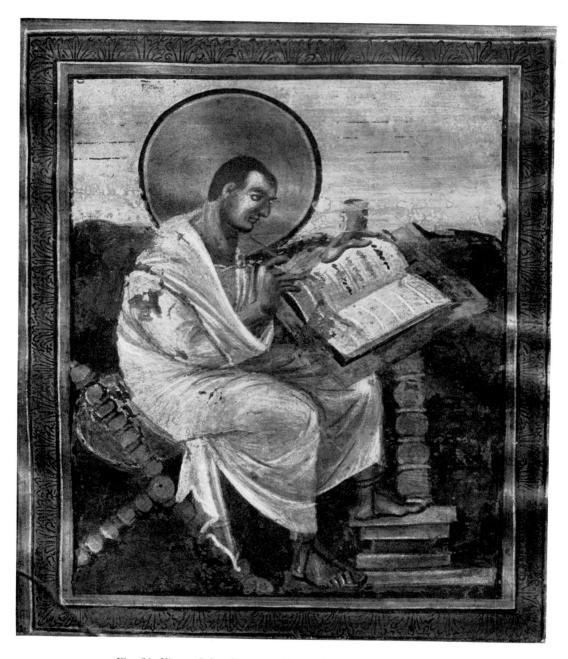

Fig. 64. *Vienna*, Schatzkammer, Coronation Gospels. Evangelist.

It differs from the Gospel Books of the Palace School in almost every aspect of its pictorial decoration to such a degree that Koehler at first placed it, along with its cognates in Aachen, Brussels, and Brescia, a good deal later, after the death of Charlemagne. This dating was, however, corrected by

Koehler himself, who (mainly by textual analysis) proved irrefutably that the foreign artists who produced the Vienna Gospels worked at the same time and probably even side by side with the painters of the Palace School. The athletic figures of the Evangelists are seated in the open; the background is formed by a rudimentary landscape or an exedra, with the horizon placed rather high. The sky is a miracle of rich and, at the same time, subdued coloring, with soft atmospheric effects which also tinge the white, classical garments of the Evangelists. There are no ornamental or linear trappings to these garments; no crumpled silk effects, no transverse cuts heighten the exquisite simplicity of the modeling.

Another Gospel Book, written and illuminated a few years later but still in Charlemagne's lifetime, shares with the Vienna Gospels the background landscape and the iridescent modeling of the Evangelist's white garments. Instead of isolated portraits, however, this manuscript, which is kept in the cathedral treasure at Aachen shows all four figures united on one page, in a hilly landscape which is divided into four compartments. Moreover, the Evangelists are now accompanied by their symbols. The coloristic effect is a bit sharper and less subdued. These features make it quite clear that the Aachen painter, though following the lead of the Vienna artists (there were probably two of them), was a distinct personality. Still another artist was responsible for the Evangelists' portraits (again on one page) of a third Gospel Book, an unfinished codex in the Royal Library of Brussels; he was the weakest of the group and seems to have been something of an outsider. More important and interesting than the four-figure composition of the Brussels codex is an unfinished purple leaf inserted after the binding, which shows a single Evangelist with the background left empty and the frame only lightly delineated (Fig. 65). The figure corresponds to the St. Matthew in the Vienna Gospels, although it is by a different hand. It is, in a way, the most puzzling production of the whole group of pictures connected with the Vienna Gospels, so enigmatic in its impressionist freshness that at its discovery it was actually mistaken for a genuine late antique painting. This opinion has now been discarded and I mention it only to underline one of the most striking characteristics of the whole group namely, their astonishing proximity to late antique or early Christian art.

Indeed, the pictures of the Vienna Gospels and their relatives have no known parallels in the art of their time. This is, first of all, true of the figure types, the costumes and the landscape elements. If we are to inquire into the date of origin of these elements we must go back to the early Christian period, certainly to a time before the sixth and possibly even as far back as the late fourth century. It is in fact quite likely that a very early Gospel Book of,

62

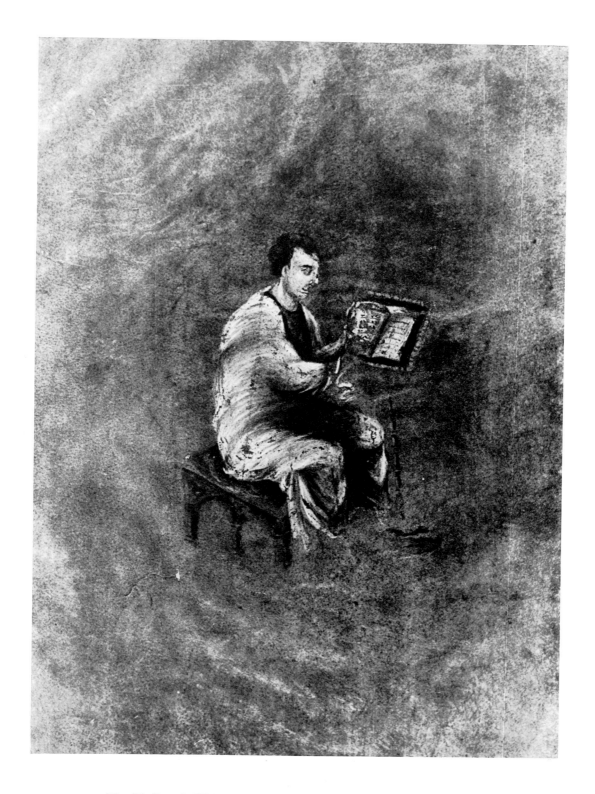

Fig. 65. *Brussels*, Bibl. Royale, ms 18723, Gospel Book. Seated Evangelist.

perhaps, Roman origin was the actual model which the Vienna painters used. But how was it possible for these painters to enter so perfectly into the spirit of early pictorial illusionism that they did not in any way betray their connection with contemporary, that is, late eighth century art? Where could they have received the training that enabled them to cope so successfully with their late antique models? And who chose the early models and was responsible for this retrospective trend? What was its aim? In the twilight of these question Koehler's reticence becomes understandable.

Strangers, foreigners, these artists certainly were; this is one thing of which we can be certain. Another is that they must have received their training in a school in which Hellenistic forms were still alive, and this school must have been connected with Byzantium, that center of perennial Hellenism. Thus they could only have come either from Byzantium itself or from Byzantine Italy. Was there in Byzantine art a brief period of unconditional return to the Hellenistic sources of Christian art, an experimental and perhaps abortive renascence preceding the revival of the late ninth century? If so, it must have been the period immediately after Nicaea, directly following the reestablishment of religious figurative art in Constantinople. It is just conceivable that a style which sought an unqualified return to early Christian Hellenism was one of the many paths tried out in this brief period that was again followed by a resurgence of iconoclasm (which, however mild, may have put a stop to some of the bolder experiments).

The second possibility, which was likewise envisaged by Koehler and which is favored by Professor Schapiro, is Byzantine Italy. Naturally, there was no need, in Italy, for an experimental groping in order to find new paths for religious art after the Council of 787, since images had never been forbidden there. Thus a strong and uninterrupted evolution did exist in Italy, an evolution which, as has been pointed out earlier, followed a very definite trend toward the linear and had, by the end of the eighth century, reached a very high degree of schematization. No artist who had grown up in this tradition and who was rooted in this development could have painted the Vienna Evangelists. It is, however, not impossible that one or another of the painters who participated in the experiments of the late eighth century in Constantinople had actually found his way to Rome—and was invited to Aachen soon afterwards.

A reexamination of the Vienna Evangelists in the light of these considerations may help us in choosing between the two alternative possibilities, Constantinople or Rome. There is one feature in the Vienna miniatures, the least admirable feature of all, which seems to point directly to Byzantium: the lack

64

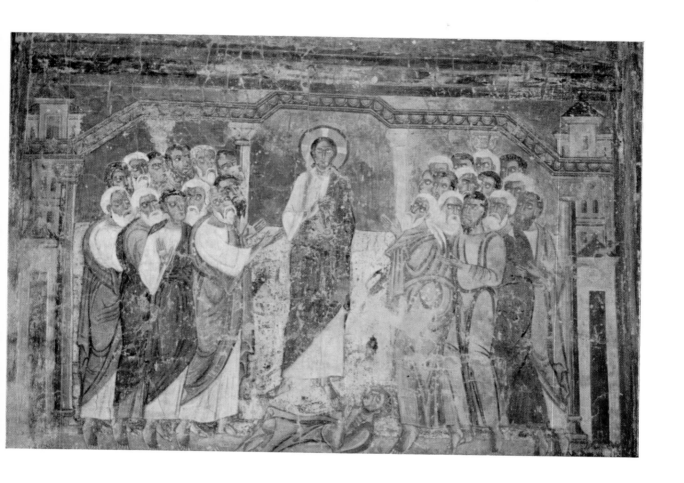

III   *Lambach,* Austria, Wall Painting. Christ in the Synagogue.

of adhesion of the colors to the ground. There is considerable flaking—a phenomenon which is only too well known to all students of Byzantine manuscripts. Byzantine miniatures are quite often in a ruinous state—something which practically never happens in Western manuscripts. Another feature is the big hands with their bold contours and strong modeling. These too occur in Byzantium: they are among the hallmarks of Byzantine ninth century arts. I am sure a Byzantine Morelli would find yet a few more features of this kind, so that the Constantinopolitan origin or training of the Vienna painters might become very plausible indeed. In any case, whether arriving in Aachen directly from Constantinople or after a more or less protracted residence in Italy, the "strangers" of Professor Koehler must have been Greeks. It is possible that one of them actually inscribed his name—Demetrius presbyter—on the margin of the Luke page of the Vienna Gospels (although some scholars believe this inscription to be somewhat later).

The painters of the Aachen and of the Brussels Evangelists did not add much that was new to the style imported by the Vienna painters, but they adapted its monumental grandeur to the scale of miniatures and, as must be said of the Aachen painter, even refined its coarseness. For our admiration of the Hellenistic freedom of the style of the Vienna pictures should not blind us to the defects of the rough and ready art of their painters.

Although the actual output of the "foreigners" was not at all large, the style introduced and fashioned by them had a great future, greater, in a way, than that of the Palace ("Ada") School. The Palace style was, it is true, copied, developed, reduced to its essentials and elaborated again, right down to the Romanesque period. Its offspring are legion, but most of them belong to archaizing trends. As the leading principles of the style were stately decoration and ornamental surface differentiation, it tended to evolve toward the precious, the complicated, the elaborate. It offered to skillful artisans wonderful possibilities of hiding essential weaknesses under yet a few more garlands of undulating folds and zigzag seams. Thus it does not seem to have led to anything new. The "Hellenistic" style of the Vienna Gospels, on the other hand, appears to have provided the basis for a most interesting and lively development. It is odd that this development should have begun only about twenty years later; at least we do not know anything about possible links between the Vienna Gospels and the Gospel Book of Ebbo, Archbishop of Reims, a book that was probably completed shortly before 820 (Fig. 66).[49] However, all of this difference in date is needed to explain the staggering change to which the style of the Vienna Gospels was subjected by the Reims painter: the quietly draped classical garments have become rotating, whirring cocoons, the close

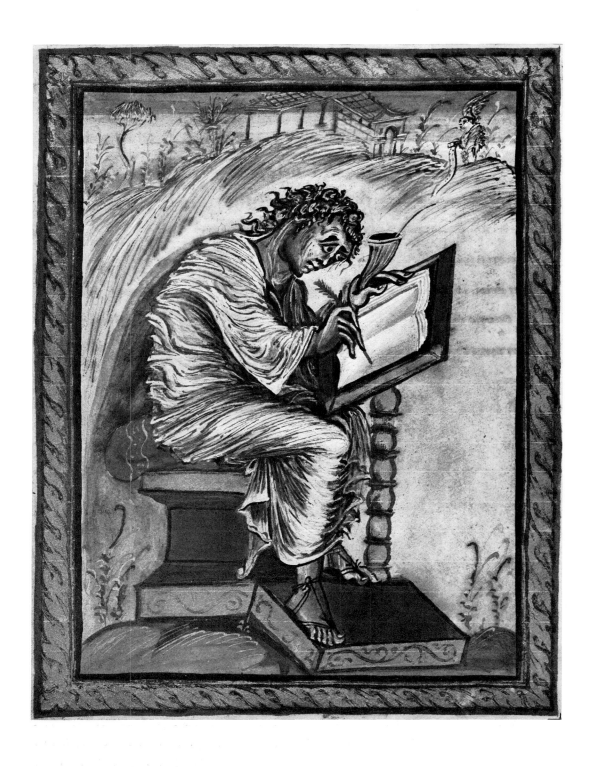

Fig. 66. *Epernay*, Bibl. Municipale, MS 1, Ebbo Gospels. St. Matthew.

caps of hair have been turned into nests of snakes, the sturdy pugilists have been replaced by hysterical visionaries or poets. All the same, there can be no doubt that the Vienna Gospel Book not only was the model for the composition, figure types, landscape and coloring of the Ebbo pictures, but also provided the technical and stylistic means which the Northern painter used in his magnificent and near-blasphemous reinterpretation of his classical model. It is unthinkable that the style of the Palace School could have served as a point of departure for this new agitated art: the picturesque expressionism of Reims, which later on bore fruit in England, could only grow out of an art which had as its underlying principle the painterly freedom of Hellenistic painting. Professor Tselos has argued that the Vienna Gospels was not the only source of this kind from which the school of Reims derived its raw material and its inspiration. He pointed at the very strong Greek elements to be found, for instance, in the Utrecht Psalter (Fig. 67), elements of Hellenistic illusionism which must have entered the Latin tradition of psalter illustration between its origin in early Christian art and its reception by Carolingian artists. That the sketchy illusionism is actually found in Greek works, has lately been corroborated by the engravings of the Moses Cross in Saint Catherine on Mt. Sinai, published by Professors Weitzmann and Ševčenko (Fig. 68).[50]

The integration of Greek and Latin elements which became so important for the Reims style must have happened in some Greco-Italian center, most likely in Rome itself. For the art of Reims and for the later developments inspired by Reims, namely the art of northern France, the Meuse country and England, these Greek elements were a kind of leaven, which seems to have had the effect of fermenting the inert mass of the Latin legacy.

For it was with resuscitating and reactivating this legacy, the legacy of Christian Rome, that Carolingian art was primarily concerned—and by the art of Rome we mean an art which includes that of Ravenna as well. A case in point is Charlemagne's palace in Aachen. He gave it the Roman name of the "Lateran" but he actually copied San Vitale in Ravenna in his palace church; and San Vitale is a Byzantine building. It is true that both these statements have been challenged. But even if San Vitale should be the work of a Latin architect, as Professor Krautheimer has very convincingly argued, this master must have studied Constantinopolitan architecture so profoundly that his work presents itself as an extension of metropolitan art rather than as a provincial copy.[51] As regards the second question, no extant building anywhere is so close to Aachen as San Vitale; stylistic differences should not blind us to the fact that there is a definite connection between the two buildings.[52] We know, further, that Charlemagne stayed in Ravenna in the time

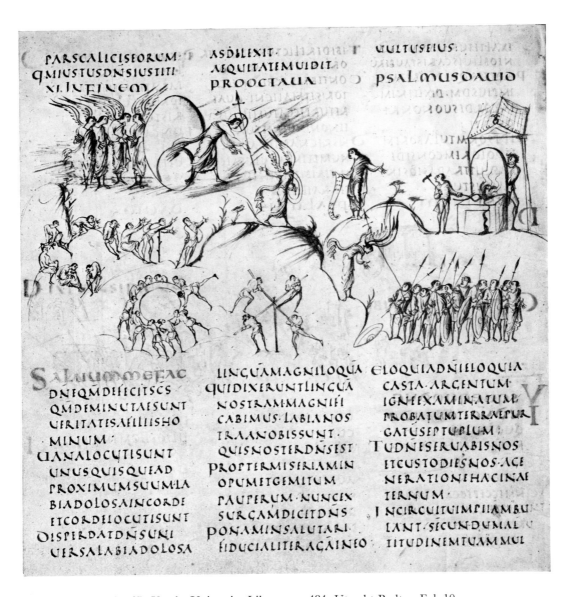

Fig. 67. *Utrecht*, University Library, MS 484, Utrecht Psalter, Fol. 10 v.

between 787 and 801, and that he stripped the Exarch's Palace of precious building material to have it shipped to Aachen, together with the presumed equestrian statue of Theodoric. In the light of these facts it is surely gratuitous to look for other prototypes, in the Chrysotriklinos of the Sacred Palace of Constantinople, in Asia Minor or in Milan.

Another question is why the scheme of San Vitale was adopted for the Palace Chapel. The general attraction must have been the regal or, rather, the imperial character of the building, but there may have been an additional

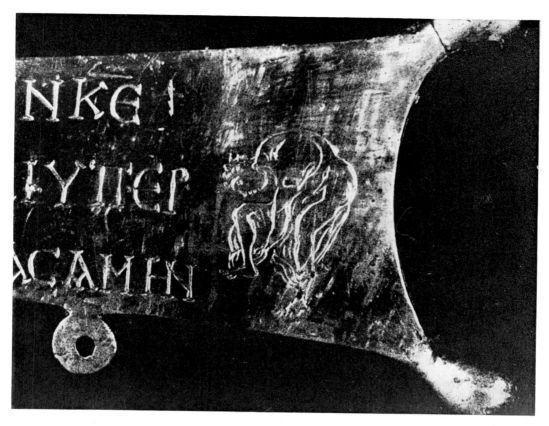

Fig. 68. *Sinai*, Monastery of St. Catherine, Engraved Cross. Moses taking off his shoes.

reason, for which the translocation of the equestrian statue may be the key: it is very likely that Charlemagne believed San Vitale to have been the palace chapel of Theodoric, in whom he saw his forerunner, perhaps even his model as a Germanic ruler of Italy. However, there is no reason to believe that San Vitale was actually begun before Theodoric's death in 526; and even if it were, it was certainly never meant to become his palace chapel. Furthermore, if Agnello's hints are justified, the equestrian statue was not Theodoric's either, but the Byzantine emperor Zeno's, usurped by Theodoric. It would be an ironic *quid pro quo* indeed if it turned out that Charlemagne twice made the mistake of choosing for his Aachen residence Byzantine works which were masquerading as creations of Theodoric.

Generally speaking, Ravenna must have been very much in the foreground of Charlemagne's thoughts—it seems to have occupied the place immediately after Rome in his mind. Miss Rosenbaum has shown that at least one of the models of Palace School illumination was a Ravenna Gospel Book; the closest parallels to the style of the Godescalc Gospels have been found in frescoes of

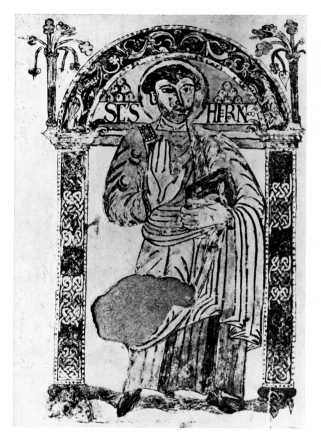 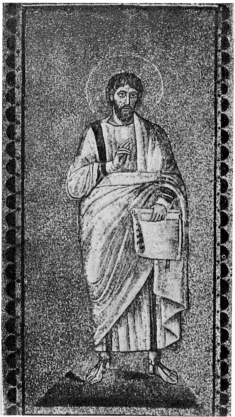

Fig. 69. *Vienna*, Nat. Bibl., Cod. lat. 1332. St. Jerome.

Fig. 70. *Ravenna*, Sant'Apollinare Nuovo, Mosaic. Prophet.

the eighth century in San Vitale. Influences from the mosaics of Sant Apollinare Nuovo were discovered by Dr. Holter and Professor Wright in the provincial scriptoria of Salzburg and Mondsee (Fig. 69, 70),[53] and it is very likely that Ravenna also provided the prototypes, iconographical and stylistic, of some of the best Carolingian ivory carvings.

There is no doubt that most Carolingian ivories were inspired—directly or through book illumination—by Italian fifth century art. The proximity of some copies to their models is—or was believed to be—so close that no consensus has been reached as to whether certain works, such as the Andrews diptych, are early Christian originals or Carolingian replicas. However, not all Carolingian ivories followed Western prototypes; there are a few which took their cue from Constantinopolitan ivory carvings of the early sixth century. About one of them, the Monza Diptych, opinion is again divided: some scholars like Mr. Beckwith think it a Carolingian imitation, while most authors

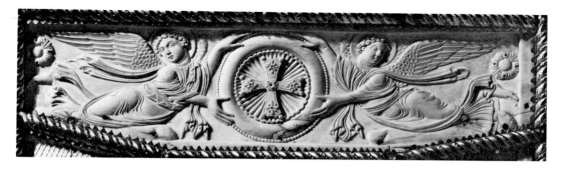

Fig. 71. *Rome*, Bibl. Vat., Lorsch Diptych. Upper part.

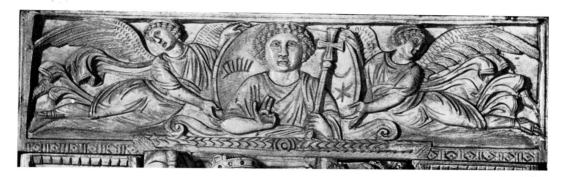

Fig. 72. *Paris*, Louvre, Barberini Diptych. Upper part.

see in it a pair of reworked early Byzantine originals.[54] A similar doubt clings to a part of the most elaborate Carolingian ivory diptych, the book cover of the Lorsch Gospels, which is divided between the Vatican and the Victoria and Albert Museum.[55] The top part of the Vatican leaf (Fig. 71), which shows two flying Angels carrying a medallion with the Cross, was thought by the late Professor Morey to be an early Byzantine original of about 500 and it figures as such in his Vatican catalogue. Damage at an early date was thought to have been responsible for the odd shape of this part, whose form and technique are said to have inspired the style of the rest. Ingenious as this hypothesis is—it would seem to account for the irregular structure of the whole which differs from all known early Byzantine diptychs—it has been abandoned by most scholars and rightly so, because the rhythmic, form-defining outlines have no true parallel in the art of the late fifth or the early sixth century. This feature is already an elaboration; its medieval and Northern character becomes quite clear if we compare it with the plastic boldness and the painterly, almost illusionistic quality of an early Byzantine original such as the top part of the Barberini Diptychon in the Louvre (Fig. 72). The two leaves of the Lorsch diptych (Figs. 73, 74) must have been carved in a rather large studio

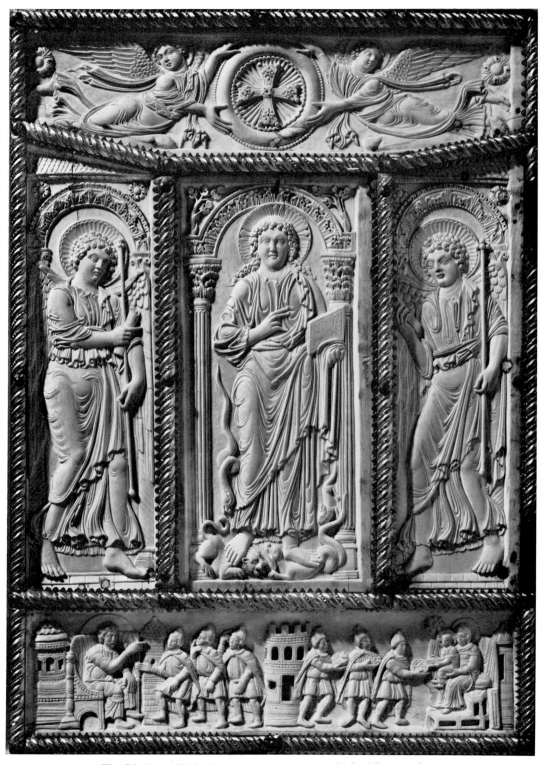

Fig. 73. *Rome*, Bibl. Vat., Lorsch Diptych. Christ between Angels.

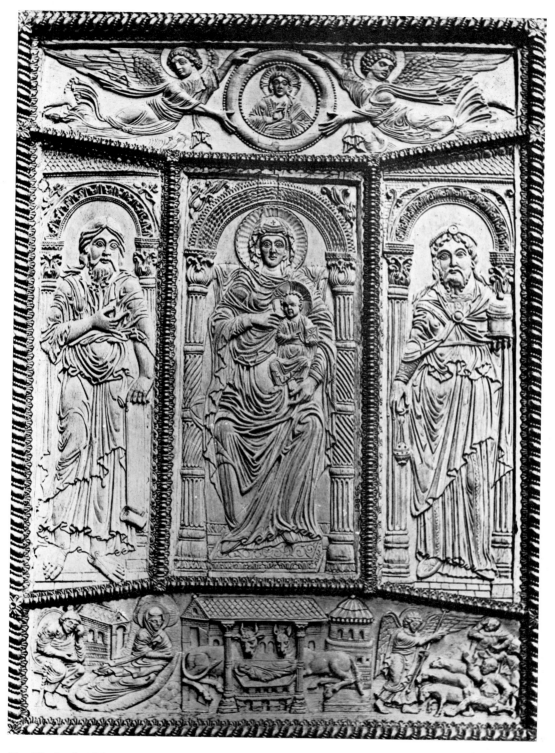

Fig. 74. *London*, Victoria and Albert Museum, Lorsch Diptych. The Virgin between St. John the Baptist and Zacharias.

where several artists worked side by side, using a number of models of ~~varoius~~ dates. It has been claimed, for instance, that the composition of the left wing, with the youthful Christ treading on the Beasts in the center and two Angels turning toward Him, follows an earlier or, at least, more "classical" model than the right wing, with the enthroned Virgin and the two almost frontal figures of the Baptist and Zacharias. While this does not seem entirely convincing, it is certainly true that different models were used for the two halves and that this led to a difference in carving technique. The drapery of Christ and the Angels is composed of thin, linear folds which not only follow the relief of the body but overemphasize it with sharply bent curves; the whole looks more like a delicate drawing then a plastically differentiated relief. In contrast, the folds of the right wing are deep furrows which form a more angular pattern, cutting up the surface rather than shaping it. The model of the left wing may have shown a style even more classical than that of the Vienna diptych with the allegorical figures of Roma and Constantinopolis, of the sixth century (Figs. 75, 76); the sensitively modeled relief of the body and the linear design of the drapery is strikingly similar in both. Even details, such as the hanging folds over the thighs seem to be prefigured in the early prototype, with which the Carolingian relief also shares details of costume; as a matter of fact, in the left Angel the artist seems to have combined the gathered-up seams of the upper garment of Roma with the diagonal hem of the toga of Constantinopolis. This does not mean, of course, that he actually used the Vienna diptych as a model, but that he must have seen something like it. What is, however, more interesting and more important than the agreements between the style of the model and that of the Carolingian derivative, are the misunderstandings, creative and otherwise. The three figures, though they all exhibit the imprint of a common workshop style, show different interpretations of the model's plastic vocabulary. In the left Angel, the best of the three and somewhat akin to the Angels of the top part, the form-defining lines that emerge from the smooth relief of the thigh curve to the right and disappear into "space," implying in this way the three-dimensional, statuesque quality of the figure. There is no such implication in the figure of Christ; there, the curving folds which accompany the left contour, turn back, as it were, to complete their hook-shaped course on the front side. The drapery of the right-hand Angel is again different: it is much straighter and thus lacks the form-defining vigor of the two other figures' draperies. This variety of handling discloses an experimental attitude on the part of the late eighth century carvers, a catch-as-catch-can grappling with a model whose true qualities were still beyond their abilities—not only of assimilation but also of understanding.

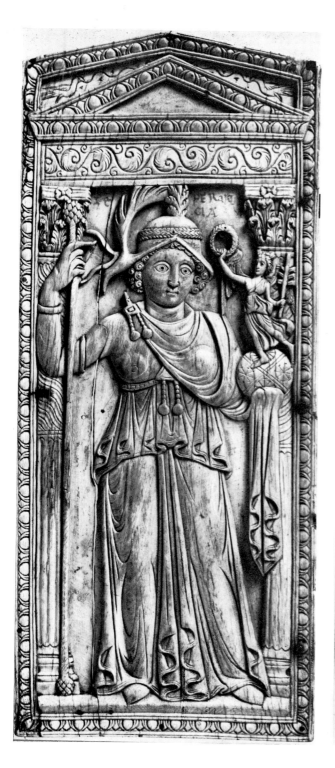 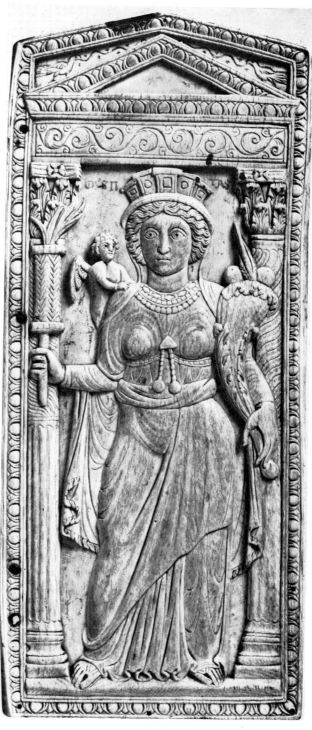

Fig. 75. *Vienna*, Kunsthistorisches Museum, Ivory Plaque. Roma.

Fig. 76. *Vienna*, Kunsthistorisches Museum, Ivory Plaque. Constantinopolis.

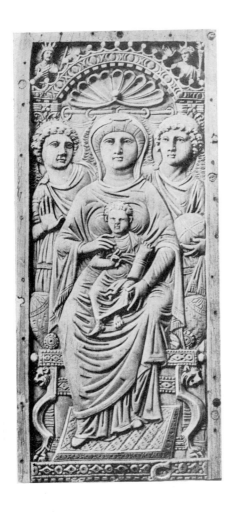

Fig. 77. *Berlin*, Staatliche Museen,
Ivory Plaque. The Virgin.

The model which served for the figure of the Virgin in the center of the second leaf—the back cover of the Lorsch Gospels—seems to have been easier for the Carolingian carvers to understand. It must have been a Constantinopolitan work of the second quarter of the sixth century, somewhat akin to, but probably even later than, the relief of the Virgin of the Berlin diptych (Fig. 77). In this prototype, the folds apparently did not twine round the body as closely as in the models used for the front panel; they had already lost something of their organic quality; three-dimensional effects were sought not through suggestive curves but through a play of light and shade in patterns which approach the abstract; the folds are carved into the surface rather than rising from it. The model must have been one akin to those reliefs on the Cathedra of Maximinianus in Ravenna in which the strained illusionism of the earlier reign of Justinian is suddenly "turning abstract." Again, many of the subtleties of this critical style must have been beyond the Carolingian interpreters; in order to hide the defects of their translation, they covered them with multiple folds and seams, thus creating a pattern at least as rich as that of the painted Evangelists of the Gospel Book to which the ivory plaques belonged. Thus the plaques are true works of the court style of the Palace School, typifying the general attitude of Carolingian art toward the art of Byzantium.

Now, what was this attitude, and what does the Byzantine element in Carolingian art amount to? What was its rôle in the formation of the first official Christian art of the Western Middle Ages?[56] There is the octagonal scheme of the Palace Chapel at Aachen, the center and symbol of the Sacrum Imperium; it had a certain effect on Ottonian building, but did not really influence the main trends of Western architecture. In wall painting, the impact of Byzantium on Frankish art may at first have been rather negative, working as it did against the development of a full Christological cycle and, perhaps, even against the monumental representation of the Deity. Carolingian book illumination and ivory carving profited more from Byzantine models. Certain figure types, schemes and attitudes were taken over together with specific methods of modeling, surface differentiation and coloring. A closely knit texture of minute forms which, in book illumination, can be interpreted as the play of light and shade and, in ivory carving actually produces this play, was substituted with the help of contemporary Byzantine models for the desiccated linear schemes provided by Italian prototypes. This must have been the first initiation of Western medieval artists into the mysteries of illusionism. A second and even more thorough initiation was provided by the art of those Greeks or Graeco-Italians who painted the Evangelists of the Vienna Gospels, with their soft modeling and the atmospheric effects of their setting. A third initiation, finally, was offered by the Italo-Greek models of the Utrecht Psalter or the Bern Physiologus, which combined late antique illusionism with the temperamental sketchiness of an inspired linearism.

These three lessons contained the most important leads which Byzantine art was able to give to Carolingian artists. Some of them were disregarded because they came too early and without proper preparation. But others bore fruit which was to ripen in later times. But these influences, however important, seem to have occurred without actually being intended. So far as the attitude of the leading men was articulated at all, it was directed against the Byzantine conception of sacred art. It would, on the other hand, be a mistake to interpret this attitude as a conscious and consistent rejection of everything Byzantine in art and in all other things. The break of 787 between Charlemagne and Byzantium had lost its edge a decade later and it is very likely that this was the time when Koehler's mysterious strangers arrived. Charlemagne's coronation by the Pope in the year 800, which at first seemed to have caused a complete rupture between the two empires, actually led Irene to seek an understanding with the dangerous new power in the West. There were again legations coming and going. It was even rumored in Constantinople that Irene contemplated a marriage proposal, a very unpopular attitude which may have contributed to her downfall. Her successor soon renewed hostilities: between 805 and 811 there was war in the Adriatic. However, the threat of the Bulgars soon forced Byzantium to come to an arrangement with Charlemagne even at the price of recognizing his imperial title: an embassy of Michael I arrived in Aachen in 812 to conclude a treaty which for a long time remained the basis of the relationship between the two empires.

Thus there was plenty of opportunity for Byzantine works of art to reach Aachen, and even for artists, since they quite often accompanied embassies of this kind. Some of the gifts they brought, such as the silver table with the plan of Constantinople, were thought important enough to be mentioned in Charlemagne's will. Other Byzantine works came to Aachen by way of Italy, such as the two carved ivory doors which the Patriarch Fortunatus of Grado brought to France in 803.[57] There must have been a great deal of this, and it is actually surprising that the influence of Byzantine art was not greater. As a matter of fact, the Carolingian system seems to have had little use for Byzantine art as such. What Charlemagne and his circle were really after was the art of the Roman Christian Empire, an art which fitted the all-pervading idea of the *Renovatio Imperii Romani*. Of course, their notion of what this Roman art really was, must have been rather hazy: they looked for it in Rome itself, in Ravenna, perhaps also in Milan, but not in Byzantium where they would have found its only legitimate and living continuation.

If in spite of this quest for the art of Christian Rome—perhaps seen as the art of Constantine, Theodosius or Theodoric—certain Byzantine elements actually did take root in Carolingian art, they came there almost by chance and were accepted by mistake. It was an odd *quid pro quo* and yet one in which we can now see a deeper meaning: for Byzantine models—their true nature mostly unrecognized—were used because of their "antique," their classical qualities which assisted Carolingian artists and their patrons in promoting the great revival they were seeking to achieve. Thus their mistake was, after all, one of the most fruitful mistakes in the history of Western art.

3

Towards the Romanesque

It was about 200 years after Charlemagne, that Byzantine art again came to play a part in the Western development. This time, however, there was no *quid pro quo* about it, no mistake, however fruitful. Byzantine works of art recommended themselves to Western potentates—especially to the Saxon emperors of the Ottonian period—not because they were regarded as Roman, but just because they were Byzantine.[58] Greek ivories—almost contemporary products of Constantinopolitan art—were set in golden covers to enclose imperial Gospel Books; they were thought to be at least as precious as the gems that surrounded them. An itinerant Byzantine artist was commissioned to paint the most holy parts of the two holiest pictures in a Gospel Book which Henry III ordered to be produced in the scriptorium of Echternach about 1045 as a gift for Speyer cathedral: heads, hands and feet of Christ and the Virgin (and an Angel's head) in the dedicatory images of the Codex Aureus Escurialensis stand out in technique (the flaking is a sure sign of genuine Byzantine technique), in color and in form from the rest of the miniatures (Fig. 78).[59] These details are painted in a style which is still reminiscent of that of the Menologium of Basil II, in Rome (Fig. 79), although it is half a century later and, consequently, somewhat harder and drier. The contrast between the oily looking heads and the pastel shaded colors of all the other forms apparently did not seem as jarring to eleventh century eyes as it does to ours. It is even likely that this contrast was intended or, at least, welcome: the Byzantine heads were treated like rare gems to be set in the center of the picture—like those gems with antique heads which form the centerpieces of golden crosses, such as the so-called Lothar Cross of Aachen. The heads in the Escorial miniatures are meant to look foreign or, rather, to look specifically Byzantine, just as some Ottonian miniatures parade Greek inscriptions. It does not matter that their Greek is often faulty—this is even the rule; it is enough that they look Greek. The new enthusiasm for things Byzantine

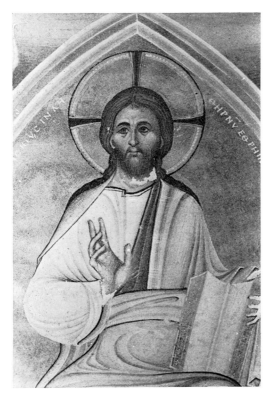

Fig. 78. *Escorial*, Codex Aureus.
Christ, Detail.

was more than a matter of fashion: it involved a change of attitude, deep enough to have an archibishop of Cologne represent himself in the Byzantine posture of proskynesis, prostrated in front of the enthroned St. Peter, or to make patrons, such as Meinwerk of Paderborn, boast about employing Greek artists even if these *operarii graeci* only came from Apulia.

It goes without saying that this new attitude, which is not entirely devoid of snobism, came from the top, from the ruler. With the *renovatio* of the *Imperium* and its title in 962, Otto the Great put in his claim for equality with the Eastern Empire.[60] The awe in which the latter was held in the West, because of its age and its unbroken tradition from Augustus and Constantine, made it desirable to have this claim recognized by the reception of the Western ruler into the imperial family. Thus Liutprand of Cremona, one of the most observant and most inept of envoys, was sent to Constantinople in 968, to ask for the hand of a royal princess for Otto's son, Otto II. How and why Liutprand was snubbed and sent packing—after having had to unpack his luggage and leave behind silks and other valuables under export embargo— makes excellent reading even today, when sudden departures of unsuccessful ambassadors are daily occurrences. Success came, however, in 972: Otto was acknowledged as Emperor of the Franks, and the hand of a princess was granted to his son, a princess who was not a *porphyrogenita* but a near relative

80

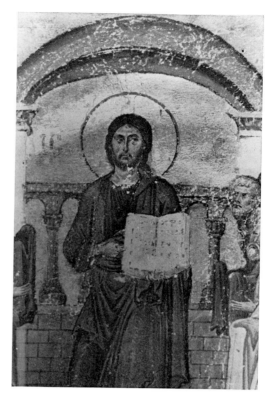

Fig. 79. *Rome*, Bibl. Vat., Cod. gr. 1613, Menologium of Basilius II. Christ, Detail.

of the reigning emperor, the usurper John Tzimiskes. However, the bride, Theophanou, seems to have been something better than a "purple-born" princess, namely, a born empress. When her husband Otto II died in 982 just after having proclaimed himself *Imperator Romanorum* (not *francorum!*) (thus invading the jealously guarded preserve of the Byzantine emperor, which inevitably led to war with the Greeks) Theophanou took up the reins of government for her infant son, the later Otto III, until her death in 991. She certainly convinced the Germans that Greek princesses made good empresses and that the two empires had to find a *modus vivendi*. So, four years later— the differences had been patched up in the meantime—an embassy was again sent to Constantinople to ask once more for the hand of an imperial princess, this time for Otto III who was just coming of age. Considering Otto's policy of the *Renovatio Imperii Romani*, the negotiations proved as difficult as might be expected. When, after legations in 997 and 998, a Byzantine princess, this time a member of the legitimate dynasty, finally arrived in Bari in 1002, the young suitor, half Greek, half Saxon, was already dead.

It would be idle (but attractive) to speculate on the course which events might have taken, had Otto lived, and had a son of Otto and of his Byzantine bride, an emperor three-quarters Greek and only one-quarter Saxon, ascended the throne of the West. For the arts, the outcome might have been

81

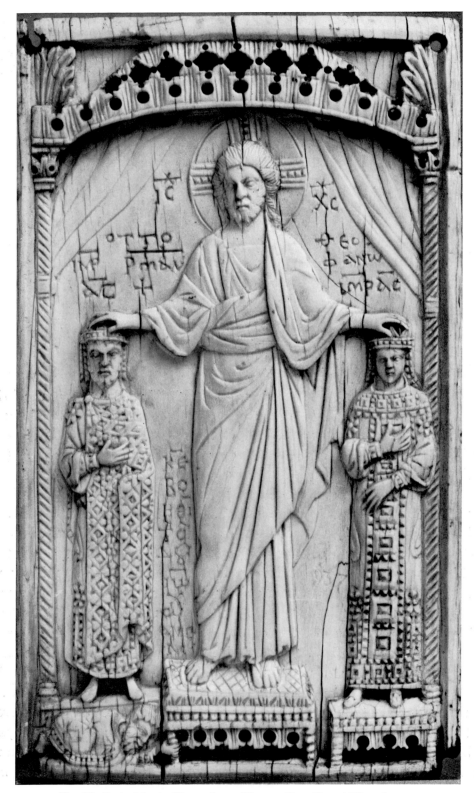

Fig. 80. *Paris*, Musée Cluny, Ivory Plaque. Otto II and Theophanou.

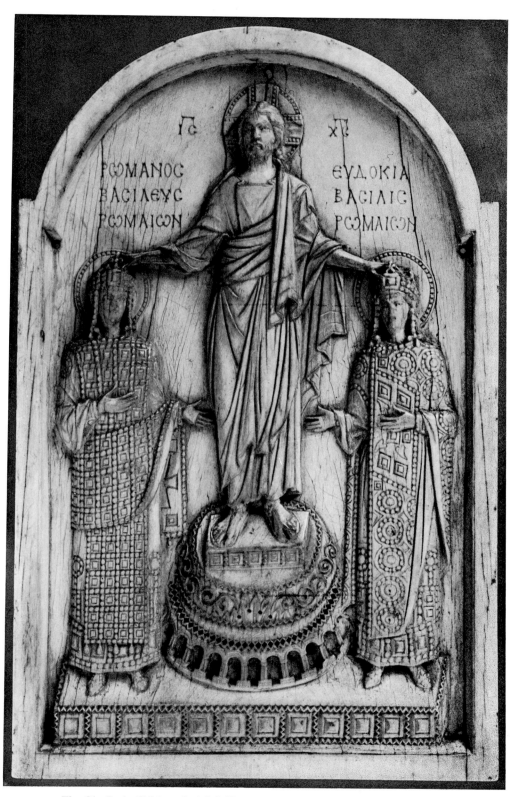

Fig. 81. *Paris*, Cabinet de Médailles, Ivory Plaque. Romanos and Eudokia.

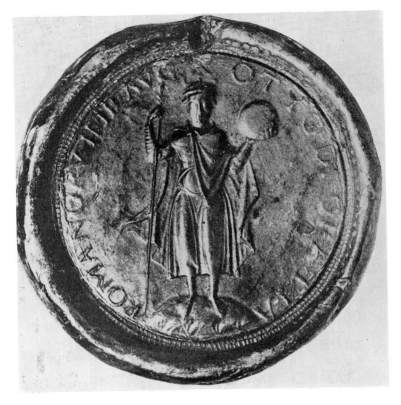

Fig. 82. *Heidelberg,*
Universitätsbibliothek,
Original diploma D.O.
III 249 for St. Stephen
in Mainz, of 15. 7. 997:
Seal of Otto III, of 997.

a real amalgamation of Western and Eastern traditions, leading to the establishment of a truly European art, connected with its classical past by an unbroken tradition. As it was, the Greek element, which was introduced in the West by the rapprochement of the late tenth century, was not strong enough to produce a synthesis, but it did serve as a catalyst, triggering and conditioning a development the outcome of which we call the Romanesque, while our great-grandfathers called it the Byzantine style. The earlier designation is no more incorrect than is ours. In German art at least, the Greek element appears to have been as strong as the Roman, and in certain currents even stronger. How difficult it is to tell Eastern and Western works apart is shown by the somewhat mysterious ivory representing Otto II and Theophanou (Fig. 80). It was first regarded as a marriage present given to the young couple by the Greek emperor; subsequently, however, it was pointed out that the title of *Imperator Romanorum* which appears above Otto's head would certainly not have been accorded to him by any Byzantine functionary, let alone the emperor himself, and that no Constantinopolitan Greek would have made the grammatical error of calling Theophanou *Augustos* (Alpha Sigma) instead of *Augusta* or *Auguste*. So the opinion of historians and art historians shifted toward the hypothesis that the inscription was a later Western addition to a

84

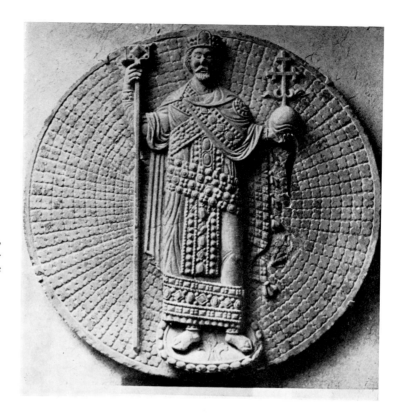

Fig. 83. *Washington*, D.C., Dumbarton Oaks Collection, Roundel. Byzantine Emperor.

Constantinopolitan relief, originally representing a different, namely, a Greek, imperial couple. More recently it has been pointed out that the relief itself contains some errors of costume and also a certain roughness of texture and design which, in comparison with an indubitably Greek relief like that of Romanos and Eudokia (Fig. 81), makes a metropolitan origin unlikely. The correct solution seems to have been suggested by Professor Schramm, who sees in the tiny figure of the donor at the feet of Christ the Calabrian monk Joannes Philagathos, later bishop of Piacenza and teacher of Otto III, and for some time even an antipope. The provincial peculiarities both of figures and inscriptions may be explained by proposing that the work was actually made in a Greek workshop in southern Italy.[61]

It is thoroughly in keeping with the political aspirations of the Saxon rulers, including Henry II, that like the Byzantine emperors, they had themselves represented as crowned by Christ and that in general, they modeled their official portraiture, at least in part, after that of their Eastern counterparts. Seals of Otto III show him standing frontally with orb and tall scepter (Fig. 82), very much in the manner of Byzantine emperors—Byzantine examples are found in seals, coins and reliefs, like the one in Dumbarton Oaks or its companion piece in Venice (Fig. 83).

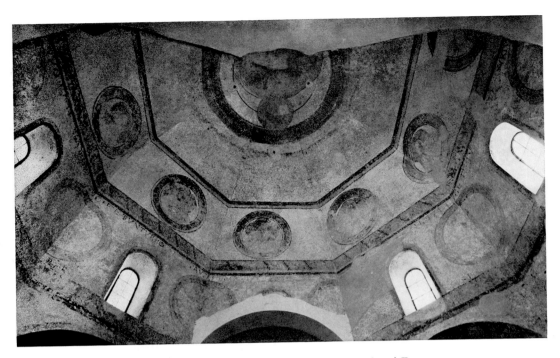

Fig. 84. *Wieselburg*, Austria, Parish Church, Painted Dome.

Small wonder, then, that the imperial coloring of Byzantine religious iconography[16] also obtained a firm hold on Ottonian ecclesiastical art. Christ as Pantocrator, enthroned or represented in half-figure enclosed in a medallion, the most sacred representation of Byzantine monumental art, which so far seems to have figured in the West only in the minor arts, now turns up, if our dating is correct, in German monumental painting: the cupola paintings in Wieselburg, Lower Austria (Fig. 84) or, rather, the elusive shadows of them which have lately come to light, seem to be the remnants of a decoration that may well go back to Wolfgang, the sainted Bishop of Ratisbon and prime minister of Otto the Great.[62] Better preserved works, such as the newly discovered preparatory drawings of Angels in the Porch Chapel of Frauenchiemsee in Bavaria (Fig. 85),[63] still show something of the hieratic magnificence of their Byzantine prototypes, which must have looked somewhat like the great ninth century mosaic figures in the bema of Hagia Sophia in Constantinople (Fig. 86). The new and, for the West, revolutionary quality of these models and their Ottonian elaborations is their monumental grandeur, their solemn strength, their "awful symmetry." Compared with these stern shapes, Carolingian figures look elegant—and almost frivolous.

Middle Byzantine art offered a lesson not only in monumentality of form but also in expression. This is not to say that Carolingian art was lacking in expression. But it was either sentimental, lyrical concentration, or explosive excitement and both these qualities are felt as moods of the artist rather than

86

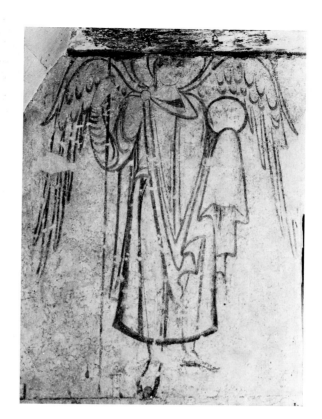

Fig. 85. *Frauenchiemsee*, Bavaria,
Porch Chapel. Angel.

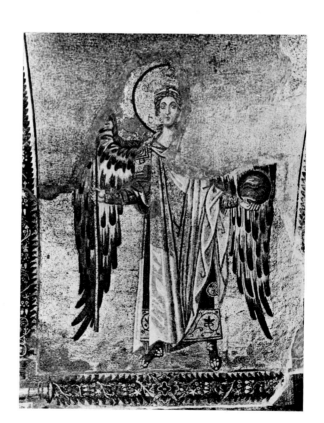

Fig. 86. *Istanbul*, Hagia Sophia, Mosaic.
Archangel.

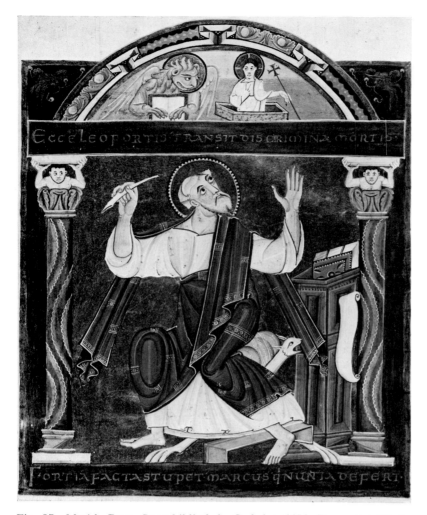

Fig. 87. *Munich*, Bayr. Staatsbibliothek, Cod. lat. 4454. Evangelist Mark.

those of the figures themselves objectively manifested in their bodies and faces. The excitement of Ebo's Evangelists (Fig. 66) is a product of the painter's temperament, while the ecstasy of the Reichenau visionaries is their own. (Fig. 87).

The lesson leading to these results may have begun with the representation of the crucified Christ. We know now that the representation of the dead Christ who still shows the signs of his suffering originated in Byzantium, not in the late eleventh century, as Dr. Grondijs would have us believe, but as early as the tenth.[64] The image must have impressed itself very early on the West. We find very moving renderings well before the turn of the century—the Gero Crucifix in Cologne Cathedral for instance or the engravings of the so-called Lothar Cross, a gift of Otto III to Aachen Minster.

88

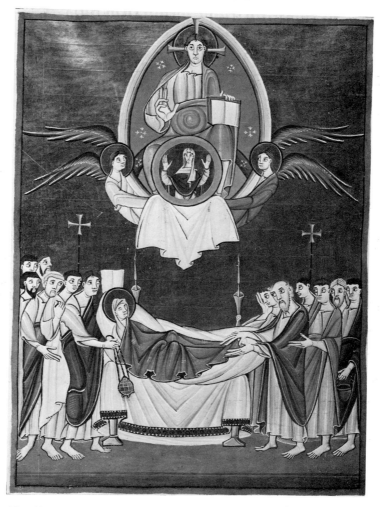

Fig. 88. *Munich*, Bayr. Staatsbibliothek, Cod. lat. 4452, Death of the Virgin.

New iconic and iconographic formulas for both single figures and compositions were, on the whole, copied and adapted avidly: there is nothing left of
the reserve with which Carolingian theologians and artists regarded narrative
representations of the life of Christ. Some models, it is true, were furnished
by late antique Italian manuscripts, but the richest and most systematically
exploited source of Gospel scenes were Byzantine lectionaries of the tenth
century. At least one of these lectionaries, possibly two, were used in the most
important production center of imperial manuscripts—which we still believe to
have been Reichenau, in spite of the doubts expressed by Messrs. Dodwell
and Turner.[65] Not only did they furnish novel (and specifically Byzantine)
themes such as the death of the Virgin (Fig. 88), or Christ sending out his
disciples for the ass and its colt, they served also as pointers toward a new

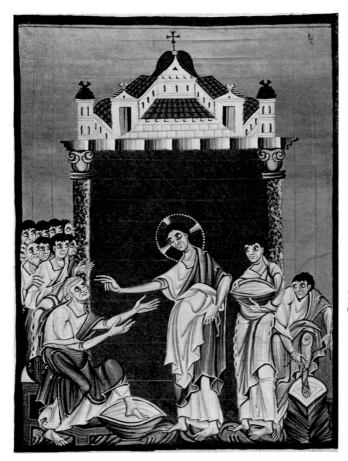

Fig. 89. *Munich*, Bayr. Staatsbibliothek, Cod. lat. 4453. Washing of the Feet.

understanding and a new interpretation of scenes and compositions that had been known before in the West. The Washing of the Feet in the Munich Gospel book of Otto III (Fig. 89) is quite different in composition from that in the narthex of Hosios Lukas (Fig. 90). Two figures, however, are so close in their attitudes—St. Peter and the disciple who puts his foot on a stool to loosen his sandals—that a common metropolitan source has to be assumed to explain this relationship. What is more important, however, is the common psychological atmosphere, the centering of all the figures' attention on the main group, the converging of the glances and gestures towards the focal point of the scene. There is, of course, the typical overacting of the Ottonian figures, who seem to exhaust their whole being in their gestures—figures that are really gesture and nothing else. This intensity goes far beyond anything Byzantine. But the development which culminated in this millennial expressionism was inaugurated by Byzantine models.

However, the most important result of the study of Byzantine models was the adoption of a new format in book illumination, or rather something more

90

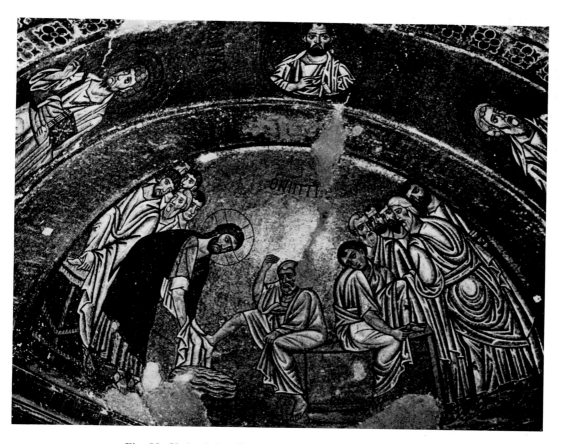

Fig. 90. *Hosios Lukas*, Greece, Mosaic. Washing of the Feet.

than a new format, a new conception of the image. Carolingian and early Ottonian book illumination had used, with few exceptions, two schemes: the scenic strip inserted between lines of text or placed on top of the page and the pseudo-architectural arch framing a single figure or a scene. Sometimes, as in the great Carolingian Bibles of Tours and other examples, several strips had been arranged on top of each other to fill a vertical rectangular frame. What is not found, however, is just that kind of image which became the most important form of the entire Middle Ages, namely, the vertical rectangle enclosing a unified composition which consists of a comparatively few large-scale figures. This pictorial form was quite new, even in Byzantium. Professor Buchthal has traced its growth in his work on the Paris Psalter; he sees the positive achievements of the Byzantine painters of the tenth century "in the isolation of the single scenes from the flow of the continuous narrative, the attempt to create a unified composition and pictorial self-consistency." This presupposed "a new interpretation of the subject with its main emphasis on the spiritual content of the scenes."[66]

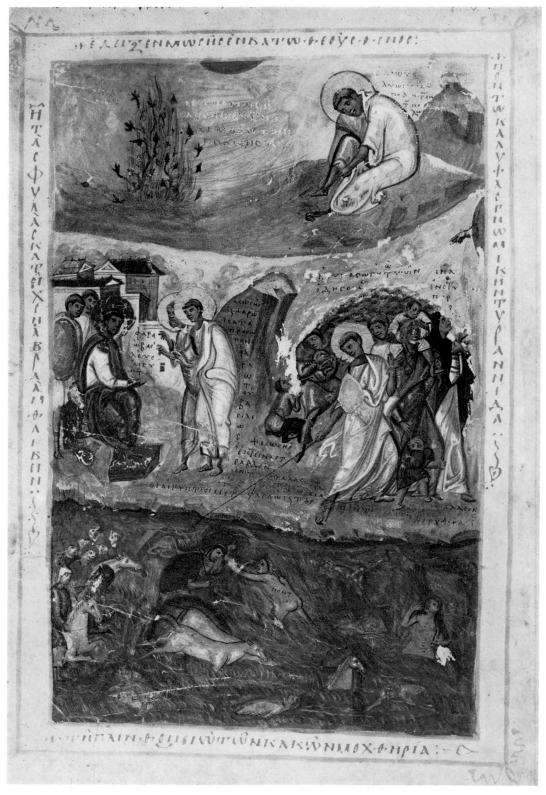

Fig. 91. *Rome*, Bibl. Vat., Cod. Reg. gr. 1, Leo Bible. Scenes from Exodus.

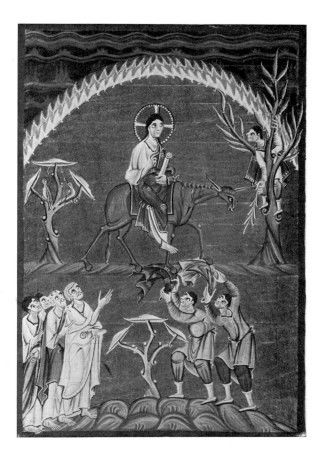

Fig. 92. *Munich*, Bayr. Staatsbibliothek, Cod. lat. 4453. Entry into Jerusalem.

At the root of it all there was a new idea of the function which the image was to fulfill in the framework of the sacred book. After the iconoclastic controversy, and as a result of it, new types of sacred books were coming to the fore in Byzantium, as Professor Weitzmann has shown, such as the lectionary, in which the images were meant not so much to illustrate the text but to serve as evocative icons in their own right.[67] Some of them were taken out of their original narrative context and arranged in autonomous sequences, cycles of the great feasts of the ecclesiastical year or the Easter Passion. It must have been quite a problem for Byzantine artists to give up the format best adapted to depicting an event, namely, the horizontal strip, and to arrange the participating figures in a vertical rectangle without cramming them (Fig. 42). And, indeed, the problems connected with this new format were not solved in one single attempt. We find tentative and intermediary solutions in the East as well as in the West. One of these was to place two strips above one another and to take out the horizontal dividing line, as in some paintings of the Paris Psalter or the Vatican Bible (Fig. 91); the experiment was repeated in the West in the Munich Gospels of Otto III, for instance, where ingenious artifices were used to fuse the two superimposed halves into one pictorial whole (Fig. 92).

93

The completely integrated vertical composition is realized in the same book and then in the Book of Pericopes of Henry II (Fig. 88); it actually came to dominate Ottonian book illumination after the turn of the millenium except for the scriptorium of Echternach in which the Carolingian practice of filling the page with a number of narrow strips pasted one above the other was continued.

The new format inaugurated a new style, a decidedly medieval style in Byzantium as well as in the West. It called for the radical elimination of practically all stage property, scenery and even atmosphere, of everything, in short, which was not necessary for the clear and impressive presentation of the spiritual core of the event depicted. If the theme required a great number of figures, they had to be bundled together in tight groups, clearly separated from the protagonists whom they oppose or follow, while all figures were set off clearly from the golden ground instead of being merged with an atmospheric ambient. It is, above all, this golden ground which brings out the timeless quality of the events and their exemplary importance and which underscores the regularization of compositions, the simplification of contours and the clear distribution of colors. If one had to name a single element which contained most of the germs of the later development, in the East as well as in the West, it would, in fact, have to be the golden ground.

In comparing Ottonian and Byzantine miniatures one cannot help feeling that the Western artists were forever overdoing the specific characteristics of their prototypes—or what they took for these specific characteristics. They were by no means all seeking the same things. They saw and imitated different qualities in the same prototypes or, more often, selected, from the very beginning, different prototypes from the vast storehouse of Byzantine art. This did not, however, happen at random: there is a definite pattern in the selective approach of Western artists towards their Byzantine models. Reichenau painters were attracted by the hieratic and the expressive, Regensburg miniaturists chose the gorgeous and the splendid, and Cologne artists—to name only the three most influential "schools"—extracted from their models the picturesque and the lively qualities. That they came to prefer just these qualities was due not only to the chance distribution of models, although this too may have played a part, but also to certain predispositions which go back to the Carolingian antecedents of these centers. The predilection of Reichenau and its dependencies for stately narrative and solemn representation was surely fostered, if not engendered, by the close connection with northern Italy, especially Verona and Milan;[68] but it was certainly also nourished by the fact that the monastery possessed Carolingian manuscripts of the Palace School and of Tours. The Byzantine models which answered this predisposi-

94

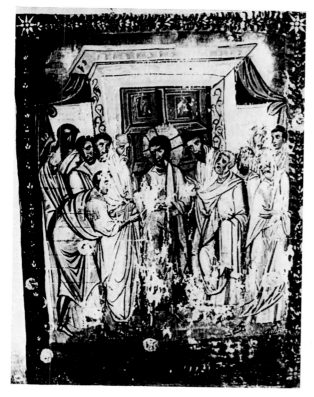

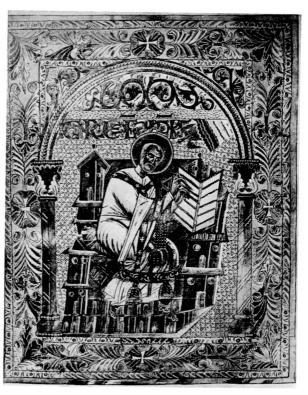

Fig. 93. *Leningrad*, Public Library, Cod. gr. 21. Washing of the Feet.

Fig. 94. *Munich*, Bayr. Staatsbibliothek, Cod. lat. 4456, Sacramentary of Henry II.

tion best were manuscripts akin in style to the Leningrad Gospels No. 21 (Fig. 93). The specific prototype has not yet been detected in spite of the heroic efforts of the late Professor Boeckler of Munich and of Professor Buchthal, but it must have been a lectionary similar to the Leningrad Codex. Regensburg went a different way (Fig. 94).[69] The style of its scriptorium, which rose to prominence under Henry II, was conditioned by the fact that Saint Emmeram possessed a famous Carolingian book, the Codex Aureus of Charles the Bald, which somehow became damaged and had to be restored. It is not too much to say that the Regensburg school actually began its life with the restoring of the Codex Aureus; in any case, when, a decade or more later, Henry II had a splendid sacramentary written and illuminated there, the scriptorium could do no better than fill six pages of the new book with copies after the Carolingian model. Some of these pages follow their prototypes so closely and are, at the same time, so characteristically different, that the comparison of the two has become a favorite theme of art historical seminars. Certainly some of the differences are due to the knowledge of Byzantine forms and techniques acquired during the interval, not only in the field of

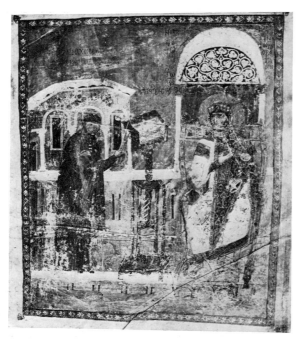

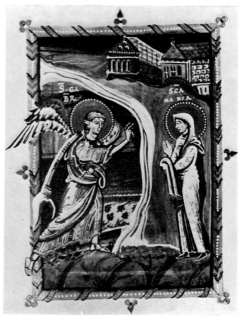

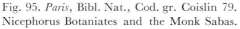

Fig. 95. *Paris*, Bibl. Nat., Cod. gr. Coislin 79. Nicephorus Botaniates and the Monk Sabas.

Fig. 96. *Darmstadt*, Landesbibliothek, Cod. 1640, Gospel Book of Hitda. Annunciation.

illumination but also in goldsmith's work and especially enamel. Conversely, the choice of Byzantine prototypes of just this gorgeous and precious kind was certainly conditioned by the point of departure of the school, the copying of the Carolingian Codex Aureus. The fact that the Regensburg artists followed the lead not only of Byzantine miniature painting but also of goldsmith's work makes it difficult to point to the precise kind of model; but later works such as Coislin 79 (Fig. 95) give us an inkling of what kind of prototypes helped to shape not only Regensburg illumination but also the styles of the Hildesheim and, in part, also the Salzburg scriptoria which took their cues from Regensburg.

A greater contrast can hardly be imagined than that between the gorgeous, metallic style of Regensburg and the free and painterly idiom of Cologne (Fig. 96).[70] Here again, the general trend was conditioned by the Carolingian heritage; the tradition of the Vienna Coronation Gospels (Fig. 64) was kept alive at the lower Rhine and led Cologne artists to look for kindred Byzantine models when it became *de rigueur* to follow Byzantine prototypes in general— and very much so in Cologne, where Theophanou spent her last years. The empress herself must have possessed illuminated Greek books, of which one or two may have been illustrated in the painterly manner that was one of the pictorial styles cultivated in Constantinople around the middle of the tenth century. Whether in this or in some other way, Cologne artists obtained just those models which emboldened them to follow their traditional bent toward the picturesque and which gave them the technical means to develop it further, even beyond the possibilities of their Byzantine prototypes. The sketchy and liquid brushwork, the finely shaded, mysteriously veiled color, the picturesque motifs of architecture, landscape and cloud, the vivid and flowing compositions—all this, in addition to figure types and iconographic patterns, the Cologne artists derived from their Greek models, from works which must have been akin in style to the Paris Psalter (Fig. 97) or the Vatican Leo Bible.

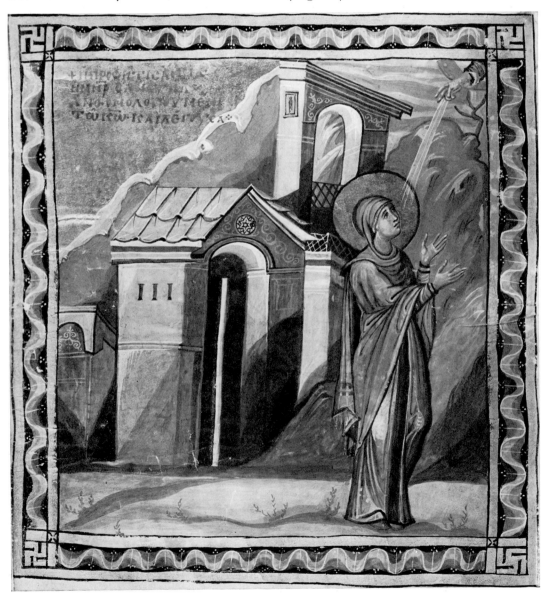

Fig. 97. *Paris*, Bibl. Nat., Cod. gr. 139, Psalter. The Prayer of Hannah.

97

What they added from their own traditions and what flowed into their work from the depths of their psychological make-up, was the fantastic splendour of pure form and the intensity of expression, the wonderful synthesis of the skilfully artistic and the mysterious. With Byzantine painters, those heirs of Hellenism, every form meant something, quite objectively depicted something, however freely. In Cologne miniatures, the seething forms that surge up diagonally across the picture may signify hill or cloud; but they are in the first place pure forms, gloriously irresponsible as regards objective meaning and, at the same time, free of the narrow bonds of ornament. This is something quite foreign to Byzantine art where hills remain hills and clouds remain clouds. But it could never have been achieved without the help of that Greek tradition of pictorial freedom which was revived in Byzantium during the Renaissance of the late ninth and the tenth centuries.

The heyday of Ottonian art was brief, but the firm systems of form which were developed in the late tenth and the early eleventh century with the help of judiciously selected and freely interpreted Byzantine models became the basis of the Romanesque. Ottonian artists developed some of the possibilities contained in Byzantine art further than that art was ever able to develop them; they created forms that were more painterly, more hieratic or more expressive than any of their models. But the possibility itself of painterly, hieratic and expressive art was derived from these models. Of course, the effective radius of these models was more or less restricted to the territory of the Ottonian Empire, that is, to Italy, Germany and parts of Burgundy. Neither France nor England had any appreciable part in this movement and they worked out their own styles mainly on the basis of pre-Carolingian and Carolingian forms. The Ottonian Renaissance was more or less a German affair.

It took another half century or more, and it required a new start, to make Byzantine influence that all-pervading leaven that was necessary for transforming early medieval art into Romanesque. The new start was preceded by a period in which it seemed that the Byzantine element would be altogether eliminated from the body of European art. In Cologne the painterly freedom derived from Byzantine prototypes was replaced, after the middle of the eleventh century, by the sterile forms of a highly schematized style, with parallel lines in cold colors. The figures in the Abdinghof Gospels (Fig. 98), for example, do not appear as integrated wholes but seem to be compounded of flat shapes cut out of a striped material. In spite of its abstract and almost ornamental cast, this style is not yet Romanesque; it lacks the coherence, the inner tension, the organic rhythm which only Byzantine art could give to a Europe that had lost all memory of classical art.

98

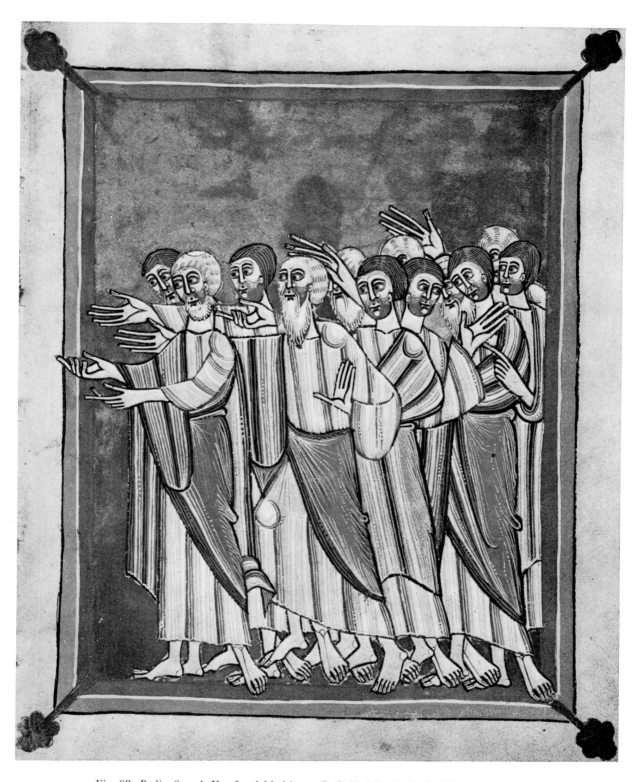

Fig. 98. *Berlin*, Staatl. Kupferstichkabinett, Cod. 78 A 3, Abdinghof Gospels. Apostles.

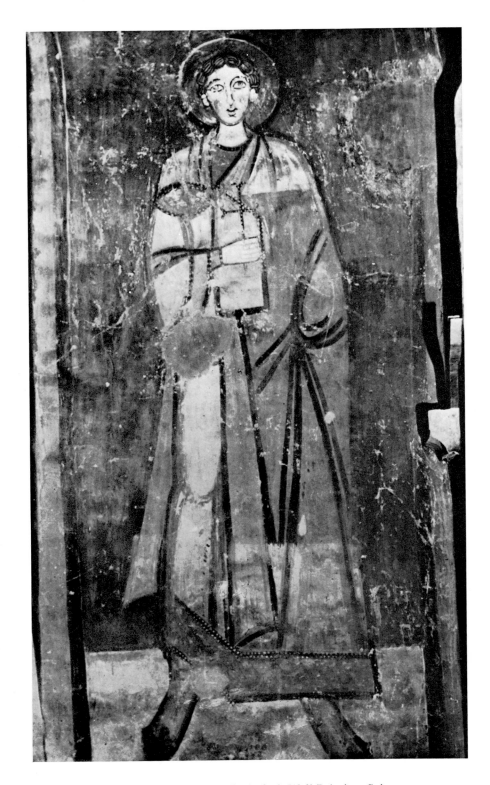

Fig. 99. *Le Puy*, France, Cathedral, Wall Painting. Saint.

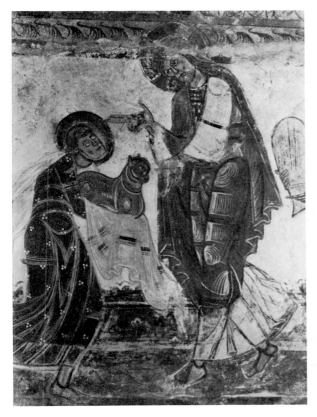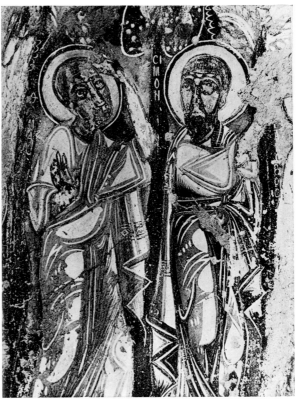

Fig. 100. *Saint-Savin sur Gartempe*, France, Wall Painting. Sacrifice of Abel.

Fig. 101. *Göreme*, Cappadocia, Chapel No. 6, Wall Painting. Apostles from Ascension.

Of course, there were still two enclaves of Greek art in Italy: one in the North, of which we shall speak later, and one in the South, where the Basilian monasteries preserved a tradition of provincial Byzantine art (Fig. 4), a kind of koiné which, because of its popular character and in spite of its meager artistic value, may have exerted some influence along the pilgrimage roads leading from Mont Saint-Michel to the Archangel's shrines in Apulia and Campania. The rather crude frescoes of the north gallery in Le Puy cathedral[71] seem to be an outcome of this infiltration (Fig. 99), and some of the unusual practices of modeling in the frescoes of Saint Savin in the Poitou (Fig. 100), which have been catalogued so amusingly by Messrs. Deschamps and Thibaut as ships' sails, ears of maize, bundled reeds, etc., may have been derived from this sub-Byzantine *vulgata*.[72] This would explain their disconcerting similarities with details of modeling in Cappadocian frescoes (Fig. 101) and it would, on the other hand, account for the fact that among all these similarities there is not one single case of complete identity of motif or technique.

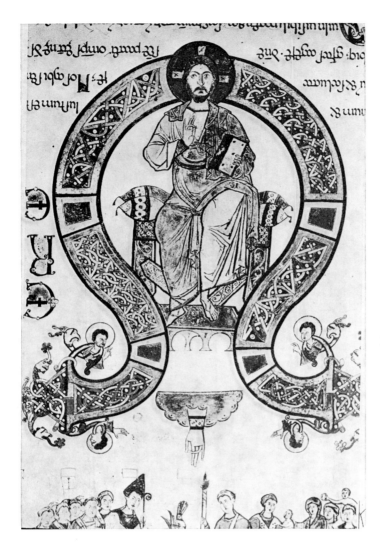

Fig. 102. *Bari*, Archive of the
Cathedral, Exultet Roll.
Enthroned Christ.

In addition to the provincial Byzantine art of Basilian monasticism, there existed a strong Byzantine ingredient in the art of the rich towns of Campania and Apulia,[73] whether or not they were under Byzantine domination (the extent and the intensity of Byzantine control was subject to great fluctuations), a Byzantine ingredient that was at times so strong as to let this art appear as an Italianized Greek art. A work like the Exultet Scroll of Bari of about the turn of the millennium (Fig. 102), while "Apulian" in iconography, technique and some stylistic features of the main cycle of illuminations, shows almost purely Byzantine types and forms in the medallions (with Greek inscriptions) and in the ornamentation of the borders. This and kindred works should warn us not to underrate the importance of the "endemic" Byzantine element in

102

the art of a country which had once borne the name of Magna Grecia and which was still half Greek, with most of its trade being directed toward the Byzantine shores of the eastern Mediterranean, and especially to Constantinople itself. It was in the capital of the Byzantine Empire that Maurus and Pantaleon of Amalfi ordered the bronze doors which they donated to San Salvadore of Atrani, the cathedral of their home town, to Saint Michael on Monte Gargano, even to San Paolo fuori le mura in Rome and finally to Monte Cassino. The last mentioned fact ought to make one wonder whether the great Benedictine house of Monte Cassino did not perhaps owe more to the Byzantine art of the Apulian and Calabrian towns than has hitherto been believed and, consequently, not everything to the Greek artists whom Desiderius called upon for the mosaics of the basilica or to the Byzantine training of the abbey's own artisans. That these Greek artists brought with them the knowledge of a recent linear style and of up-to-date Byzantine iconography (both apparent in the pen drawings of manuscripts Nos. 98 and 99), has been pointed out in the first chapter (Figs. 25, 26, 27). That there is also something new in the surface treatment and the modeling of figures and drapery in Cassinese art can be seen in a comparison between the Exultet of Bari and the Life of St. Benedict and Maurus, Vat. lat. 1202 (Fig. 29), of the time of Desiderius. The graphic arrangement of light in a comblike hatching, framed by double contours—a transformation of Byzantine *chrysographia*—clearly to be seen at the knees of the seated figure, is characteristic of a Byzantine manner which seems to have turned up first in the late tenth century (Fig. 103) and became one of the styles of the eleventh and twelfth centuries especially favored in the provinces and the colonial regions (Fig. 104). It was a rather showy style reminiscent of goldsmith's work and enamels and has, in fact, been named the "cloisonné" style. Its range stretches from Cappadocia to Cologne and from Russia to South Italy. Very much in keeping with the reforming and modernizing tendencies of Desiderius, this style was adopted as one of the official styles of the abbey not only in miniatures but also in wall painting (Fig. 105) where some of its characteristic forms turn up, with slight modifications, in Sant' Angelo in Formis, the most important fresco decoration of the time of Desiderius.[14]

Cloisonné effects are not, however, the only Byzantine element to be found in Cassinese art. The coloring, with complementary colors used for modeling, brilliant blue and purplish brown, for instance, with the lighter colors in abstract patterns on the darker tones, and also compositional schemes such as that of the raising of Lazarus, Christ and the Samaritan Woman, or the Last Supper, are orthodox Byzantine. In figures of large scale such as the im-

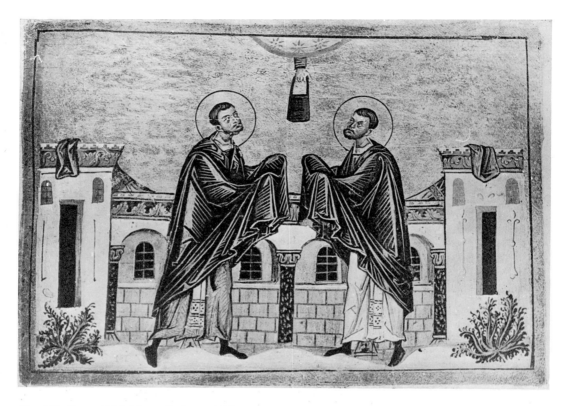

Fig. 103. *Rome*, Bibl. Vat., Cod. gr. 1613, Menologium of Basil II, fol. 152. Cosmas and Damian.

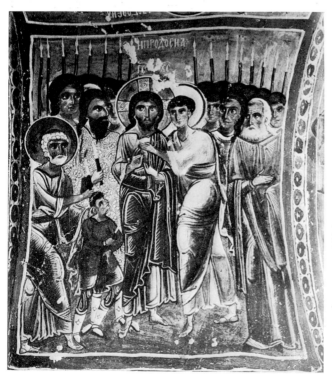

Fig. 104. *Göreme*, Cappadocia, Chapel No. 23 (Quaranleq Kilise),Wall Painting. Betrayal of Judas.

104

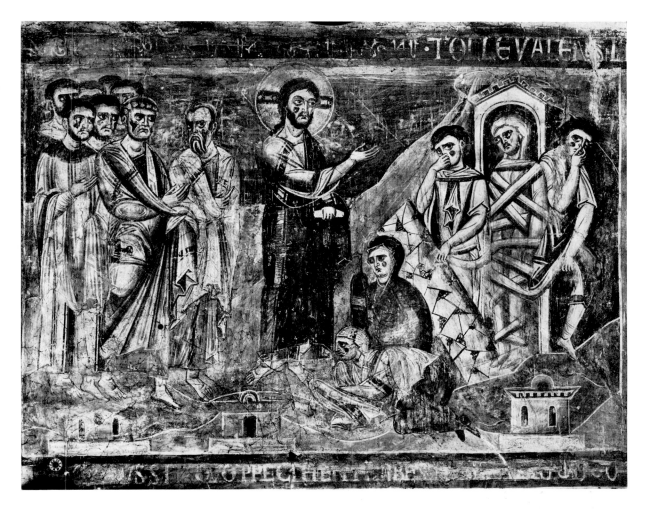

Fig. 105. *Sant'Angelo in Formis*, Italy, Wall Painting. Raising of Lazarus.

age of the Pantocrator in the apse (Fig. 106), the hard and broken forms in sharp tonal contrasts have the flavor of mosaic and may in fact have derived from the mosaic Christ which we know was executed by Byzantine workmen in the apse of Monte Cassino itself. On the other hand, this figure cannot by any stretch of terminology be called Byzantine. Type, gesture, costume (with golden clavi) and drapery (with agitated zig-zag seams reminiscent of Carolingian forms) are not Byzantine but Campanian. Thoroughly anti-Byzantine too are the bodily shapes and movements of a good many figures in Sant' Angelo—some of them have a kind of reptilian shape and movement. Much of the iconography is Campanian.

Thus, what the Byzantine artists called in by Desiderius did—in addition to their contributions in the technical field—was to bring up to date and, per-

105

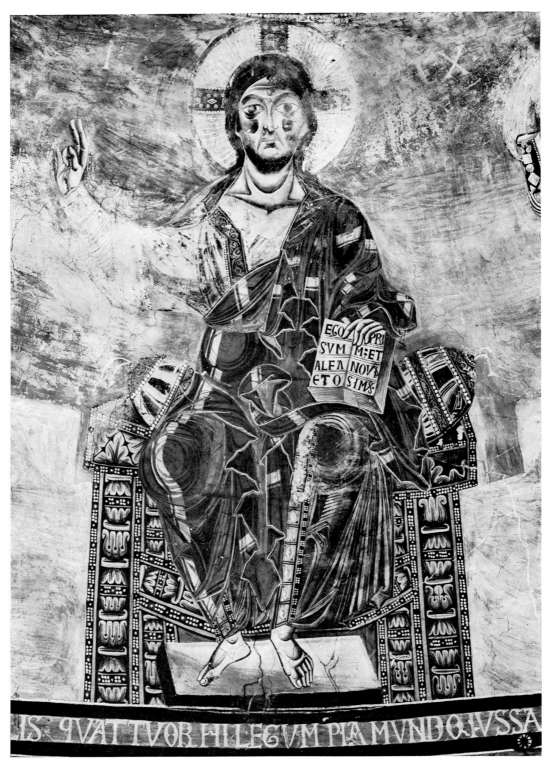

Fig. 106. *Sant'Angelo in Formis*, Italy, Wall Painting. Enthroned Christ.

106

haps, to strengthen the Greek component of Campanian art and to introduce elements of a new metropolitan style. They made the figure style of Campanian art more elegant, more plastically suggestive, more pliable and thus better adapted to cope with the many new tasks with which it was confronted in this period of the greatest artistic activity which southern Italy had seen since the end of the early Christian era.

It seems that Rome[75] experienced a revival in the field of painting at approximately the same time as, or perhaps a little later than, Monte Cassino. The fact that Abbot Desiderius became pope in 1086 makes it extremely tempting to see in the Roman development not just a sequel to but a consequence of the Cassinese movement and to regard it as the second stage in the triumphal progress of a new "Benedictine" art,[76] inaugurated by the Byzantine artists of Desiderius. This historical perspective has been severely criticized and passionately defended, the more so since the evolutionary vista which seemed to open up in this way, did not end in Rome but included further perspectives reaching as far as Cluny and even further. Actually, the reign of Victor III (Desiderius) was so short—it lasted only for a few months—and so tumultuous that there was neither time nor opportunity for any patronage of the arts. The work in which the Roman revival culminated, the fresco decoration of the lower church of San Clemente (Fig. 107), seems to have originated about twenty years later. These frescoes contain, it is true, certain more modern Byzantine elements than those found in other contemporary Roman paintings. The main difference is that the local artists, as they can be seen at work in the pictorial decoration of Sant'Elia at Nepi in Latium (Fig. 108) (signed by three Roman painters), used simple parallel lines for working out the little there is in the way of modeling and otherwise covered the surface with a busy system of ornamentation, while in the new pictorial style visible in San Clemente sharp white highlights are introduced as the chief means of modeling, setting accents and building up form-designing patterns. Now, to use highlights in this manner is not only a specifically Byzantine technique, it is also reminiscent of the cloisonné style of Monte Cassino. However, a confrontation of the two styles, that of Monte Cassino and that of Rome, shows their intrinsic difference: Monte Cassino is much nearer to the Byzantine cloisonné than Rome, which follows a much less specific line. Nor do we find in Rome any of the idiosyncracies of the Monte Cassino style, for instance the comblike or the zigzag shapes of the highlights. Rome has its own types of figures, faces, architectural motifs, patterns of costumes, etc., which are so decidedly Roman that the influence from Monte Cassino must have been very slight indeed, if there was any such influence at all. It seems,

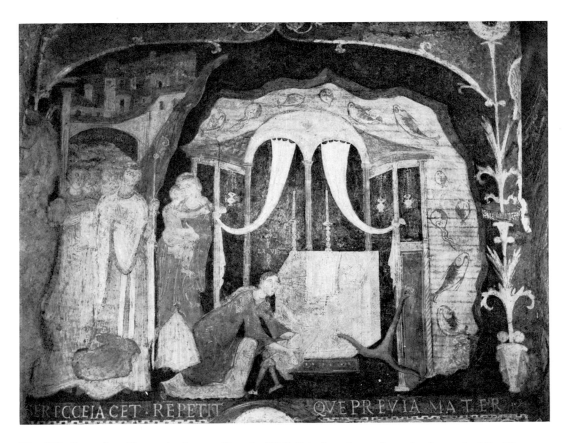

Fig. 107. *Rome*, San Clemente, Lower Church, Wall Painting. Scene from the Legend of St. Clement.

rather, as if Rome had had its own source of Byzantine art. Roman and central Italian painters must have known the Byzantine cloisonné style a good deal before the time of Desiderius. By the turn of the century this style was firmly established in Roman book illumination, especially in the scriptorium of Santa Cecilia whose production paralleled that of Monte Cassino in many ways, but was certainly not a filiation (Fig. 109).[77]

The next wave of Byzantine influence seems to have reached Rome in the forties of the twelfth century. Among the three painters of the busts of Patriarchs, the only remaining part of the pictorial decoration of Santa Croce in Gerusalemme (ca. 1144), there is one who must have been trained in one of the centers of Byzantine painting (Fig. 110). His style is free and painterly, with an entirely new color scheme—green is modeled with blue, brown with purple—and with bold white highlights as accents; the sudden appearence of this genuinely Greek style seems to have had a certain effect on the conservative art of this painter's colleagues or at least on the style of one of them, whom we meet again in San Pietro in Tuscania[78] around the middle of the

108

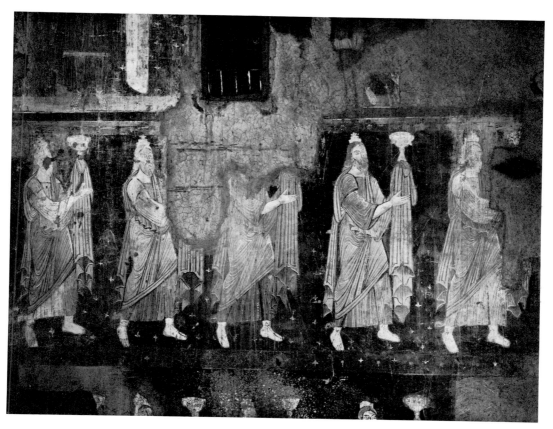

Fig. 108. *Nepi*, Castel Sant'Elia, Italy, Wall Painting. Elders of the Apocalypse.

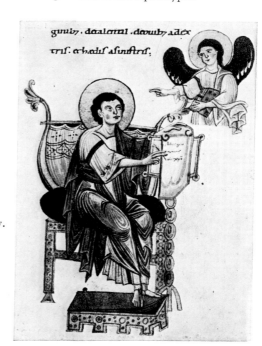

Fig. 109. *Florence*, Bibl. Laurenziana, Cod., 1727, fol. 6 v.
St. Matthew.

109

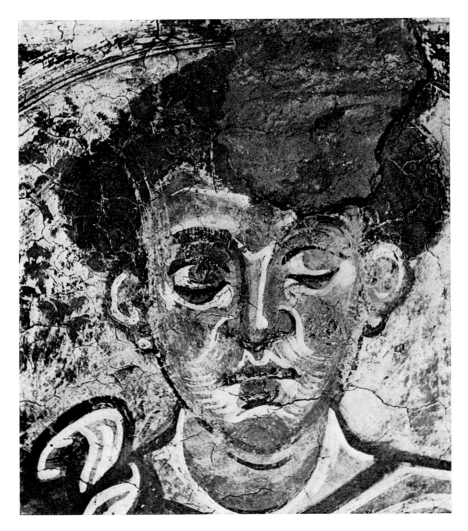

Fig. 110. *Rome*, Santa Croce in Gerusalemme, Wall Painting. Patriarch.

century. There is a new rhythm in the movement of the Apostles and Angels in the Ascension of the main apse of Tuscania (Fig. 111), a new tension in the lineament of the draperies. The joints of the figures are accentuated by light forms, islands as it were, which are surrounded by the vivid flow of the drapery. The fundamental pattern is still provided by the multilinear style of Roman painting, but the lines are not as strictly parallel as they used to be; they have come to life.

However, this new style does not seem to have obtained a firm hold on Roman art; it remained an episode. Generally speaking, the Byzantine element does not seem to have played a very important part in Roman painting

110

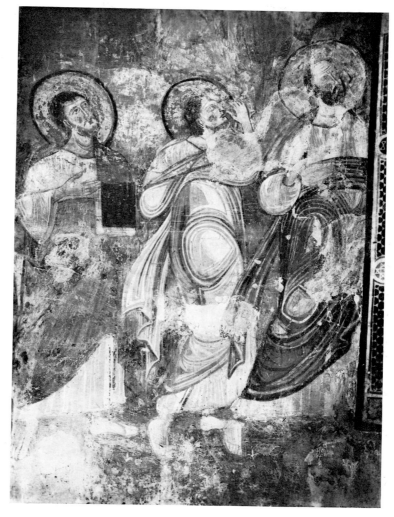

Fig. 111. *Tuscania*, Italy, San Pietro, Wall Painting.
Apostles from Ascension.

at any time. Roman art had its own tradition which was extremely strong. It could and did draw on its own Christian heritage, and for decorative details and architectural motifs on its own pagan, classical past. Thus, the most powerful incentive for the use of Byzantine prototypes—namely, the dearth of indigenous models—did not exist in Rome.

It is, therefore, not very likely that Rome was the only or even the main source of the powerful current which transformed Western art in the late eleventh and early twelfth centuries. Campanian art seems to have been at least as important in providing France with the new Byzantine schemes of composition and modeling. The swelling volumes and the plausible movement of

111

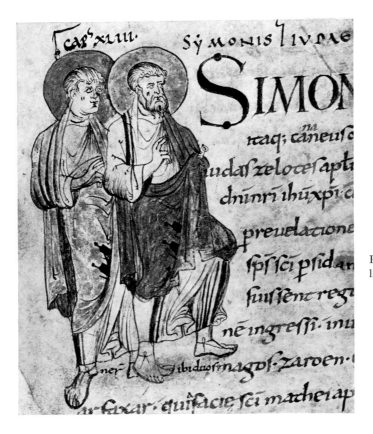

Fig. 112. *Paris*, Bibl. Nat., Cod. lat. 5301, Lectionary of Limoges. Two Apostles.

the figures in the Passionary (Fig. 112) and the Bible of Saint-Martial of Limoges seem to mirror successive stages of Campanian miniature painting, in part pre-Desiderian.[79] Indeed Limoges may have been one of the most important receiving centers of Italo-Byzantine forms, more important perhaps than the great Abbey of Cluny which, owing to its unique role in the history of the medieval church, has almost monopolized the attention of art historians in this field.[80] Professor Meyer Schapiro has shown in his study of the *Parma Ildefonsus*, a Cluny manuscript of about 1100, that the Italo-Byzantine style (Fig. 113) with its organic modeling resulting from a painterly use of shading and highlights and from the division of the draperies into cloisons whose contours curve broadly with the convexities of the limbs—to paraphrase Professor Schapiro,—was neither a monopoly of Cluny nor the only style to be found in Cluny at this period. As a matter of fact, only two of the 35 miniatures of the Parma Codex are painted in the Italo-Byzantine style, the others (Fig. 114) being very provincial offshoots of late Ottonian painting, possibly derived from Bavaria; they remind us of the fact that Cluny belonged to the Holy Roman Empire. There is no doubt, on the other hand, that the Byzan-

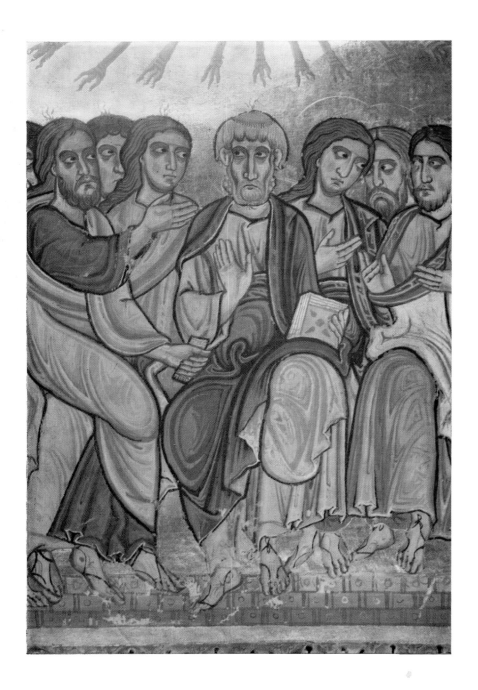

IV *Vienna*, National-Bibliothek, Antiphonary of St. Peters, Miniature. Pentecost, Detail.

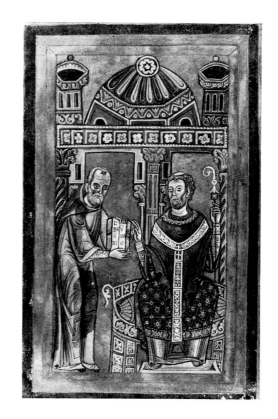

Fig. 113. *Parma*, Bibl. Palatina, MS lat. 1650,
Ildefonsus. Presentation of the Book
to Bishop Gotiscal.

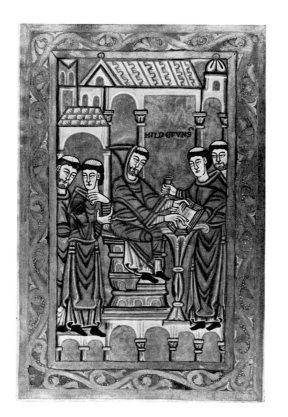

Fig. 114. *Parma*, Bibl. Palatina, MS lat.
1650, Ildefonsus. Ildefonsus writing.

113

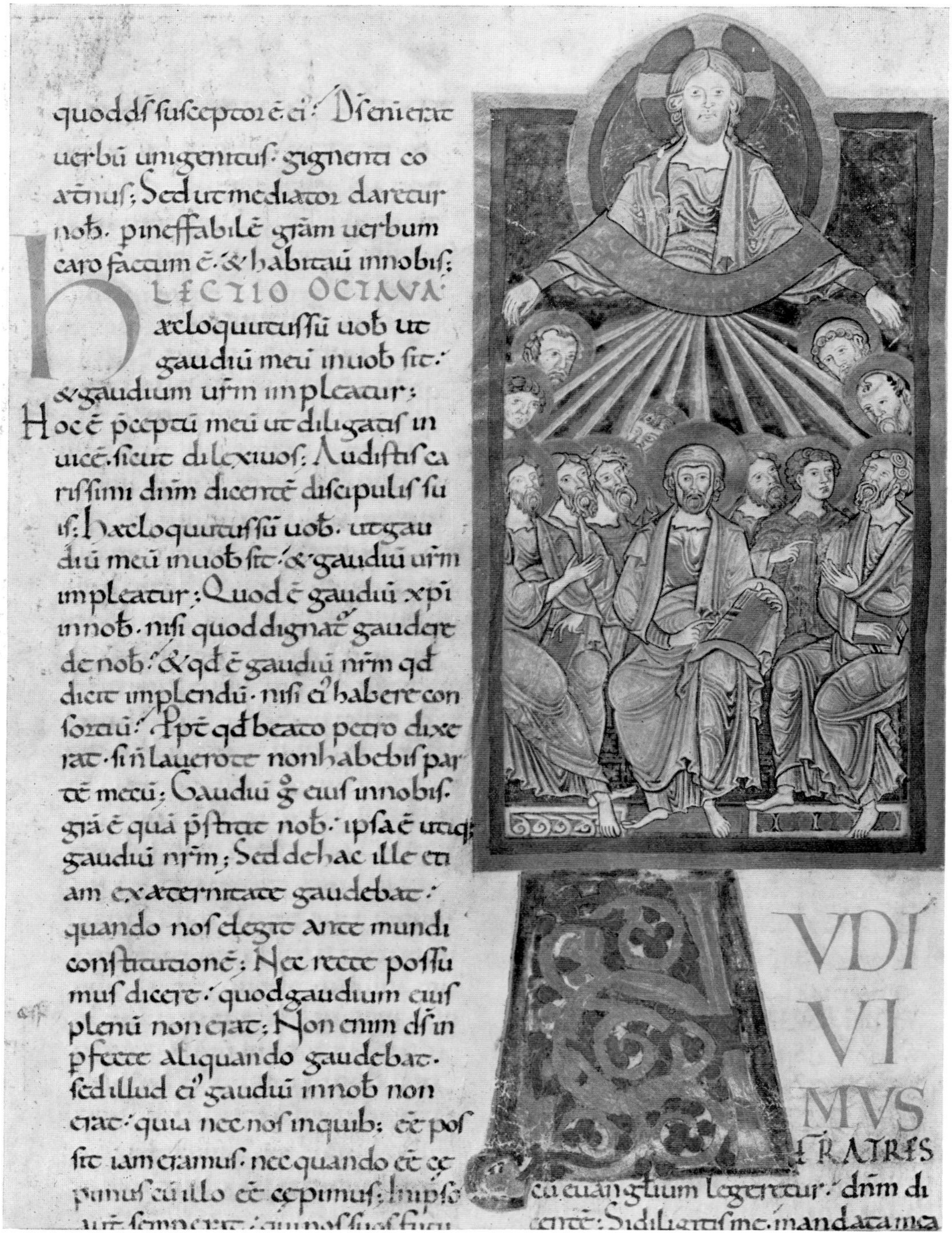

quod dñs susceptor é ei. Dseniet
uerbū unigenitus. gignenti co
aternus; Sed ut mediator daretur
nob. pineffabile grām uerbum
caro factum é. & habitau innobis;

LECTIO OCTAVA

Hxcloquutussū uob ut
gaudiū meū inuob sit.
& gaudium uřm impleatur;
Hoc é pceptū meū ut diligatis in
uice. sicut dilexiuos. Audistis ca
rissimi dñm dicerē discipulis su
is. Hxcloquutussū uob. utgau
diū meū inuob sit. & gaudiū uřm
impleatur; Quod é gaudiū xpi
innob. nisi quod dignat gaudere
de nob. & qd é gaudiū nřm qd
dicit implendū. nisi cū habere con
sortiū. Apt qd beato petro dixe
rat. si n lauerote nonhabebis par
tē mecū; Gaudiū g eius innobis
grā é quā pstitat nob. ipsa é utiq;
gaudiū nřm; Sed dehac ille eti
am exaternitate gaudebat.
quando nos elegit ante mundi
constitutione; Nec recte possu
mus dicere. quodgaudium eius
plenū non erat; Non enim dš in
pfecte aliquando gaudebat.
sed illud eius gaudiū innob non
erat. quia nec nos inquib; ee pos
sit iam eramus. nec quando ee ce
pimus cū illo ee cepimus; Inipso
aut semper erat. cum nos sui ssū.

VDI
VI
MVS
FRATRES
cū euāgelium legeretur. dñm di
cente; Si diligitis me. mandata mea

Fig. 115. *Paris*, Bibl. Nat. ms nouv. acq. lat. 2, 246, Cluny Lectionary. Pentecost.

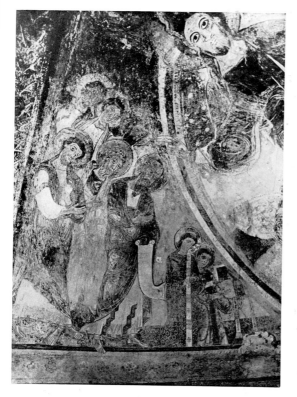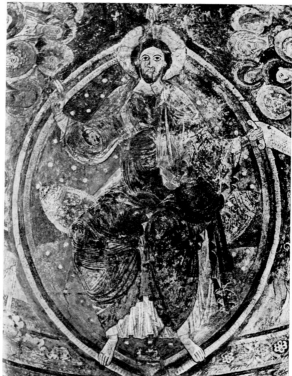

Fig. 116. *Berzé-la-Ville*, France, Château des Moines, Wall Painting. Group of Apostles.

Fig. 117. *Berzé-la-Ville*, France, Château des Moines, Wall Painting. Enthroned Christ.

tinizing style took root in Cluny and that it became the most important mode of expression in Cluniac painting. It is to be found in other miniatures—the best is the Cluny Lectionary of the Bibliothèque Nationale (Fig. 115), with most convincing modeling by form—designing lines and elastic cloisons—and, above all, in the magnificent early twelfth century apse frescoes of the Château des Moines, at Berzé-la-Ville, a few miles from Cluny itself (Fig. 116). The Berzé-la-Ville style was not a recent creation but had already had time to develop very special and somewhat mannered idiosyncracies which are seen in the way locks of hair are represented, in the curious loops, like cross sections, which terminate drapery folds, in the almond shaped—sometimes double—nuclei of drapery configurations surrounded by multiple lines, and especially in the highly complex technique of glazes and hatchings. There is nothing experimental about this art—an art which is absolutely sure of its means and effects, in spite of the complexity of its components. Among these components various Byzantine layers can be discerned. One of them, the oldest, can be traced back to Carolingian times: the enthroned Christ (Fig. 117),

115

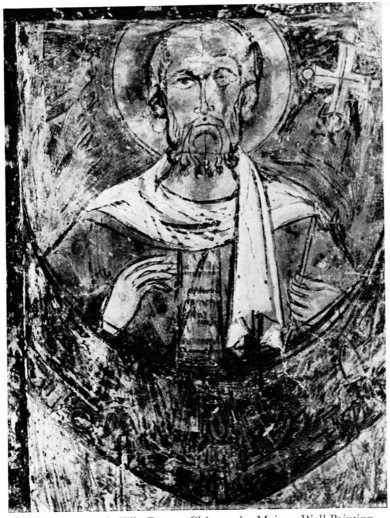

Fig. 118. *Berzé-la-Ville*, France, Château des Moines, Wall Painting.
Bust of Saint.

its proportions and its modeling with some parts curiously bulging and others rather flat, the drapery with hanging folds and zigzag seams, continues the tradition of the Palace School of Charlemagne (Fig. 62). The preparatory drawing of some heads, especially those of the saints in the lower part of the decoration (Fig. 118), owes its classical cast to Byzantine prototypes of the tenth century—a confrontation of St. Sergius in Berzé with St. Ignatios from one of the tenth century tiles from Constantinople (Fig. 119), which are shared by the Louvre and the Walters Art Gallery, shows the similarities and the dissimilarities of the two. The most recent Byzantine influence can be seen in the agitated movements and the "damp-fold-draperies" of the figures in the two martyrdom scenes of the apse of Berzé-la-Ville (Fig. 120). The

116

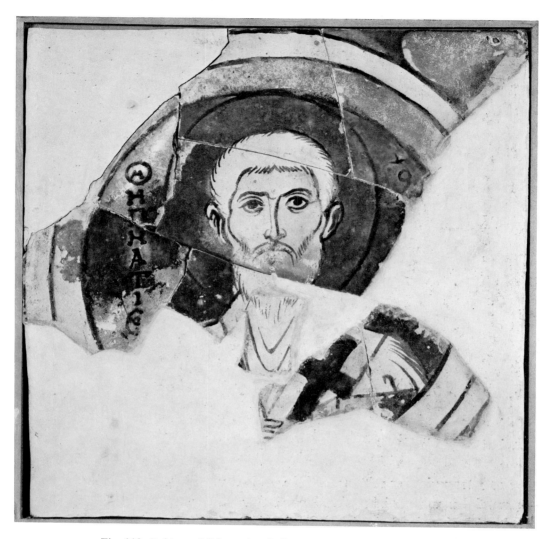

Fig. 119. *Baltimore*, Walters Art Gallery, Painted Tile. St. Ignatius.

Byzantine models of this style, which was graphically described by Professor Koehler and Mr. Garrison, have to be looked for in eleventh century Byzantine painting; a characteristic, if provincial, example is provided by the frescoes of Hagia Sophia in Ohrid (Fig. 121), which have been dated in the fifties or sixties of the eleventh century.[81]

Among the various Byzantine influences which played roles in the formation of the style of Berzé, there may have been some which were transmitted to Cluny by way of Rome—one might think that the tendency towards multiple linearism crept in this way—and others which were passed on by Campania and Monte Cassino; the latter may have furnished models for the cloisonné technique which can be seen in some parts of the Berzé frescoes—in the comb-

117

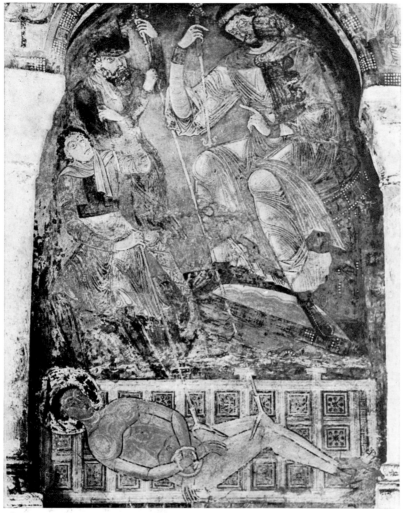

Fig. 120. *Berzé-la-Ville*, France, Château des Moines, Wall Painting.
Martyrdom of St. Lawrence.

shaped treatment of the lights in the body of the beheaded St. Blasius, for instance (Fig. 122)—a treatment which is reminiscent of Sant'Angelo in Formis. But these were rather secondary influences. The main current must have come from Byzantium itself, where the accession of Alexius Comnenus to the throne in 1081 had inaugurated a new era of political and cultural consolidation and expansion. The echo of this revival can be felt in Cluny; in the course of the twelfth century the radiation of the new art of Constantinople became so strong that it led to the establishment of veritable bridgeheads of Byzantine art in the West: those great centers of colonial art which originated in Venice and Sicily and which helped to shape high and late Romanesque painting.

118

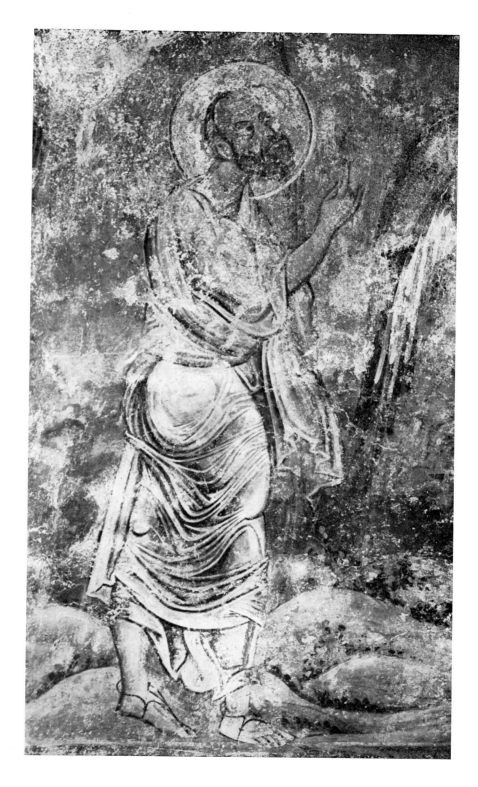

Fig. 121. *Ohrid*, Yugoslavia, Hagia Sophia, Wall Painting. Apostle from Ascension.

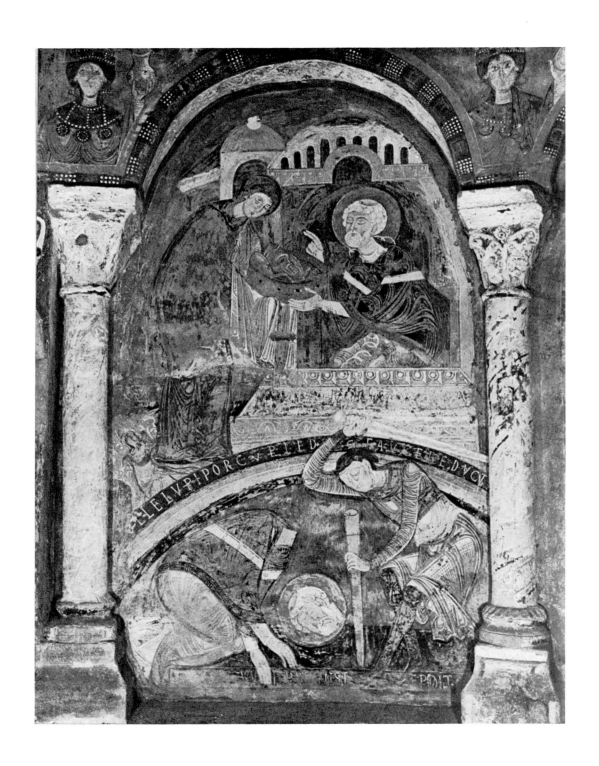

Fig. 122. *Berzé-la-Ville*, France, Château des Moines, Wall Painting. Martyrdom of St. Blasius.

120

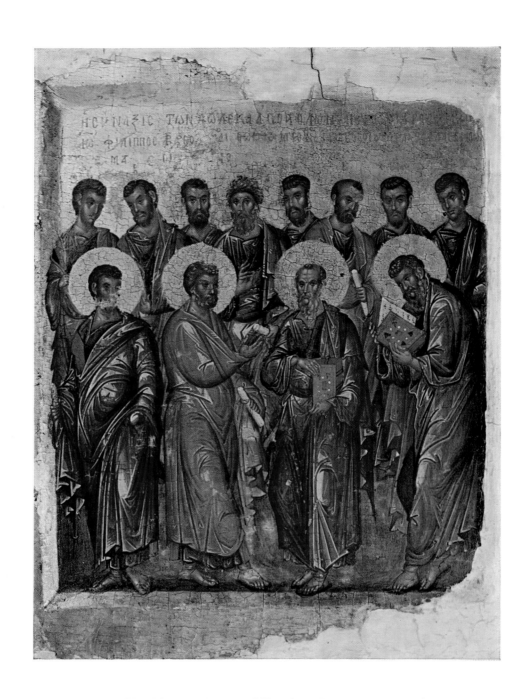

V *Moscow*, Museum of Fine Arts, Icon. Twelve Apostles.

4

Colonial Art

The rise of two great powers in the western Mediterranean—the Venetian and the Siculo-Norman states[82]—created a new demand in the field of the arts: mosaic as the imperial art par excellence was regarded as the only art that could do justice to the grandeur with which the two governments, the aristocratic and the monarchical, surrounded themselves. Now, mosaic was virtually a Byzantine monopoly; both material—especially the gold cubes—and technicians had to be imported from Byzantium. It is one of the most fruitful coincidences in the realm of art that the new demand coincided with a spectacular increase in the quantity and the quality of mosaic production in Byzantium itself, in the late eleventh and the twelfth centuries. Thus, Byzantium was able to meet this new demand. Furthermore, it was willing to do so, much more so than in the middle of the eleventh century, when Yaroslav of Kiev had to be content with third-rate mosaicists for his church' of Hagia Sophia.[83]

The uncouth figures of the church in Kiev (Fig. 132), with their heavy proportions and schematic draperies, look distinctly provincial compared with the elegant, slender saints of the Sicilian churches, true representatives of Constantinopolitan court art (Fig. 137). Of course, a very essential part of this difference is one of date and style, but something of it is certainly due to conscious selection on the part of the exporters: it must have made a great difference, who it was that asked for mosaic artists and how much he was able to pay.

It is very interesting to see how the social and financial status of the "importers" found their expression in the quality of the art they acquired and how even the special nature and structure of the government at the receiving end influenced the nature of the transmission. Thus, there is a profound difference between the ways in which Venice and Sicily went about the importation of mosaic art. San Marco[84] in Venice, which was really the palace chapel of the

121

doge, was looked after by the procuratori, the highest authority of the state after the doge, the primicerius, the chief ecclesiastic of San Marco, and, finally, the doge himself—a complicated pattern of oligarchic government which is mirrored in most Venetian representations of the doge, who, at least in the early period, was never shown alone but always surrounded by the representatives of the governing bodies, lay and ecclesiastical (Fig. 139). As regards the decoration of San Marco itself, this multiplicity of officials entailed, as it invariably does, slow progress and a lack of unity. Several workshops or artists were active side by side or one after the other, each following its own models and realizing its own style. Changes of plan occurred; periods of complete inactivity alternated with periods in which gaps were filled and missing cycles or subjects fitted in, so that the whole presents a rather motley aspect. In Sicily, on the other hand,[85] it was one will, that of the ruler, which controlled all decisions about the mosaic decorations of Cefalù, the Palatina and Monreale. Entire workshops were transported to the island and set to work at the royal enterprises. They produced decorations which are not only homogeneous but uniform, bearing the unmistakable imprint of official and of royal art. The emphasis is very much on the royal character. Professor Kitzinger has shown how ardently Roger aspired to emulate the majesty of Byzantine emperors, down to the minutest details of costume, and how he and his successors consciously aimed at creating an art that could vie in splendor with the aulic art of Byzantium. They succeeded only to a certain extent for there is something about the Sicilian mosaic decorations that makes them inferior to Constantinopolitan work, something second hand, something that makes them appear as what they are, imitations, produced in a highly competent manner, with a systematic division of labor. Theologians prepared the program and the layout; leading masters provided the models, which followed current metropolitan prototypes; several draftsmen sketched the figures and compositions on the walls, which were then covered with mosaic by a host of technicians, some of them specialists in heads, others in figures, others in landscapes and architecture. Finally, there was the lowest grade of workmen who executed the ornamental parts and the golden grounds. Especially in Monreale, the entire work was ruled by the strictest artistic economy: frequently recurring figure types, such as the seated Creator or the seated Christ (Fig. 123), were almost mechanically reproduced according to a pattern set by the leading artist. The resulting effect is, of course, one of cool perfection.

In Venice, we find the opposite—with its negative and its positive aspects. Workshops and artists seem to have worked on their own, without the slightest effort at integrating their various styles or even their compositional patterns.

122

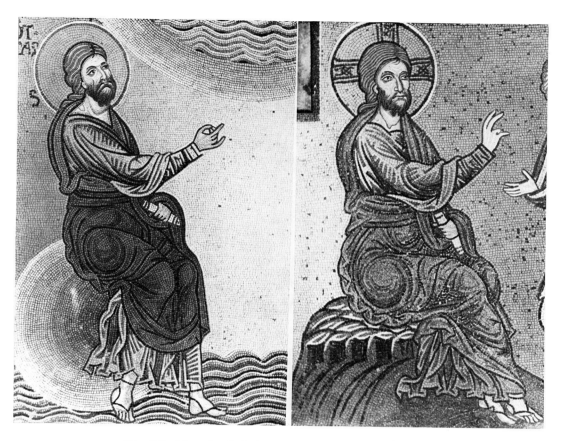

Fig. 123. *Monreale*, Cathedral, Mosaic. The Creator, Christ.

In some instances we find two or even three individual artists at work in one dome: the easternmost cupola with prophets surrounding a central medallion of Christ Emmanuel is an extreme example of this multiplicity of styles (Fig. 124). One of the artists copied the much older figures of the apse, another developed a highly mannered, jagged style, and a third (and probably a fourth) produced a somewhat provincial version of the current mannerism of the second half of the twelfth century with its overemphasis on plastic differentiation (Fig. 125). There was so little unity of planning that the two transept domes were filled with what appear as leftovers from the overall decorative scheme, miniature-like scenes of the legend of St. John the Evangelist in the north dome and four lonely figures of saints in the south dome.

True, the vaulting system of San Marco did confront Byzantine iconographers and mosaicists with problems which were not easy to solve with the means of twelfth century art. This art knew only three different schemes of cupola decoration—the Pantocrator with prophets, the Ascension, and the

123

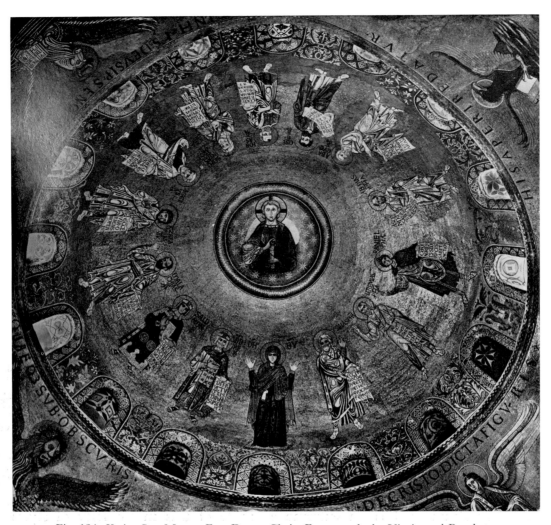

Fig. 124. *Venice*, San Marco, East Dome. Christ Emmanuel, the Virgin and Prophets.

Pentecost, of which the first two were interchangeable and hardly ever occurred side by side. This restricted number was quite sufficient for eleventh or twelfth century churches which had only one or, at the most (as in Hosios Lukas), two domes not counting the secondary cupolas in the angles. Thus, the mosaicists of San Marco were at a serious loss when they had to provide for five domes—and, it must be owned, they did not make a success of it. But this was not the only difficulty: Greek mosaicists were used to working on comparatively small surfaces—including those of the domes, which were much smaller in medieval Byzantine architecture than in San Marco; and all these surfaces were firmly framed, were, in fact, niches that called for single figures or for centered compositions. In San Marco, however, there are no framed niches; there are hardly any articulations, for the golden ground stretches unbroken over the entire vaulted surface of the interior, smoothing over edges and corners and asserting itself, generally speaking, as the primary element, the universal background against which the colored mosaic figures are silhouetted. The scenes are not conceived as "pictures" but as more or less complicated assemblies of figures in rhythmic juxtaposition.

All this must have been rather bewildering for Byzantine artists, but hardly more so than the conditions they found in Sicily. There, the domes—in the Palatine Chapel and in the Martorana—were small enough, it is true, but their shapes, especially those of the squinches with their multiple framed recesses, are entirely un-Byzantine. If the surfaces in San Marco were not articulated enough, those of the Sicilian domes were cut up too much, forcing the decorators to use all kinds of tricks if they wanted to house their programs (Fig. 126). In the other two mosaic churches of Sicily there was another difficulty: the fact that they have no domes made a complete rearrangement of the decoration necessary, with the apse assuming the rôle of the dome as the place of the most sacred representation. The conch had to take the half-figure of the Pantocrator (Figs. 127, 128)—at a scale much larger than any

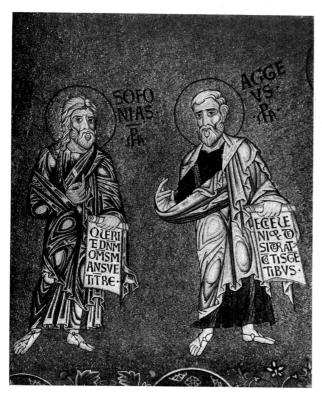

Fig. 125. *Venice*, San Marco, East Dome, Detail of Mosaic. Zephaniah.

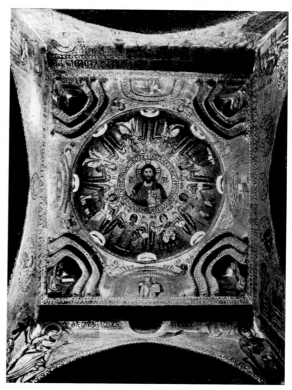

Fig. 126. *Palermo*, Cappella Palatina, Dome. Pantocrator and Angels.

125

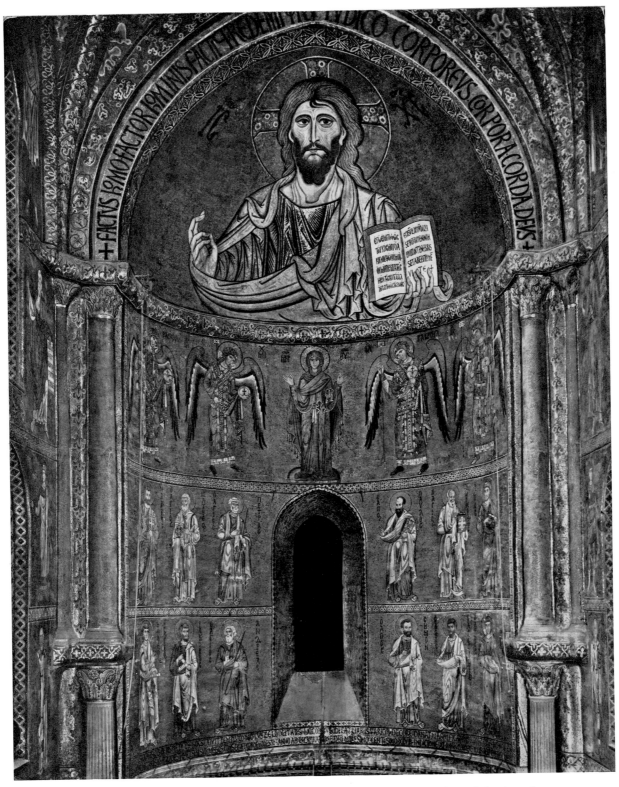

Fig. 127. *Cefalù*, Cathedral, Main Apse. Pantocrator, Angels, the Virgin and the Apostles.

126

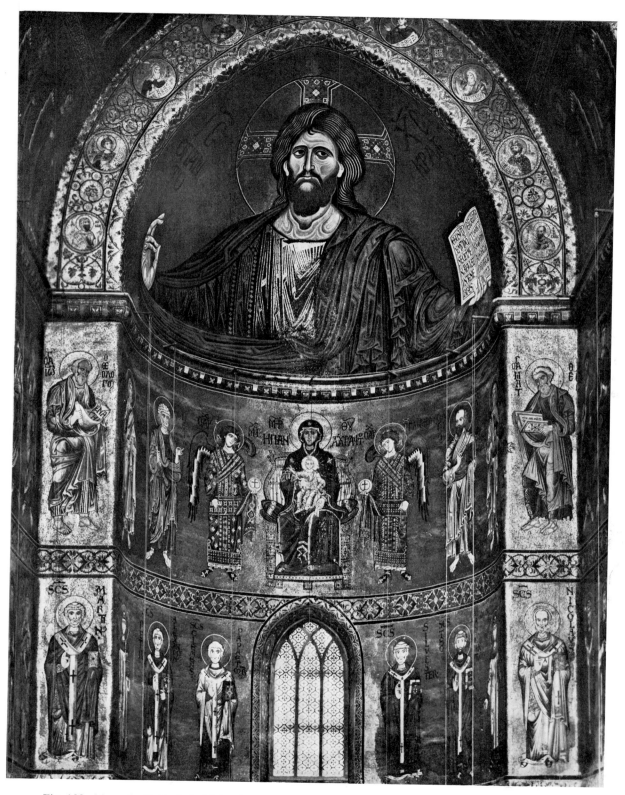

Fig. 128. *Monreale*, Cathedral, Main Apse. Pantocrator, Angels, the Virgin, the Apostles and Saints.

127

Byzantine mosaic—and places for angels, apostles, prophets and saints had to be found on the vaults and the walls of the apse or the presbytery. In order to preserve something of the unity of the program, a complicated system of formal relationships between the figures had to be worked out. Apart from the domes, the apses and some secondary vaults, the Sicilian churches (and with them other basilican churches in the West such as Torcello) offered only flat surfaces—something that hardly occurs in Byzantine buildings. These flat surfaces were subdivided into strips to take a great number of scenes from the Old and New Testaments (Monreale) or the numerous episodes and motifs of composite images such as the Last Judgment of Torcello. Thus, what Greek decorators and their Western pupils had to learn in order to do justice to their tasks in Western buildings, was to marshal large programs and scenes on large surfaces, to work in widely differing scales, gigantic and almost miniature, and to instill a new rhythm into the rows of figures displayed on flat surfaces, in order to hold together the loosened, unframed compositions. Surely, it was a difficult assignment, which required great elasticity and versatility on the part of those artists who were called to Venice and Sicily at

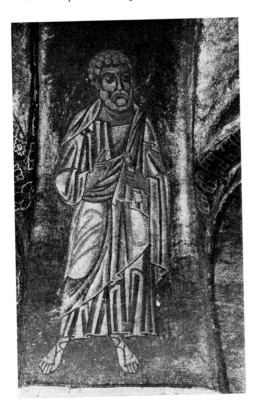

Fig. 129. *Hosios Lukas*, Greece, Narthex, Mosaic. St. Peter.

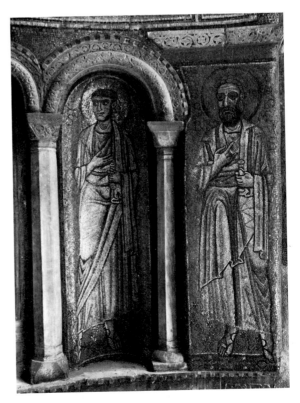

Fig. 130. *Venice*, San Marco, Main Porch. Two Apostles.

128

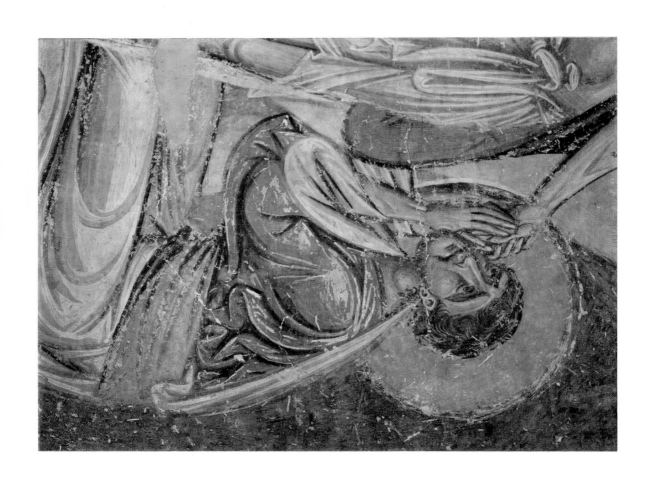

VI *Nerezi*, Yugoslavia, Wall Painting, St. John from Lament of Christ.

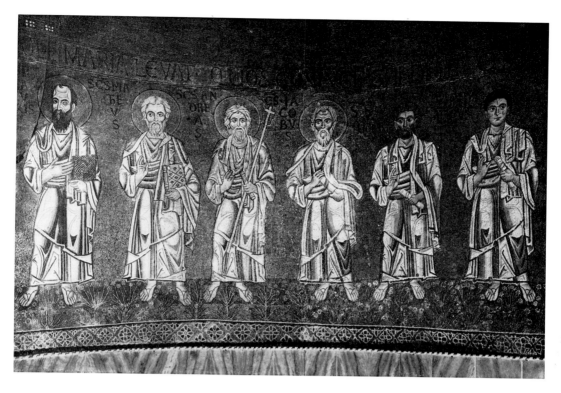

Fig. 131. *Torcello*, Cathedral, Main Apse. Apostles.

various times during the late eleventh and twelfth century. As they arrived, they brought with them habits of form which corresponded to certain phases in the stylistic development of Byzantine art. The interaction between this development and the rhythm of activity in the West set the pattern for the succession of styles or stylistic phases in Venice and Sicily, and their radiation from these centers to the North and to the West. Not every phase of the Constantinopolitan development can be found in Venice and Sicily: some styles were transmitted to Venice only, while others can be found only in Sicily, and one or another important phase of the Byzantine evolution cannot be exemplified at all in either of the two centers.

The series of transmissions began in the second half of the eleventh century with an ascetic style very much like the style of the mosaics of Hosios Lukas (Fig. 129).[86] This style manifested itself in Venice in a series of apostles in the niches surrounding the main entrance from the narthex into the interior of San Marco (Fig. 130). Straight lines, seeking the vertical, articulate the austere draperies of these figures; the only features to enliven this pattern are folded seams zigzagging obliquely across the legs, one of which is usually accentuated by framing contours and a triangular shadow under the knee. Within these

129

contours there are abstract elements, stemming, in the last analysis from late antique illusionism. The style appears in Venice in several of its varieties, one of which can be seen in the apostles of the main apse of Torcello cathedral (Fig. 131),[87] also of the second half of the eleventh century, a rather rich, overcharged version, which recalls the heavy, provincial idiom of the Kiev mosaics (Fig. 132).

The second phase, at the turn of the eleventh century, is represented by the four monumental figures in the main apse of San Marco (Fig. 133). The figures are livelier, more personal as it were, and freer in attitude, gesture and expression. Contours, seams and folds are somewhat curvilinear and the modeling is more comprehensive, giving body and weight to the figure as a whole. Close parallels to this style, which appears also in the mosaic fragments of the Basilica Ursiana of Ravenna, dated 1112, are difficult to find in Byzantium—we have nothing from this period in Constantinople; and the frescoes of Hagia Sophia in Ohrid, usually dated soon after the middle of the eleventh century, show much more animated drapery patterns, as befits the

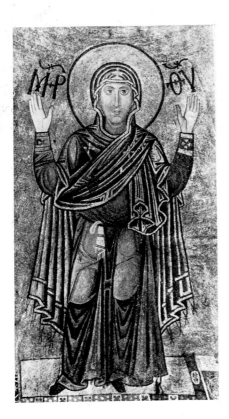

Fig. 132. *Kiev*, St. Sophia. Mosaic of Virgin in the Main Apse.

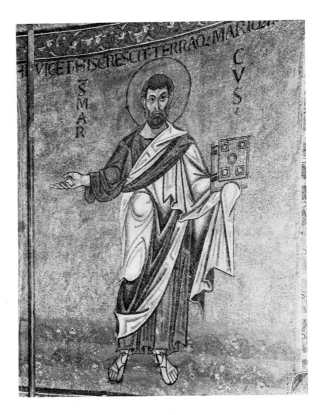

Fig. 133. *Venice*, San Marco, Main Apse. St. Mark.

130

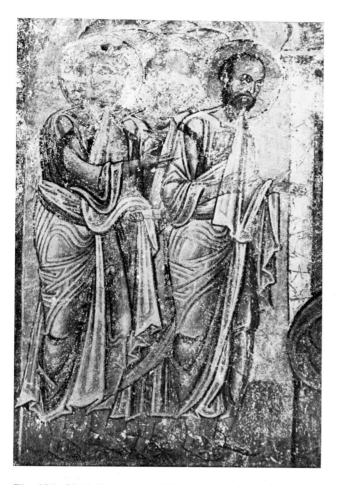 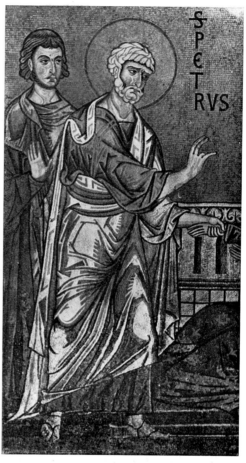

Fig. 134. *Ohrid*, Yugoslavia, Hagia Sophia, Wall Painting. Apostles.

Fig. 135. *Palermo*, Cappella Palatina, Mosaic in North Aisle. St. Peter from the Healing of Tabitha.

more pliable technique (Fig. 134). The new Comnenian style, elegant, animated and Hellenistic, as it first appeared in the mosaics of Daphni soon after 1100 (Fig. 6),[86] does not seem to have reached Venice where there is a gap of about three-quarters of a century.

The gap is filled by the mosaics of Roger II in Palermo (Fig. 135) and Cefalù (Fig. 127), roughly of the middle of the twelfth century. Compared with the classical beauty of the Daphni figures, the forms have become more complicated and, at the same time, stiffer, with a somewhat neoclassical air. Folds are not seen and rendered as plastic motifs, rising, stretching, hanging and falling, in short, conforming to the logic of the drapery; rather, they appear as incised linear designs obeying the laws of semi-abstract graphic patterns. Again, it is not easy to point to exact parallels in Constantinople; the

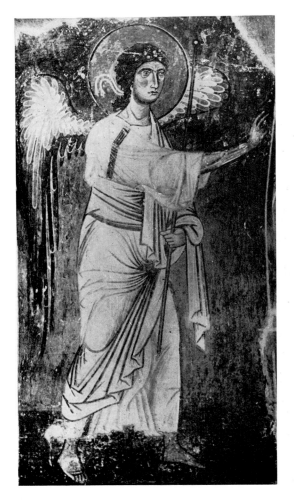

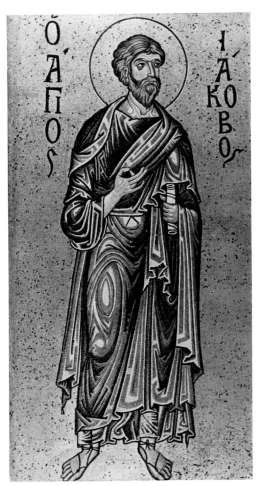

Fig. 136. *Pskow*, U.S.S.R., Cathedral, Wall Painting. Angel.

Fig. 137. *Monreale*, Cathedral, Mosaic in Main Apse. St. James.

nearest relatives, of what is already an advanced phase, are to be found in the frescoes of Pskov, of 1156, works of a Greek *équipe* working in Russia (Fig. 136). They share with the latest parts of the mosaics of the Palatine Chapel, especially those of the aisles, not only the dry, sharp and wiry outlines but also the white, form-designing arabesques which model the faces, stylized highlights which give to the features a certain linear tension and, at the same time, a certain glittering polish. Taken as a whole, this style was especially well adapted for export: its neoclassical coolness and regularity, its schematic linearism and its correct and simple compositions were much easier to copy than the classical Hellenism of Daphni. It goes almost without saying that the style of the Palatina mosaics had in fact the greatest success in the north-west.

132

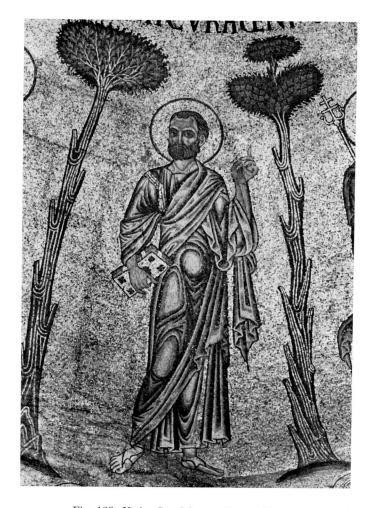

Fig. 138. *Venice*, San Marco, Central Dome.
Apostle from Ascension.

The next wave of strong Byzantine influence reached the Italian centers—
Venice as well as Sicily—in the last third of the twelfth century. It introduced
into the West the dynamic style, one of the most distinctive styles of Byzantine painting. Agitated movements, swirling draperies with plastic islands surrounded by flowing folds, distorted faces, and dynamic compositions characterize this mannerist phase, which seems to have met a deep need for expression that was felt in the East and in the West in the late twelfth century.
Monreale (Figs. 123, 128, 137) shows the style in its pure Byzantine form,
while in Venice it appears in a version which is already colored by Romanesque
tendencies (Fig. 138).

This quick assimilation is characteristic of Venice in general. Whereas
Sicily was, artistically as much as politically, a new and upstart country,

133

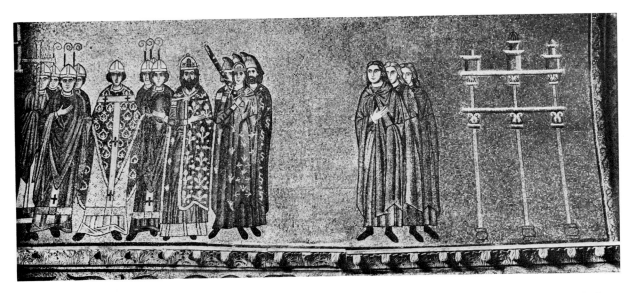

Fig. 139. *Venice*, San Marco, Mosaic in the Cappella San Clemente. The Doge receiving the Relics of St. Mark.

Venice had its traditions of form which, in the last analysis, hark back to the great period of Ravennate art in the sixth century. Some of these traditions—Byzantine traditions, of course—were exceedingly long-lived. The decoration of a vault in the Cathedral of Torcello is an eleventh century copy of the presbytery vault of San Vitale, with four angels supporting a central medallion and with the ground filled with green and golden scrolls. Even the most Venetian, the most national subject of Venetian art, the representation of the doge with his grandees, councillors and clergy triumphantly receiving the relics of the holy Mark, the state patron, in the church of San Marco itself (Fig. 139), followed the pattern of a famous Ravenna model, the dedicatory mosaic of Emperor Justinian in San Vitale (Fig. 140). This use of ancient prototypes in eleventh, twelfth and thirteenth century Venice may not be due to an unbroken tradition; it could be part of a consciously archaistic political tendency, fostered by the desire of the young city-state to create for itself something like a national past. It is even likely that it was this archaistic trend which led the Venetians to adopt a very early model for San Marco itself, the state church and receptacle of the relics of the patron saint, whose translation to Venice in 829 marked, in fact, the birth of Venice: here too it was the art of Justinian to which they resorted—the special prototype being the Church of the Apostles in Constantinople. The choice of this model (which the first San Marco, of the ninth century, already may have followed and of which the present building, of the later eleventh century, is a more or less

134

faithful copy) was certainly a stroke of genius. In this way the Venetians provided for their patron, the "near-apostle" Mark, an Apostoleion following the time-honored scheme of apostles' churches with five domes, arranged crosswise; usurped for themselves the type of the Byzantine state church; and established a link with the past—with what they took for the apostolic age. Like most strokes of genius, theirs was imitated more than once, the closest imitation being Saint Front in Périgueux (the church of the would-be apostle of the Périgord). Between them San Marco and Saint Front had a huge progeny, in Venice descending in time down to the seventeenth century, in France in space, the domed churches of the central west, such as Solignac, owing their most characteristic features to Saint Front, San Marco and thus, finally, to Justinian's Apostoleion in Constantinople.[88]

Not only the building but also the decoration of San Marco had its effects on the art of the North, especially that of the Alpine countries, not to speak of the Veneto proper. The oldest of the Byzantine styles of Venice, that of the apostles in the narthex (Fig. 130), very soon dominated wall painting and book

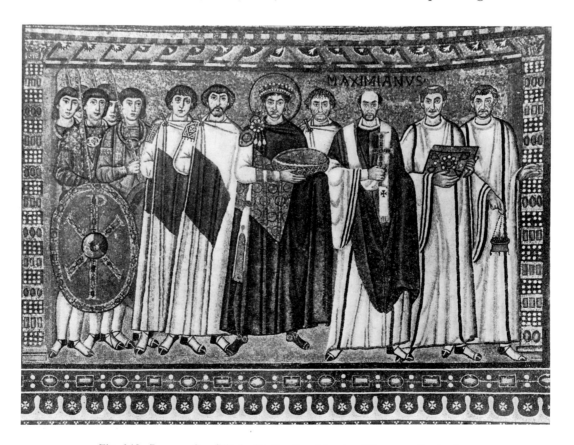

Fig. 140. *Ravenna*, San Vitale, Dedication Mosaic of Emperor Justianian.

135

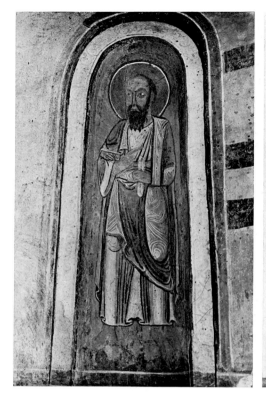

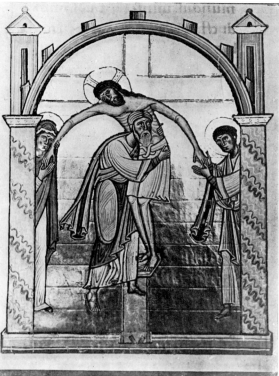

Fig. 141. *Concordia Sagittaria*, Italy, Baptistry, Wall Painting. St. Paul.

Fig. 142. *New York*, Pierpont Morgan Library MS 780, Custos Bertolt, Descent from the Cross.

illumination in those regions which belonged to the Venetian sphere of influence. The frescoes of the baptistery of Concordia (northeast of Venice) (Fig. 141), of the 1090's are quite clearly inspired by this style with its rigid parceling of the body and its ascetic contours;[89] Salzburg miniaturists, such as the painter of the Glazier Lectionary in the Pierpont Morgan Library (G. 44) or the fertile (and not very imaginative) Custos Bertolt (Fig. 142) were much indebted to this heavy style, which must have been known and used in Venice as early as 1050. And the author of the most important fresco decoration of the north Alpine region, the wall paintings of Lambach (Fig. 143), a Salzburg painter active in the last third of the eleventh century, must have been trained in Venice or in Aquileia. These newly discovered wall paintings have been a great surprise, for their painter's mastery of Byzantine composition, iconography, types and modeling, with the bodies divided up into framed, almost geometrically shaped parts, is so much greater than that of Custos Bertolt, his artistic stature so much more impressive, that we have to regard him as one of the leading masters of his time in Salzburg, the greatest religious and artistic metropolis of the German Southeast.[90]

136

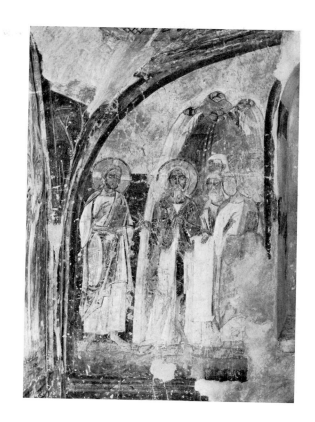

Fig. 143. *Lambach*, Austria, Abbey Church, Wall Painting. St. John Baptist announcing Christ.

The Lombard artist also learned from Byzantine models that synthesis of narrative and timeless representation which is one of the greatest achievements of post-iconoclastic art. A complicated symmetry of two interlinked compositional systems is employed as, for example, in the scene of the twelve-year-old Christ in the Temple (Fig. 144), where, though the main group is displaced towards the left, symmetry and regularity are restored by the introduction of Mary and Joseph at the right and by the subordination of the whole to the symmetrical framework of the painted architecture. This complicated composition forms, together with the firm and rigidly symmetric composition of the Healing in the Synagogue below, a highly complex unit of wall decoration; and six units of this kind, together with an apse and three domes, form the decoration of the entire chapel—a decorative system which goes far beyond the possibilities of Ottonian art and must have been inspired by Greek narthex decorations like the one in Hosios Lukas.

The style of Hosios Lukas, as it was brought to the West by the narthex figures of San Marco (Fig. 145), retained its paradigmatic importance for a long time. It must have been from these figures that a Salzburg painter

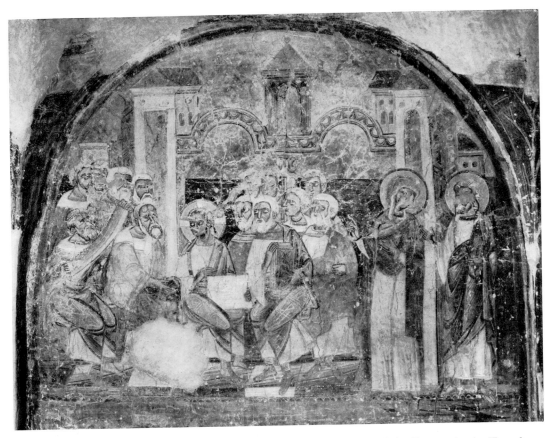

Fig. 144. *Lambach*, Austria, Abbey Church, Wall Painting. Christ and the Doctors in the Temple.

of the 1150's or 1160's took his cue for the construction (by ruler and compasses) of those magnificent heads of saints which are the only remains of a large and comprehensive decoration in the convent church of Nonnberg in Salzburg (Fig. 146);[91] of course, he overdid the geometric regularity of the faces in his desire to capture something of the timeless strength and the hieratic dignity of his Byzantine models. The Nonnberg heads are early instances of that perpetual quest of Northern artists for the regular, cogent and, as it were, definitive form, a quest which was tragically renewed, 350 years later, by Albrecht Dürer in the same Venice where the Salzburg painters of the eleventh and twelfth centuries made their first studies of mediterranean art.

The reversion of the Nonnberg painters to earlier models was not a unique case. Some of the legendary scenes in the crypt of the Cathedral of Aquileia illustrating the story of St. Hermagoras, also seem to hark back to earlier prototypes, almost certainly Venetian. The style of these lost prototypes had its effect in the North as well, in the illustration of one of the most magnificent works of Romanesque illumination, the Antiphonary of St. Peter's in

138

Salzburg (now in the National Library of Vienna) (Pl. IV), which shares with the Aquileian frescoes patterns of composition, types and forms of modeling. Since the Aquileian frescoes are later than the Salzburg miniatures, this relationship can only be explained by the assumption of common models. These Veneto-Byzantine models must have been of the highest quality, especially as regards the treatment of color, with complementary *changeant* tints in blue and pink, brown and purple, red and green.[92]

The next wave of Venetian influence is connected with the great campaign of mosaic decoration which took place in San Marco in the last third of the twelfth century and which brought the dynamic, late Comnenian style to Venice. The arrival of this agitated style with its swift-flowing forms coincided with the activity of an artist of great stature, the master of the Ascension dome (Figs. 138, 148), a Byzantine-trained Venetian, as it seems, whose style quickly became the strongest and the most expansive element in the art of Venice. He not only dominated mosaic painting in San Marco itself and in Torcello, but his style of composition and modeling set the tune for fresco painting as well: some of the frescoes in the crypt of Aquileia cathedral

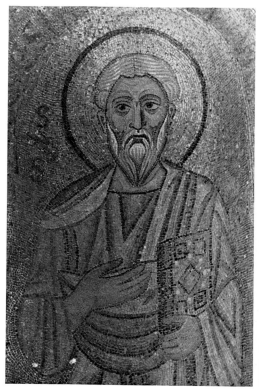 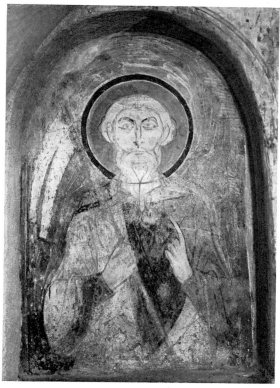

Fig. 145. *Venice*, San Marco, Main Porch. Evangelist, Detail.

Fig. 146. *Salzburg*, Abbey Church of Nonnberg, Wall Painting. St. Florian.

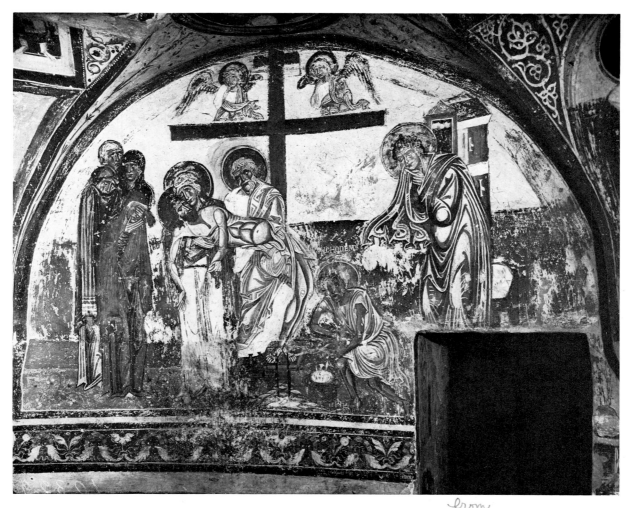

Fig. 147. *Aquileia*, Italy, Crypt of Cathedral, Wall Painting. Descent from the Cross.

(Fig. 147) are paraphrases of mosaics in San Marco. What is, however, more astonishing still, is that some of his figures, those of the Virtues in the Ascension dome (Fig. 148), which belong to the most spirited creations of late twelfth century mosaic painting, were translated more than a generation later into sculptural reliefs to decorate one of the arches of the main porch of the church (Fig. 149); even sculpture in the round was inspired by works of this style, for one of the angels placed (in the early thirteenth century) under the central dome of San Marco (Fig. 150), to stress the Parousia or Judgment aspect of the Ascension, is a translation into three-dimensional sculpture of one of the tuba-sounding mosaic angels on the west wall of Torcello cathedral (Fig. 151). The collaborators and followers of the Ascension master developed his style in the direction of an *outré* mannerism, whose near-absurdity is

140

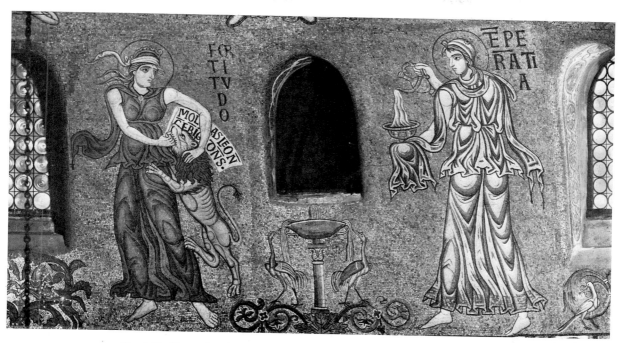

Fig. 148. *Venice*, San Marco, Central Dome. Fortitudo and Temperantia.

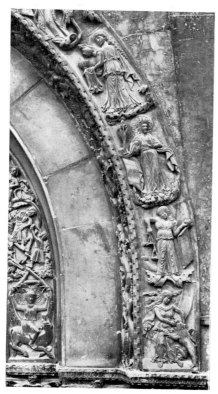

Fig. 149. *Venice*, San Marco, Main Door, Reliefs. Allegories of Virtues.

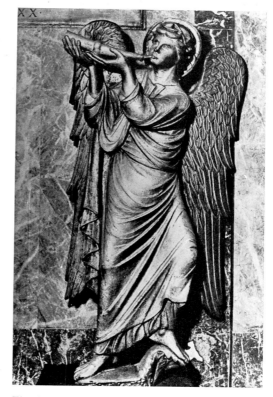

Fig. 150. *Venice*, San Marco, Sculpture of Tuba-sounding Angel.

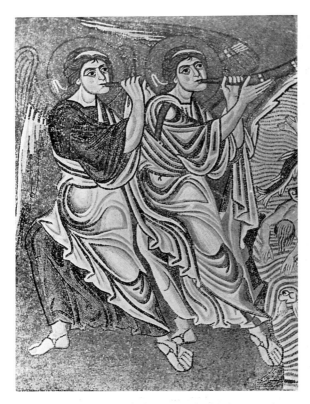

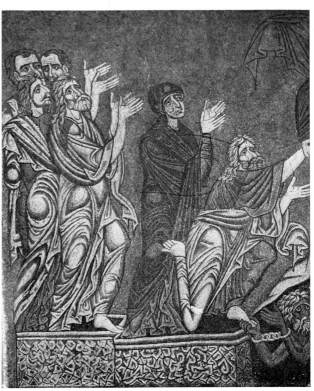

Fig. 151. *Torcello*, Cathedral, Mosaic of Last Judgment. Tuba-sounding Angels.

Fig. 152. *Venice*, San Marco, Mosaic. Harrowing of Hell, Detail.

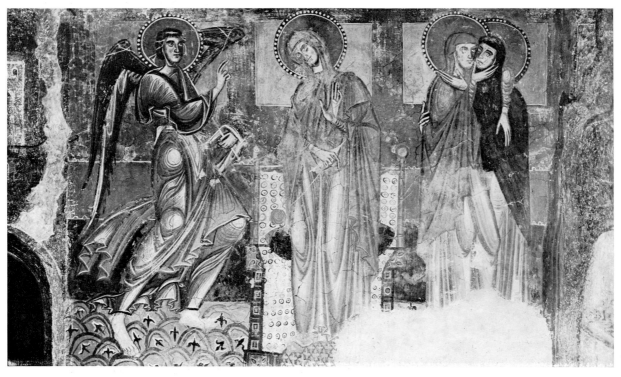

Fig. 153. *Castel Appiano* (Hocheppan), Italy, Wall Painting. Annunciation.

142

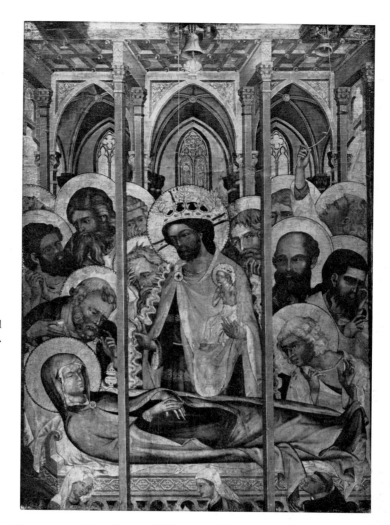

Fig. 154. *Prague*, National Gallery, Bohemian Master. Death of the Virgin.

counterbalanced by its deep emotional qualities, as in the Harrowing of Hell (Fig. 152). Both aspects of the style became effective as influences in the West and the North: its agitated mannerism in the Alps—for instance, in the fresco decoration of Castell'Appiano in southern Tyrol (Fig. 153)[93]—and its intense expressionism in France and Germany, in painting and in sculpture.

In the thirteenth and fourteenth centuries the Byzantinizing art of Venice continued to provide Northern painters with models and even with specialists. While the activity and the influence in the Austrian Alps of Veneto-Paduan artists, both illuminators and fresco painters, is by now well known and appreciated, the impact of Venetian art on Bohemian painting has not yet been properly studied. The Prague mosaics, it is true, are in too bad a state of preservation for any nicer points of style to be discussed; but the types, the modeling and the coloring in the panels of the Master of Hohenfurt, one of the leading Bohemian painters of the middle of the fourteenth century, and of his school (Fig. 154), show quite clearly that they are derived from Venetian models, in the first place from panel paintings by Paolo Veneziano, where we

143

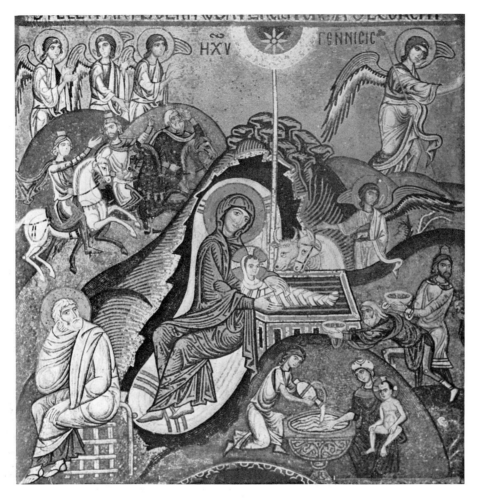

Fig. 155. *Palermo*, Cappella Palatina, Mosaic. Nativity.

find the originals of those overmodeled, darkly colored faces with their strong
Byzantine cast. The modeling technique which this Venetian influence brought
to Bohemia became a very important factor in Central European painting,
including that of the International Style. It may have been introduced by one
of those wandering artists to whom the contemporary sources allude; thus,
Tommaso da Modena (whether he was personally in Prague or not) was not
the only Italian painter to leave his impact on Bohemian art. There must have
been at least one Venetian among them.[94]

While in Venice Byzantine styles seem to have become assimilated very
quickly, to have, in fact, become Venetian styles very soon after their trans-
plantation to Venice, the styles of Sicilian mosaic art remained remarkably
pure, with little admixture of local elements with the exception of icono-

144

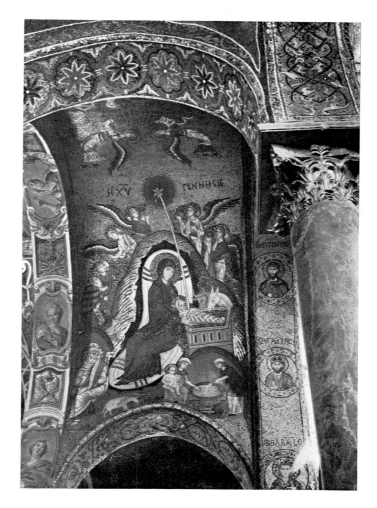

Fig. 156. *Palermo*, Martorana, Mosaic. Nativity.

graphy, arrangement and ornamentation. These factors and, perhaps, also the common source of the Sicilian mosaic styles in metropolitan art—some of the Venetian styles may have come from the provinces, especially Salonica—brought about a certain uniformity of character in works of different dates, a uniformity which might be mistaken for the effect of a local tradition. Of course, contemporary works—and three of the Sicilian mosaic cycles, those of the Palatina, the Martorana and Cefalù, are roughly contemporary—are linked with each other by workshop relationships: thus, the secondary workshop of the Martorana copied from Cefalù (Fig. 155) the monumental figures of the apostles and from the Palatina the composition of the Nativity, the latter in a reduced version (Fig. 156). But there was little or no stylistic assimilation, to say nothing of a Sicilian development proper. The develop-

145

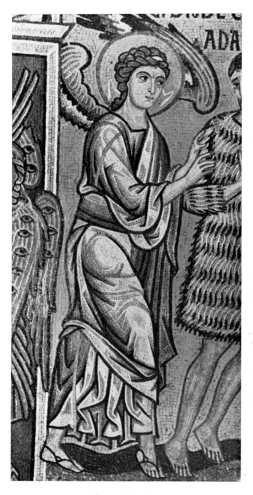

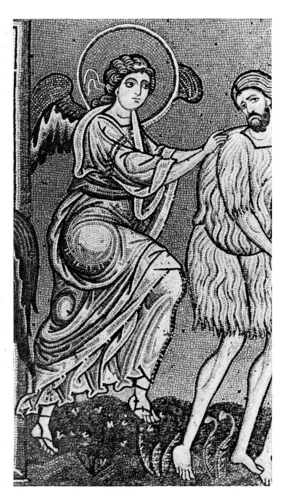

Fig. 157. *Palermo*, Cappella Palatina, Mosaic.
Expulsion from Paradise, Angel.

Fig. 158. *Monreale*, Cathedral, Mosaic.
Expulsion from Paradise, Angel.

ment took place in Constantinople itself and various phases were transferred to Sicily ready made.

Generally speaking, only two distinct phases can be discerned in the style of the Sicilian mosaics: the classicist phase of the middle and the dynamic, baroque phase of the last quarter of the twelfth century. In contrasting these two styles one can hardly do better than to follow Professor Kitzinger[95] in placing two figures side by side, the angel of the Expulsion from Paradise in the Palatina and in Monreale (Figs. 157, 158)—the juxtaposition speaks for itself; or, the Pantocrator of Cefalù, with its classicist mildness and somewhat sweet beauty, not really filling the conch and still somewhat timidly adhering to an invisible medallion frame, against the huge Christ of Monreale, who appears to embrace the entire semicircle of the apse and to fill the space

146

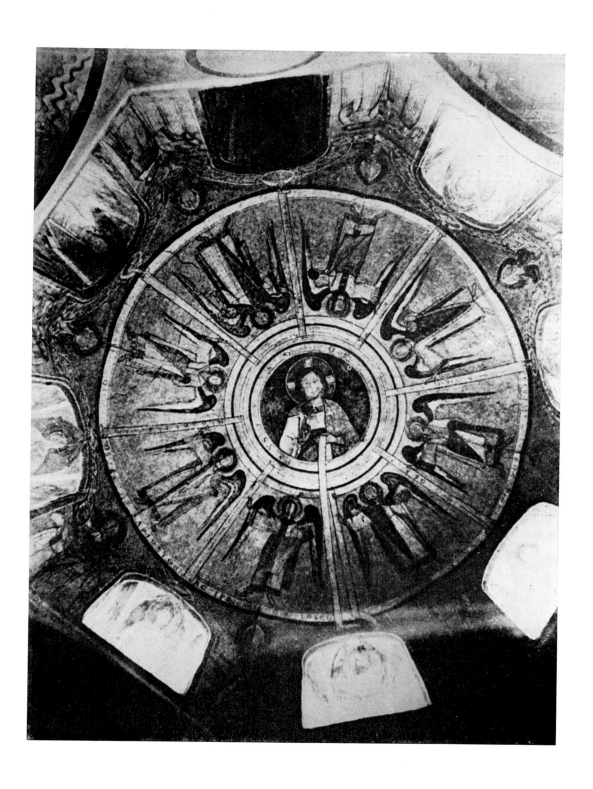

Fig. 159. *Regensburg*, Germany, All-Saints Chapel, Cupola.

with his overpowering presence. The Monreale Christ is not only very much larger absolutely, but he is also made to appear even more enormous by the tiny medallions surrounding him and by the relative smallness of the details of the drapery—typically mannerist means and features.

As the works of the first and the second Sicilian styles are separated by a whole generation, their effect outside Sicily can be differentiated into two waves, one in the third, the other in the last quarter of the twelfth century. Perhaps the most important effect of the Palatina mosaics, the crucial monument of the first phase, was the lesson in monumental composition it gave to the West. For the first time after a very long pause—since late antiquity, in fact—Western artists were furnished with an easily accessible model of cupola composition, and that at a time when domed chapels were becoming a fashion in Romanesque architecture; the Venetian cupola mosaics came later and were too large to be adapted to small-sized domes. The most direct imitation of the Palatina dome (Fig. 126) and one whose faithfulness is the more astonishing as the theological program is entirely different, is the fresco decoration in the chapel of All Saints in Regensburg, which originated around 1160 (Fig. 159); here it is not only the composition of the dome itself that was copied, but also the idea of filling the drum with half-figures in the spandrels and standing figures between the windows. Of course, as all compositional schemes derived from Byzantine models, this too was geometricized, tightened up, as it were, by regular articulations—the spokes of the wheel—and by the identical treatment of the angels' figures and costumes, a process of homogenization and abstraction which made a Romanesque scheme[96] of the Byzantine composition.

How intensively German painters studied the decorative principles governing the Palatina mosaics can be seen in the crypt of Quedlinburg where the device of allowing the figures to be cut off by the edges of the spandrels was imitated—as if the triangular surface had been cut out of a complete rectangular composition. Unfortunately, the scenes from the story of Susanna in Quedlinburg are badly restored but they still show the adherence to the Sicilian scheme.[97] More widespread even than the influence of the Palatina's principles of monumental decoration was that of Siculo-Byzantine iconography, because it concerned not only wall painting but also book illumination and the minor arts. This influence seems to have been especially strong in northwestern Europe, in the Rhineland, in northern France, the Meuse and Scheldt country and in England. Several compositions of the Palatina were copied in Mosan art, for example, the picture book now partly in Berlin, partly in London and the enameled chasse de St. Marc of Huy, a work of

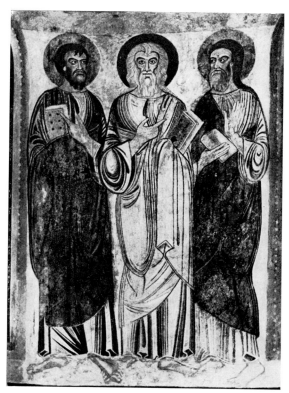

Fig. 160. *Knechtsteden*, Germany, Abbey Church, Wall Painting. Three Apostles.

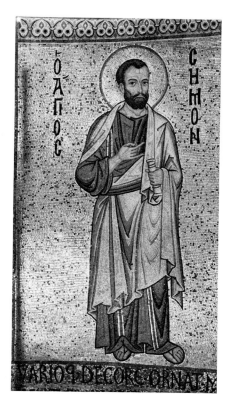

Fig. 161. *Cefalù*, Cathedral, Apse Mosaic. Apostle.

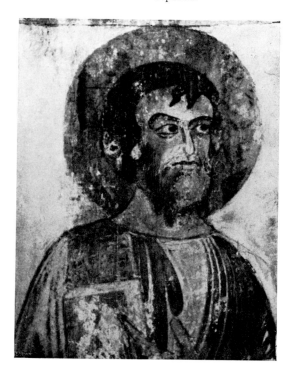

Fig. 162. *Knechtsteden*, Germany, Abbey Church, Wall Painting. Head of Apostle.

149

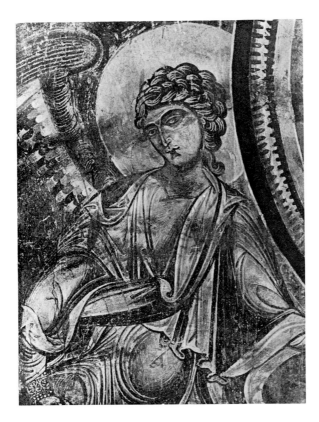

Fig. 163. *Sant'Angelo in Formis*, Italy,
Porch, Wall Painting. Angel.

about 1200.[98] Other Western artists lifted only single figures from the context of Sicilian mosaic decoration. The painter of the apse of Knechtsteden near Cologne (Fig. 160), for instance, an artist whose home was in Tournai, must have known and studied the mosaics of Cefalù (Fig. 161). More than one of the Knechtsteden apostles is an adaptation of the monumental figures of the Sicilian apse. Not only the individual motifs of the drapery, but also the entire build and stance of the figures themselves correspond so closely that a direct relationship between the two works cannot be doubted—even if the Knechtsteden frescoes have been restored almost out of existence. The same relationship holds for the heads: the one which is by far the best preserved (Fig. 162) is actually the one which is nearest to Cefalù. Of course, the Flemish painter interpreted the Sicilian model in his very rhythmical style, but this style itself owed a great deal to the Sicilian mosaics.[99]

The second wave of Sicilian influence, the effect of the mosaics of Monreale, had an even wider impact. There was, to begin with, the diaspora of the Monreale artists themselves, some of whom seem to have gone as far as Rome in their search for work after the sudden termination of their activity in Monreale. We find one of them in Grottaferrata, where he executed the mosaic representing the Pentecost, continuing, as it were, where he had left off in the left transept of Monreale. Color, technique, facial types and draperies are almost the same as in the Pentecost of the Sicilian cathedral. Grottafer-

150

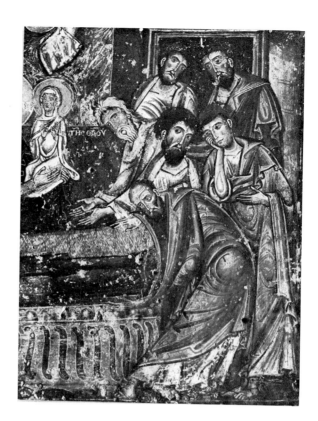

Fig. 164. *Rongolise*, Italy, Wall Painting. Death of the Virgin.

rata was a Basilian monastery; its abbot, who played an important part in the Greek monasticism of Italy, would naturally employ Greek mosaicists; and, similarly, Greek mosaicists out of work on Italian soil would naturally look for employment to one of the mightiest Greek monasteries in the peninsula. The mosaic tympanum—with the bust of St. Matthew in Salerno originated a little later. Of course, the chances of finding work in the art of mosaic itself were rather slim at the end of the twelfth century. In most cases the Sicilian masters had to be content with work in fresco. The hand of one of them can be recognized in the fresco above the main entrance of Sant'Angelo in Formis, painted after the rebuilding of the narthex in the late twelfth century (Fig. 163). The vividly swirling concentric folds, which bring out the plasticity of the body and create, at the same time, a melodious pattern of semi-abstract lines, are in the best Monreale tradition. This tradition was continued right into the thirteenth century in Campania, and it seems to have been adopted by Monte Cassino as its own official art, at least for monumental decoration. The very noble apse frescoes, formerly in the Crocefisso chapel, now transferred to Monte Cassino abbey itself, follow Monreale not only as regards the decorative scheme: the special brand of beauty of the Christ and of the saints in the medallions underneath is also strongly reminiscent of the Monreale mosaics, while the frescoes of Rongolise, still later, show the continuation of the dynamic style with its complicated, swiftly flowing and circling folds (Fig. 164).[100]

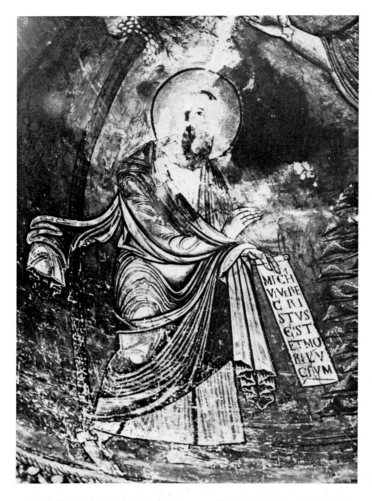

Fig. 165. *Tivoli*, Italy, San Silvestro, Wall Painting. St. Paul.

Both the new monumental form and the dynamic style of Monreale, with its mannerist overemphasis of movement and volume, seem to have made a certain impression even on those most conservative of Italian artists, the painters of Rome itself. The master of San Silvestro in Tivoli (Fig. 165), a hitherto underrated painter of the early thirteenth century, follows, it is true, the time-honored scheme of Roman apse decoration, with the standing figure of Christ, appearing from on high, flanked by Sts. Peter and Paul, with a frieze of lambs and two registers of figures and scenes beneath; but this scheme has been interpreted in a new monumental manner. The single parts not only fit together in a vertical sequence, but also constitute an architectural whole, a grand overall picture, compositionally and coloristically. Blue grounds alternate with yellow ones—i.e., golden—the arrangement of the figures

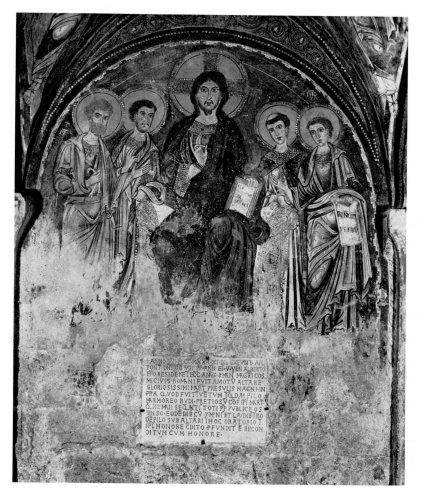

Fig. 166. *Anagni*, Italy, Cathedral, Crypt, Wall Painting.
Christ and four Saints.

takes account of the windows, and the small scenes of the life of St. Silvester are so composed as to balance each other harmoniously. That this new integration is a product of the study of great decorations like that of Monreale, is proved by the modeling of the two figures of apostles on either side of Christ: they show the unmistakable characteristics of the dynamic mannerism of Monreale, with its overemphasized joints and *points culminants* and with the swelling folds surrounding them—all developed even further. A more sketchy, less continuous kind of modeling, also to be found in Monreale, was still used as late as the second quarter of the thirteenth century by one of the pupils of the San Silvestro master, the so-called Maestro delle Traslazioni, and by his collaborators in the crypt of Anagni cathedral (Fig. 166).[101] Nor was this the latest specific effect of the Monreale style in Italy: Professor Buchthal has shown that a very

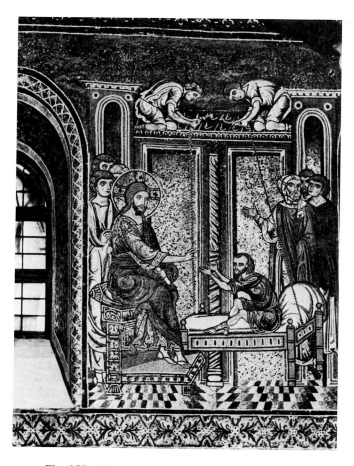

Fig. 167. *Monreale*, Mosaic. Healing of Paralytic.

curious revival of this style, which began with literal copies of Monreale compositions (Figs. 167, 168), took place in Sicily itself at the very end of the thirteenth and in the first years of the fourteenth century.[102]

However, the most important effect of the mosaic style of Monreale is to be found not in Italy but in the Northwest, especially in England, where it colored the art of Winchester in the late twelfth century. At least two of the painters who were responsible for the later miniatures of the Winchester Bible,[103] the so-called Master of the Genesis Initial and the Master of the Morgan Leaf, worked under more or less direct Sicilian influence, but the Sicilian elements are so completely integrated that they do not appear to be foreign in any way. At least one of the two masters, perhaps both, must have been in Italy and actually studied the mosaics of Monreale. The attitudes, the draperies and even more the facial types of the figures painted by these

154

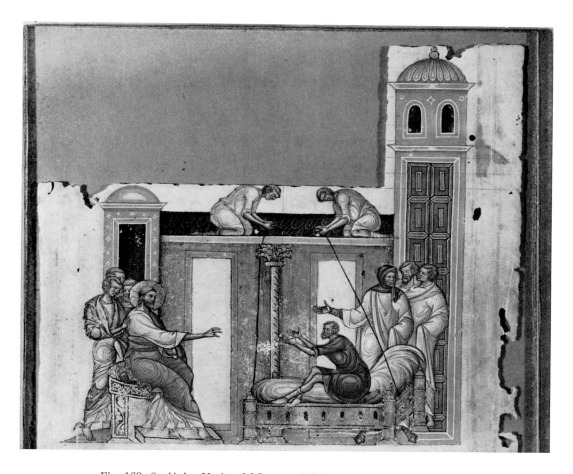

Fig. 168. *Stockholm*, National Museum, Miniature. Healing of Paralytic.

masters are more than echoes of the Monreale mosaics. Even the expression, the spiritual *habitus* of the faces, is very much the same (Fig. 169, 170).

These works of the late twelfth century mark the apogee of Siculo-Byzantine influence in England: it was the time of the closest political and cultural contact between the two Norman states. Sicilian influence must also have extended to English wall painting as is proved by the lately discovered frescoes in the chapel of the Holy Sepulchre in Winchester. In addition, we have the work of an English painter in Spain, the wall and ceiling paintings of the Chapter House of Sigena (Province of Huesca) (Fig. 171)[104]—or rather their charred remnants, since it was all but destroyed in the civil war. This artist, certainly one of the best English painters of the period, undoubtedly came from Winchester. It is extremely likely that he was none other than the so-called Master of the Morgan leaf. He brought from England a number

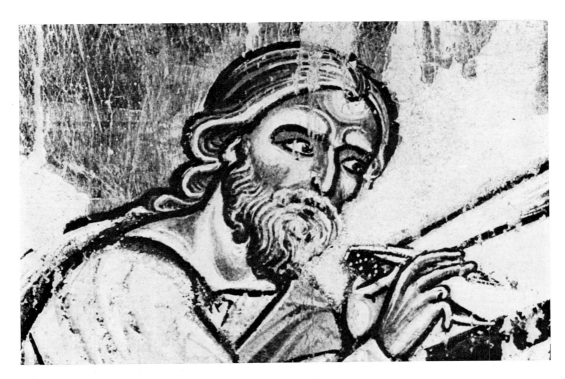

Fig. 169. *Winchester*, England, Cathedral Library, Bible Miniature. St. Jerome.

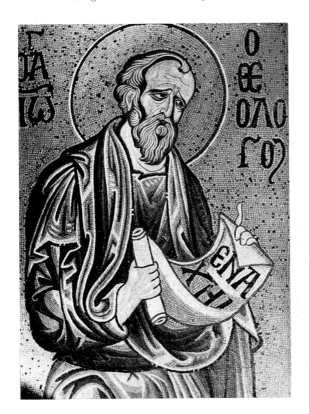

Fig. 170. *Monreale*, Cathedral, Mosaic.
St. John.

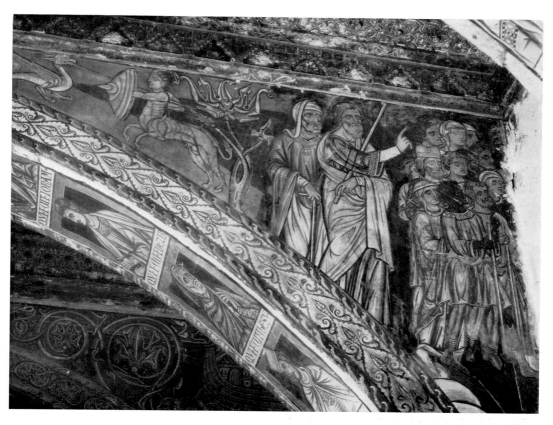

Fig. 171. *Sigena*, Spain, Former Chapter House, Wall Painting. Moses and Aaron.

Fig. 172. *Monreale*, Cathedral, Mosaic.
Healing of a Leper.

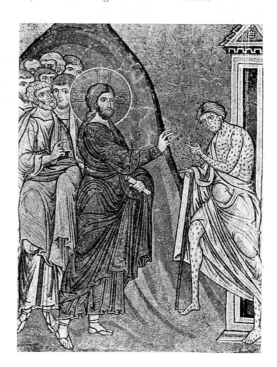

157

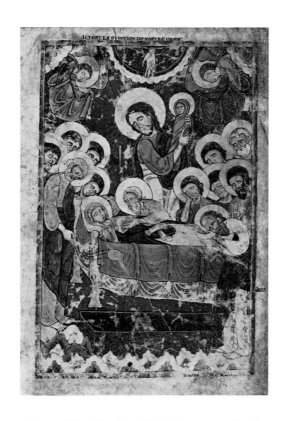

Fig. 173. *London*, Brit. Mus.,
Psalter, MS Cotton Nero C. IV.
Death of the Virgin.

of specifically English features, both stylistic—and iconographic, such as those subjects which Otto Pächt has shown to have been taken from English bestiaries. What comes to the foreground even more in Sigena than in his English works, however, is the Sicilian training of the master. His figures of Moses and attendants are *similia* of the figures of Christ and the apostles as they appear in a good many Monreale scenes (Fig. 127). But Monreale was not the only source of the Siculo-Byzantine features contained in the paintings of Sigena. Professor Kitzinger has shown (in a lecture in Athens) that he must have studied the Palatina as well. What recommended these earlier works to a Northern painter even at the very end of the twelfth century, was, in all likelihood, the purity of their style, a quality which must have made the mosaics of the Palatine chapel for twelfth century artists into something similar to the Farnese Gallery for seventeenth century painters. Thus, the two waves of Sicilian influence were not, after all, so sharply separated. There was always the possibility for artists who were primarily under the spell of the second phase, that of dynamic, late Comnenian art, to turn back to the classicist models of the first Sicilian phase, that of the Palatina.

Similarly, it is not always possible to draw a firm dividing line to separate the Sicilian from the Venetian sphere of influence. It is even possible to find

158

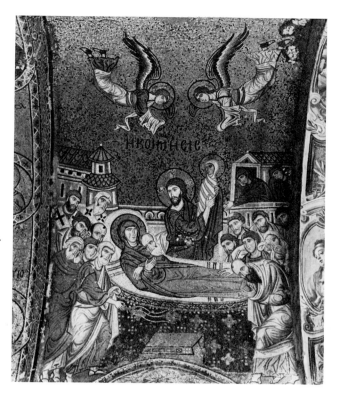

Fig. 174. *Palermo*, Martorana, Mosaic. Death of the Virgin.

in one cycle of paintings traces of both currents, as, for instance, in the Tyrolean frescoes of Castell'Appiano, which belong stylistically to the orbit of San Marco, while some of the iconographic schemes seem to have been derived from the Palatine chapel. The sequence of figures, their types and attitudes in the two representations of the Flight to Egypt, with Joseph leading the way as a kind of Christophorus, and James, the brother of the Lord, bringing up the rear and carrying the family's provisions on a staff over his shoulder, are too similar in both cycles to be due to chance. An explanation of this seeming anomaly is not too difficult to find: the Alpine painter must have used a model book which contained iconographic schemes copied from works of the mid-twelfth century, among them the Palatina mosaics—a model book the drawings of which he may have collected in his youth or inherited from his predecessor. In making use, however, of these *similia*, at the very end of the twelfth century, he translated them into the stylistic language which was that of his time and of his region, namely, the dynamic style of Venice. A similar case can be found in English art. The close alliance between England and Sicily in the second half of the twelfth century has led to the conclusion that all Byzantine elements to be found in English painting of that period must be derived from Sicily. This has been assumed, for instance, in the case of

159

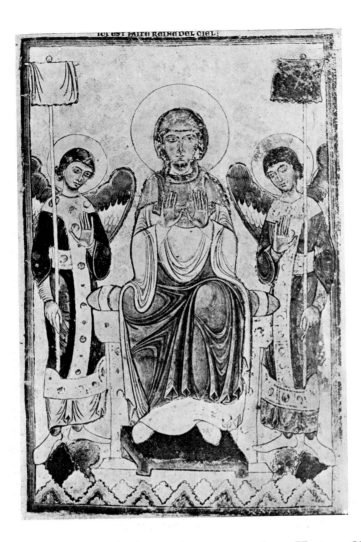

ici est faire reine del ciel:

Fig. 175. *London*, Brit. Mus.,
Psalter, ms Cotton Nero C. IV.
The Virgin and Angels.

St. Swithin's Psalter—the more so since Henry of Blois who commissioned this magnificent book was bound to Sicily by many ties. The *Death of the Virgin* (Fig. 173) in this book—one of two rather strange foreign bodies in the otherwise purely English manuscript—has been connected, therefore, with the mosaic of the same subject in the Martorana chapel in Palermo (Fig. 174). However, the relationship between the two representations is not specific enough to stand up to a critical reexamination: the composition might have been derived from any other Byzantine prototype; it is nearer, for instance, to the Melisenda Psalter of the British Museum, a splendidly illuminated book so convincingly characterized by Professor Buchthal, that originated in one of the scriptoria of the Holy Land. As a matter of fact, the *Enthroned Virgin* (Fig. 175), the only other "Byzantine" miniature of St. Swithin's Psalter, is stylistically so close to another miniature of Queen Melisenda's book (Fig. 176)

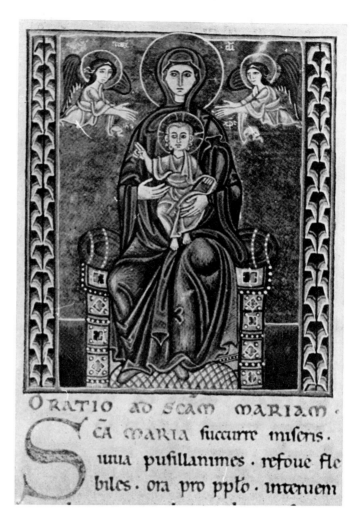

Fig. 176. *London*, Brit. Mus., Psalter, MS Egerton 1139. The Virgin.

(compare, for instance, the modeling of the draperies from the knees down) that the derivation of the two English miniatures from Crusader art becomes a virtual certainty—at least until someone finds another, still closer model.

These examples should warn the student not to look at things in too simple a way. Especially toward the end of the twelfth century we must reckon with the fact that the artist was replacing the patron as the decisive factor. Such practices as the free choice of models, the conscious selection of single features or principles, and the free translation of models into new languages of form were becoming the rule. For this selective approach to have become possible it was necessary that a great body of acknowledged models exist within easy reach: this was exactly what the mosaics of Sicily and Venice provided. Thus, they became the academies of Western artists in the twelfth century.

161

5

The Birth of Gothic

"At the middle of the twelfth century, two revolutionary ideas—that of the articulated body and that of the animated figure—are carried by the crest of the Byzantine tidal wave to northern France, where a great creative genius makes them the cornerstones of a new style, the Gothic."

These portentous words are to be found in the late Professor Koehler's inaugural lecture, "Byzantine Art in the West," delivered at Dumbarton Oaks in 1940.[106] The new integration of body and spirit, the instilling of will and personality into figures which only now become truly humanized, this was the crowning success of the long wooing of the art of Byzantium by Western artists. These artists were not content with borrowing from Byzantine art the mere vocabulary of representation or its rules of syntax; they penetrated deeper, to the very roots of this art in Hellenism. The omnivorous attitude of earlier times developed into a selective, even a critical approach which enabled Western artists to discover the classical prototypes of Byzantine art. There was a long way to go from the beginning of this process to its end. A confrontation of works separated from each other by less than one hundred years brings out the immense change that took place between the first and the last years of the twelfth century, the most fateful period in the development of European art between late antiquity and the early Renaissance. The figures of the apostles, especially St. Peter, in the Cluny Lectionary of the early twelfth century (Fig. 115) owed, it is true, a great deal to Byzantine models. The proportions of the figures, their dignity, the arrangement of the toga and the firm logic of the economically employed drapery are qualities which were derived from Byzantine prototypes. But there is as yet hardly any differentiation of body and garment. The entire figure seems to consist of some hard, homogeneous material, cast into permanent shape: no movement, no change of temper or mood seem to be possible. The figure is not even imaginable as existing apart from its surroundings which are also integral parts of the

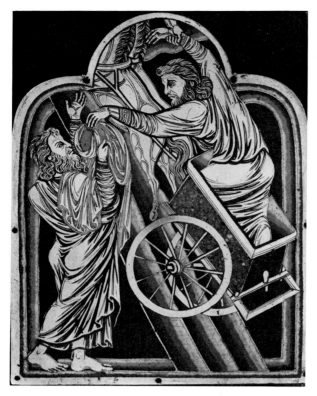

Fig. 177. *Klosterneuburg* (Vienna), Enamel Altar by
Nicholas of Verdun. Ascension of Elijah.

homogeneous whole, the entire image. In contrast to this, the enthroned
Christ by Nicholas of Verdun, of 1181 (Fig. 200), is not part and parcel of
a whole that includes the frame; it seems rather to "inhabit" the frame with
a much greater freedom, in spite of the fact that in this goldsmith's work the
figures are materially much more bound up with the framework than in the
miniature. The projection of the limbs and the modeling suggest a physical
presence that is enhanced by the dualism of the garment and the body; the
latter is felt as existing in its own right apart from the covering draperies,
which cling to the body in some places and detach themselves freely or
stretch tightly in others.

This so-called damp fold style, perhaps the most important single element
derived from classical art, could be used intelligently and convincingly only
by artists who had achieved a real understanding of the body and its movements and were able to see these movements as caused and directed by the
will of the person represented. There is no trace of this personal will in the
grand spectres of Saint-Savin (Fig. 100) whose attitudes and movements
appear as something imposed on them by a power outside and above them-

164

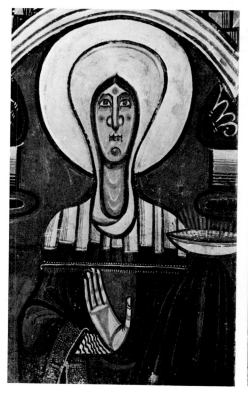 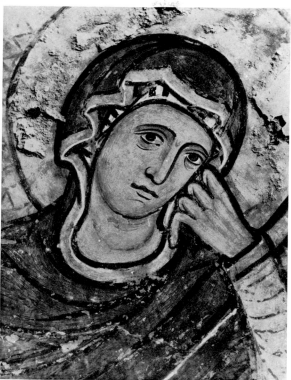

Fig. 178. *Tahull*, Catalonia, San Clement, Wall Painting. The Virgin.

Fig. 179. *Sigena*, Spain, former Chapter House, Wall Painting, Virgin from Nativity.

selves. The figures of Nicholas of Verdun's Ascension of Elijah (Fig. 177), on the other hand, move of their own volition and express their own feelings. Masks become faces, no longer set in some grand, frightening or even grotesque mold, but humane and variable. Compared with the Virgin of Tahull (Fig. 178), the work of a Spanish painter of about 1120, the face of the Virgin from the Nativity of Christ in Sigena, of the early thirteenth century (Fig. 179), seems to belong to our time or, rather, to a time near to ours, a time which ended about 1900. The same is true of monumental compositions. Crowded, expressive and turbulent compositions, threateningly explosive and difficult to unravel, such as the tympanums of Moissac, (Fig. 180), Vézelay or Conques, give way in the later twelfth and the early thirteenth centuries, to well-ordered arrangements of large figures in "natural" attitudes, following a simple design, as in the north transept portal of Chartres (Fig. 181).[107]

Now it is quite clear that all or most of the traits which distinguish the works of about 1200 from those of the early twelfth century are characteristic of the art of classical antiquity. Would it not be logical to assume that they were in fact derived directly from classical Greek or Roman models and so

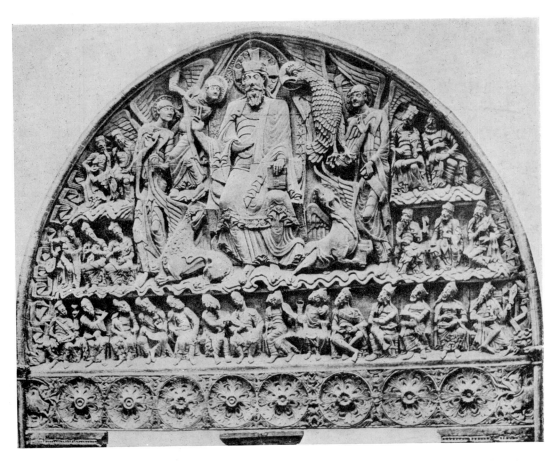

Fig. 180. *Moissac*, France, Main Porch. Christ in Majesty.

have nothing to do with Byzantium? As a matter of fact, there are works—and not only single works but entire currents—which appear to have been inspired by Roman art without the intervention of Byzantine models. One of these currents is, of course, that of the Proto-Renaissance of southern France. In Saint-Gilles (Fig. 182), for instance, the Byzantine factor is certainly not very important, although it is not entirely absent. The most important factor in the genesis of the style of this enigmatic work was undoubtedly the rediscovery of the Roman and early Christian art of Provence.

The case is even clearer in Saint Trophime in Arles (Fig. 183). The heavy figures of apostles and saints in the niches of the porch look as if they had been built up in several stories rather than grown. There is hardly any feeling for the body as something distinct from the complicated drapery, and there is certainly no feeling at all for growth, innervation and movement. Even the faces are stony—the whole is unredeemed Romanesque.[108]

Of course, something of this tectonic solidity has also gone into early Gothic, but the constitutive elements of this art of the North stem from other sources. One of the most important of these sources was the art of Byzantium, directly

166

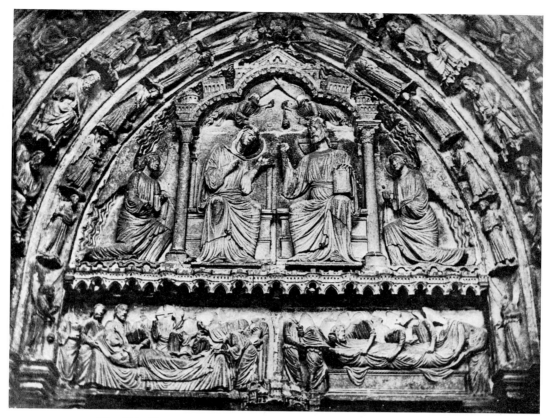

Fig. 181. *Chartres*, Cathedral, North Porch. Coronation of the Virgin.

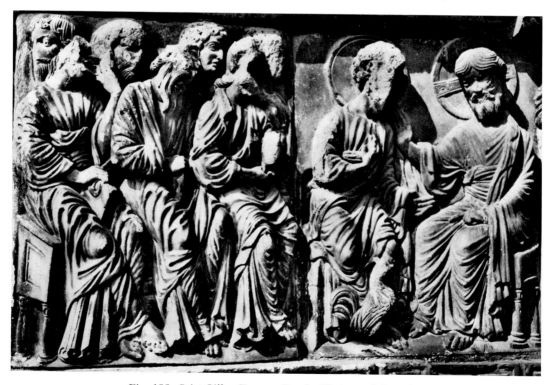

Fig. 182. *Saint-Gilles*, France, Porch. Christ and Apostles.

167

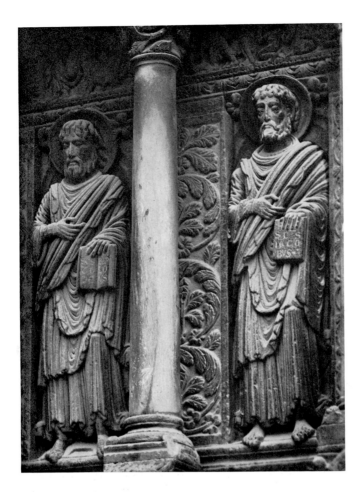

Fig. 183. *Arles*, Saint-Trophime, Main Porch. Apostles.

and indirectly. Some Byzantine elements had already been part of Ottonian classicism, which must have been of paramount importance for one of the greatest works of the first half of the century, the font of Saint Barthélémy in Liège, by Renier de Huy (Fig. 184).[109] Even more important, however, for the broad development of Romanesque art toward the Gothic were the ever-renewed contacts with the living art of Byzantium, the contemporary or almost contemporary art of Constantinople and of the colonial centers of Byzantine art in Italy.

Those values of which I have been speaking, namely, the feeling for the organic growth and movement of the body conveyed by means of damp fold drapery, the very personal dignity of the human figure, and the simple grandeur of composition, are in the last analysis classical Greek or Hellenistic qualities. All these values had again become part of a living tradition in the art of Constantinople since the late ninth century. They appear in the Paris Gregory of the late ninth and the Paris Psalter of the tenth century

168

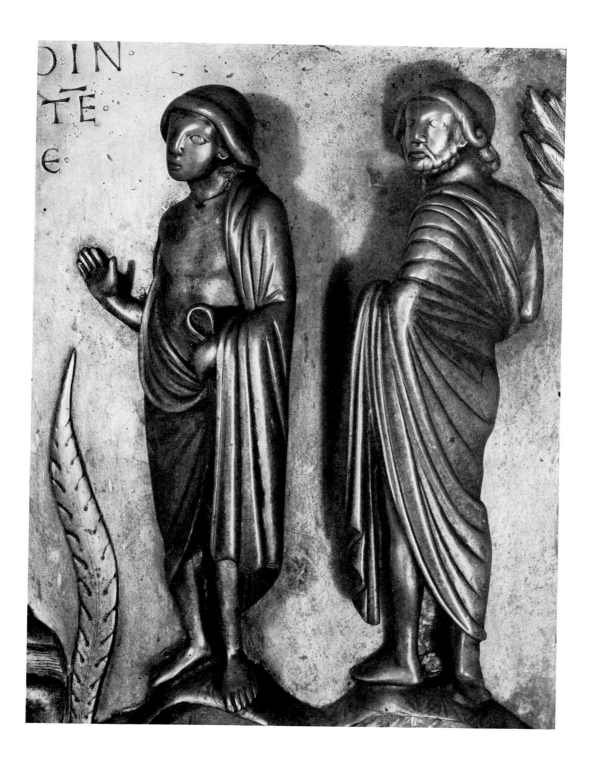

Fig. 184. *Liège*, Saint-Barthélémy, Font. Figures from Baptism.

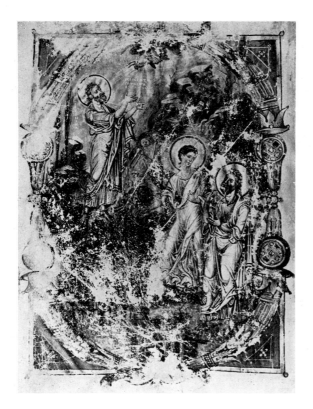

Fig. 185. *Paris*, Bibl. Nat., Cod. gr. 510,
Vision of Ezechiel.

(Fig. 185). The question, why it took the West so long—until the later twelfth century—to recognize and to assimilate these values, is thus quite legitimate. Apparently it was only step by step, layer by layer, that Western artists were able to penetrate to the core of Hellenism; only after long preparation did they succeed in seeing the Greek behind the Byzantine, the classical within the medieval. The slow but constant growth of this understanding, the increasing power of assimilation and, at the same time, the development of independence is an absorbing spectacle. At the end of this process, Western artists were no longer imitators of Byzantine models: they had become students of classical antiquity on a par with their Byzantine colleagues.

The beginning of the coherent development seems to coincide with the crystallization of Comnenian classicism around 1100. In the mosaics of Daphni (Fig. 6), the wealth of detail appears to be somewhat reduced and the pictorial freedom of the Macedonian Renascence somewhat curtailed. The body-drapery relationship is restated in linear patterns which are still those of the damp fold style, but simpler and more patently logical. It is the damp-fold style *ad usum delphini*, much easier to imitate than its painterly variety of

170

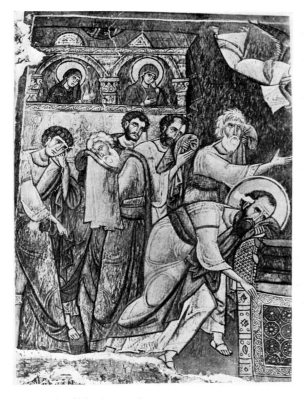

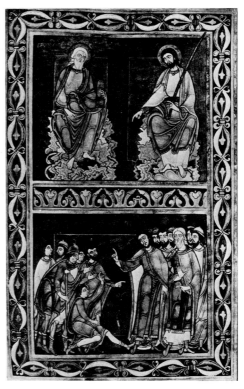

Fig. 186. *Asinou*, Cyprus, Wall Painting. Death of the Virgin, Detail.

Fig. 187. *Cambridge*, Corpus Christ College, MS 2, Bury Bible. Scenes from Old Testament.

the late ninth or tenth centuries, because it was translatable into rhythmical lines.

A still greater emphasis on linear pattern dominated Byzantine art in the first half of the twelfth century. The figures in the wall paintings of Asinou, in Cyprus (Fig. 186), of the early twelfth century, seem to be composed of lens-shaped parts, bounded and joined together by double lines which are meant to be folds but show little three-dimensional definition. The resulting effect is that of a rather flat relief, with sharply incised subdivisions and with the surfaces of the single cells looking like inflated membranes. The frescoes of Asinou are somewhat provincial, apparently transcriptions of metropolitan forms in a simplified and more primitive alphabet. For this very reason they show the prevailing trends of Byzantine art of this period more clearly, if more crudely, than Constantinopolitan work. And it is quite possible that models like these played an important part in the West, meeting Western artists halfway in their struggle to recreate Byzantine forms with their as yet limited repertory of means. In any case, some of the best paintings done in the Northwest, for instance the miniatures of the Bury Bible (Fig. 187), of about

171

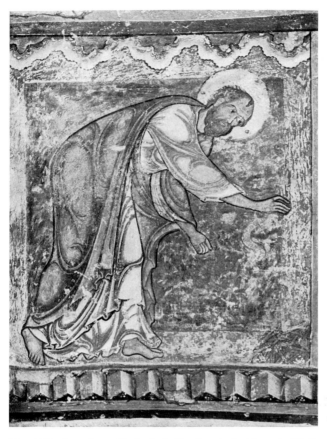

Fig. 188. *Canterbury*, Cathedral, St. Anselm's Chapel, Wall
Painting. St. Paul and the Viper.

the middle of the century, seem to have been inspired by models of the
Asinou kind or are at least astonishing parallels in interpretation of metropolitan prototypes.[160]

Only a short time elapsed between the execution of the miniatures of the
Bury Bible and the magnificent figure of St. Paul in St. Anselm's chapel in
Canterbury (Fig. 188), but a comparison with the figure of St. Paul from the
Death of the Virgin in Asinou underscores one very important change: the
movement of the Canterbury figure is much more natural, dignified and
statuesque, a movement not imposed on the figure but dictated by its own will.
Here, the Canterbury painter must have applied a lesson learned from more
recent metropolitan work, perhaps already from the mosaics of the Palatina in
Palermo (Fig. 189), where the groping figure of the blinded St. Paul—marred
by bad restoration of the drapery but authentic in contour and movement—
shows in its attitude an even more differentiated expression of inner life, the
terrified helplessness of a man suddenly struck with blindness. It is in works

172

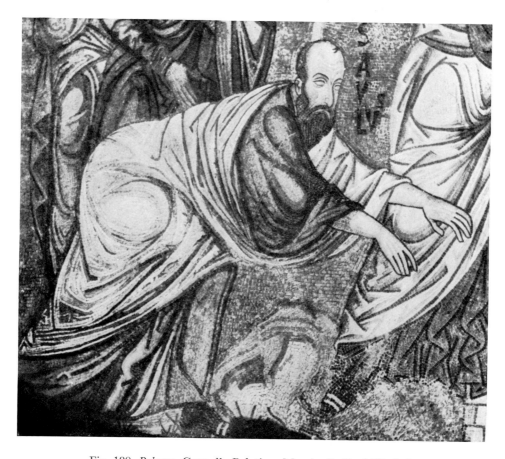

Fig. 189. *Palermo*, Cappella Palatina, Mosaic. St. Paul Blinded.

like the Canterbury St. Paul, the central tympanum of the west facade of Chartres or the wall paintings of Brauweiler near Cologne, the genuine but shadowy remains of which were recently reclaimed from under nineteenth century overpainting, that the new understanding of movement appears in the West, together with a new feeling for the totality of the body as it exists apart from the garments. It is very likely that here, too, the Palatina served as a model or, at least, as a corrective.

In the 1160's the static style of Byzantine art was gradually being supplanted by the new dynamic style of the late Comnenian era.[111] The innovation very soon made itself felt in the West as well. Swift movements, swirling and fluttering draperies and dynamic compositions were used to convey intense emotion. The new style is fully developed in the frescoes of Nerezi, in Macedonia, of 1164 (Pl. VI, Fig. 249) or soon after; and it must have reached the West about 1175, its effects persisting in certain regions well into the thirteenth century. For the growth of the style in the West, the most important quality

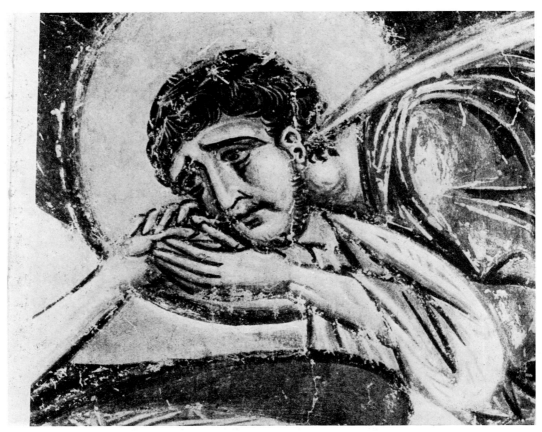

Fig. 190. *Nerezi*, Yugoslavia, Wall Painting, St. John from Lamentation.

was not that of exaggerated movement (Fig. 209) but the new depth of feeling expressed in the attitudes and the faces of the figures. And in the realm of expression it was more the lyrical depth and intensity of sentiment (Fig. 190) than the loud and stormy expression of strong emotions that helped to shape the new ideal of Gothic man. Here are the roots of the *dolce stil'nuovo* that humanized Western art.

The dynamic style was not the last phase in the development of Byzantine art before the fall of Constantinople in 1204 during the Fourth Crusade. The late Comnenian style was followed by a return to monumental grandeur and simplicity, by an ever-increasing feeling for the totality of bodily volume and by a quiet, melodious flow of line. A figure like that of the Prophet Elijah, depicted in an early thirteenth century icon from Mount Sinai (Fig. 191), shows all these qualities and something more: directness of feeling and reaction, coupled with great personal dignity. This style made its first appearance in the West in the last years of the twelfth century but it lingered on well into the thirteenth: one of the seated figures from the vault frescoes in San Giovanni

174

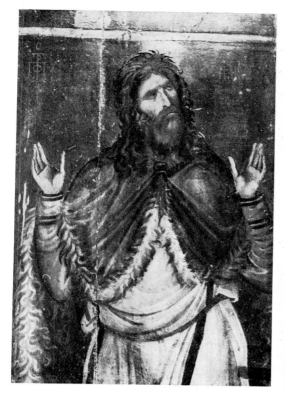 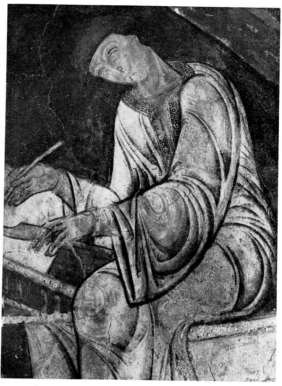

Fig. 191. *Sinai*, Monastery of St. Catherine, Icon. Fig. 192. *Tubre* (Taufers), Italy, Wall Painting
Elijah. Deacon.

di Tubre (Taufers, in South Tyrol) (Fig. 192) typifies this later phase of the
new monumental art.[112]

It is hardly to be expected that Western sculpture would show the effects of
Byzantine influence as clearly as Western painting. There would be little
direct influence from contemporary Byzantine sculpture since there was little
development in this field during the twelfth century in Byzantium itself.[113]
Nevertheless, Byzantine elements did play a part in the triumphal awakening
of sculpture in the late Romanesque and early Gothic West. On the one
hand, Byzantine painting furnished some stimuli for sculpture as well as for
painting itself, and, on the other hand, earlier works of Byzantine sculpture—
mainly in ivory and metal—actually served as models for monumental sculpture. The development of the multilinear, form-designing style of Burgundian
relief sculpture, as it appeared in the 1120's or 1130's in Vézelay (Fig. 193) or
Autun, was certainly, if not inspired, at least assisted and conditioned by
Byzantine enamels (Fig. 194) that show a very similar organization of the
drapery through a dense system of curving parallel lines which bring out the

175

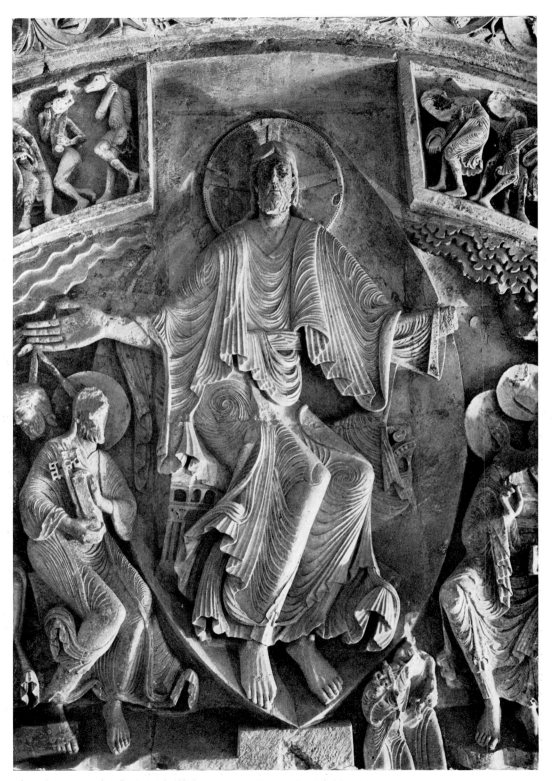

Fig. 193. *Vézelay*, Main Porch. Christ in Majesty.

176

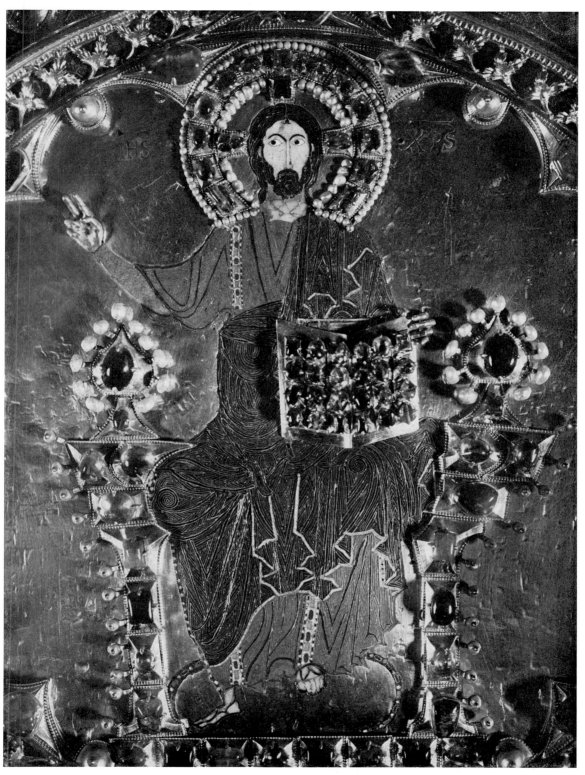

Fig. 194. *Venice*, San Marco, Pala d'Oro, Enamel. Christ Enthroned.

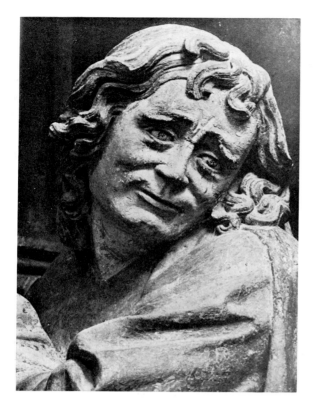

Fig. 195. *Naumburg*, Cathedral. St. John, Detail.

relief of the body. And it is perhaps not without significance that the greatest work of Byzantine enamel art ever to reach the West made its appearance in San Marco in Venice immediately before, in 1105. These enamels of the Pala d'Oro (and other Byzantine work of the eleventh and the early twelfth century) even exhibit those curious idiosyncracies that look so odd in Vézelay and which are so much more "natural" in the technique of cloisonné enamel, namely, the spiral whirls on the knees of standing and seated figures. It is hardly likely that this is a mere coincidence. It will, therefore, have to be assumed that French sculptors in their search for anything that might help to model a figure in low relief fastened, among other things, on Byzantine enamels. However, modeling techniques were not all that was derived by Western sculptors from Byzantine or Byzantinizing painting, for new dimensions of expression were also opened up to them by the study of these sources, the rendering of deep feeling, as in the sorrow-distorted face of St. John in Naumburg (Fig. 195), of the third quarter of the thirteenth century. This was made possible by the conquests of psychological terrain achieved by the painters of Byzantium a century before (Pl. VI, Fig. 190).

178

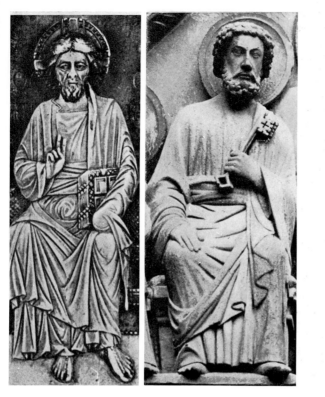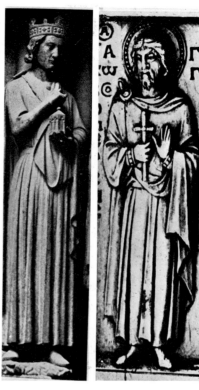

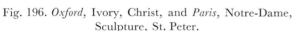

Fig. 196. *Oxford*, Ivory, Christ, and *Paris*, Notre-Dame, Sculpture, St. Peter.

Fig. 197. *Amiens*, Cathedral, King, and *Paris*, Harbaville Triptych, Apostle.

The effects of the study of earlier Byzantine sculpture on Western twelfth and thirteenth century statuary and reliefs have repeatedly been pointed out, from André Michel, Emile Male and Adolph Goldschmidt to Professor Sauer- länder. Constantinopolitan ivories of the tenth century seem to have played an important part in the genesis of the classical style of French sculpture in the early thirteenth century. Professor Sauerländer's comparison of relief figures from the Oxford book cover and the Harbaville triptych with figures in the round from Paris and Amiens seems to be completely convincing (Figs. 196, 197). The similarities concern not only the arrangement of the drapery in straight lines with predominant verticals, and the plastic treatment of the folds with recurring parallel planes, but also the entire conception of the body, its posture, weight and restrained movement, and, finally, the spiritual qualities of the figures, their cool distance coupled with a quiet awareness, as it were, qualities which are extremely characteristic of the "dehydrated" Hellenism of the Macedonian Renascence.[114]

179

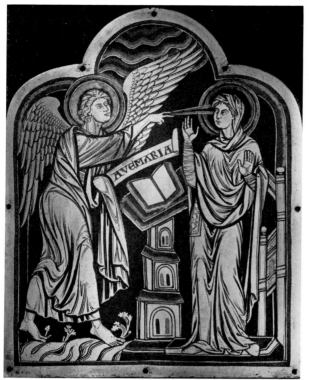 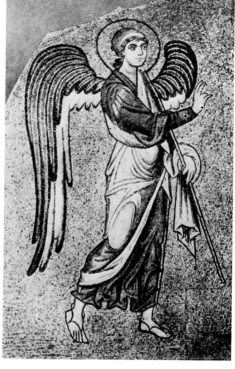

Fig. 198. *Klosterneuburg*, Vienna, Enamel Altar by Nicholas of Verdun. Annunciation.

Fig. 199. *Daphni*, Greece, Mosaic. Angel from Annunciation.

Ivories of this period were, of course, especially frequent in the West after the fall and the sacking of Constantinople by the Crusaders in 1204; before this catastrophe (or this windfall, for that matter) it must have been more difficult for Western artists to find models of metropolitan origin. They had to make use of anything that fell into their hands, which makes it very difficult for the art historian to put his finger on the exact kind of model they employed. A case in point is Nicholas of Verdun, perhaps the greatest artist of the late twelfth century.[115] One of the main sources of his earlier style, as it appears in the enamels of the Klosterneuburg Altar of 1181 (originally a pulpit revetment), was certainly the Palatina. The angel of the Annunciation (most probably, the earliest composition) (Fig. 198) is very close to analogous figures in the Palatine Chapel, for instance, to the angel expelling Adam and Eve from Paradise (Fig. 157). Both figures are stepping out in the same swift and somewhat mincing way, advancing the near foot, instead of the far one as would have been the rule in earlier Byzantine and in classical Greek art; the figures have the same build and the fall of the folds in the enamel is a most interesting interpretation of the mosaic's drapery scheme. Above the right knee there is

180

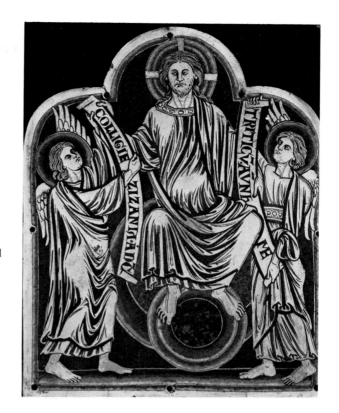

Fig. 200. *Klosterneuburg*, Vienna, Enamel
Altar by Nicholas of Verdun.
Christ from Last Judgment.

even a very specific attempt at copying the model's lineaments. The general
effect of the linear pattern is perhaps a bit richer than that of the Palatina but
it still has the sobriety of the Byzantine style of the middle of the twelfth
century. That this phase, and not an earlier one was indeed the source should
become quite clear if the Klosterneuburg angel is placed side by side with that
of the Daphni Annunciation (Fig. 199) with his entirely different gait, completely different arrangement of drapery—especially in the hollow of the
knee—and incomparable, truly Hellenic composure! However, following, as
Nicholas did, the lead of the Palatina, that is, of the style of about 1150, he
must have become aware of the more recent Byzantine development which, a
few years later, was to culminate in the Monreale style (Figs. 123, 137, 158).
Quite a few of his draperies already (Fig. 171) have something of the turgid
wealth, the swirling movement, and those bald spots which mark the joints
and the plastic protuberances of the bodies. It is, of course, difficult to say
just how specific this awareness was, whether it was based on a definite knowledge of contemporary Byzantine works or simply participated in a general
trend which dominated Western as well as Byzantine art in the latter part of
the twelfth century.

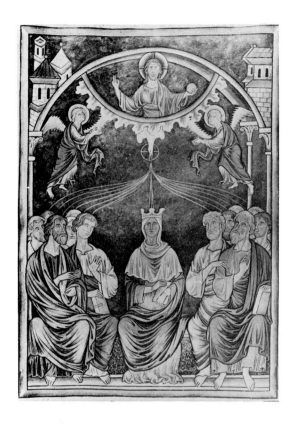

Fig. 201. *Chantilly*, France,
Psalter of Queen Ingeborg. Pentecost.

The farther Nicholas progressed in his work, the farther he moved away
from any direct contact with contemporary Byzantine prototypes. The later
parts of the Klosterneuburg Altar are already imbued with the classical spirit
that became the dominating quality of his later work. Toward the end of his
work in Klosterneuburg, when he made the last six enamels, among them the
Last Judgment (Fig. 200) it may even have looked as if Nicholas would then
and there become a classicist, like one of the illuminators of the Ingeborg
Psalter (Fig. 201), younger by about two decades. But the prophets of the
Shrine of the Magi in Cologne (Figs. 202, 203) show a new upsurge of
feeling and vigor, of expression, possibly derived from the study of Carolingian
illumination, and, at the same time, a new plastic style, the origin of which
is still one of the great riddles of the history of medieval art.

Is there anything Byzantine at all in these figures? Surely not their three-
dimensional qualities and not their fervor or their psychological refinement.
But the drapery style could not have originated without the help of Byzantine
models. An attempt has been made to trace these models in Byzantine goldsmith's work, of which so very few metropolitan specimens have come down
to us that we must try and fill the gap with peripheral works such as those

182

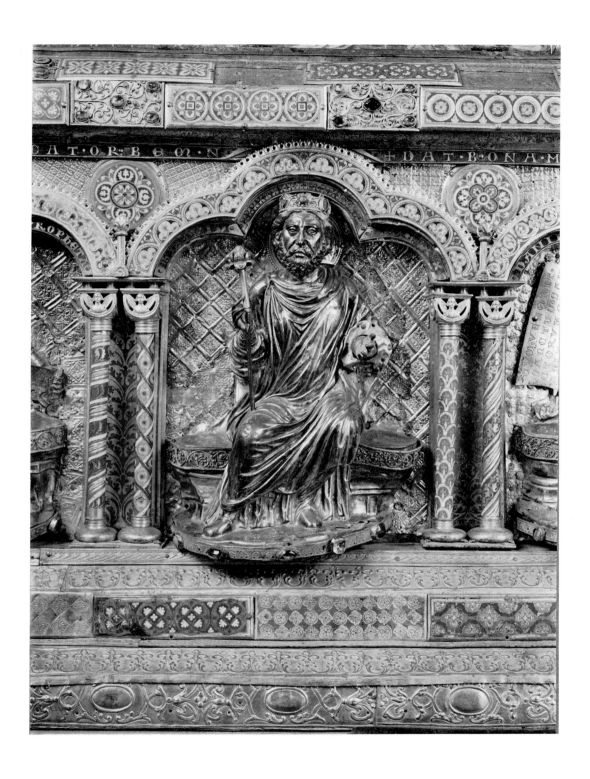

Fig. 202. *Cologne*, Cathedral, Dreikönigschrein by Nicholas of Verdun. David.

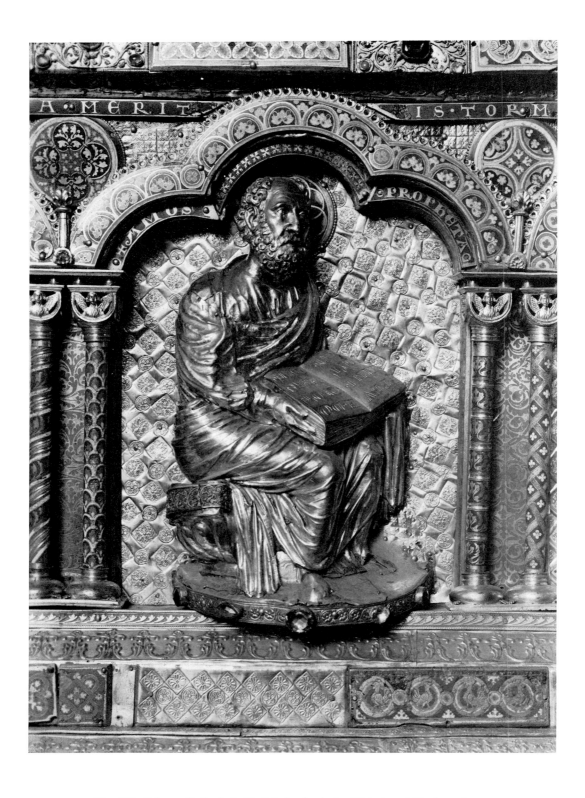

Fig. 203. *Cologne*, Cathedral, Dreikönigschrein by Nicholas of Verdun. Amos.

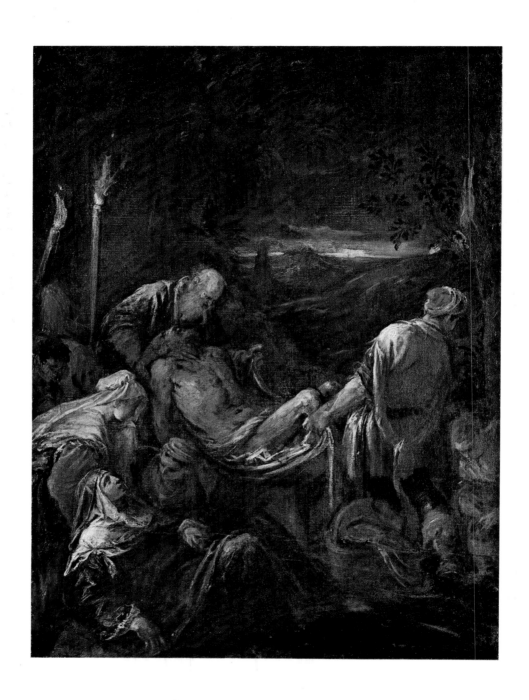

VII   *Vienna*, Kunsthist. Museum, Jacopo Bassano. Entombment of Christ.

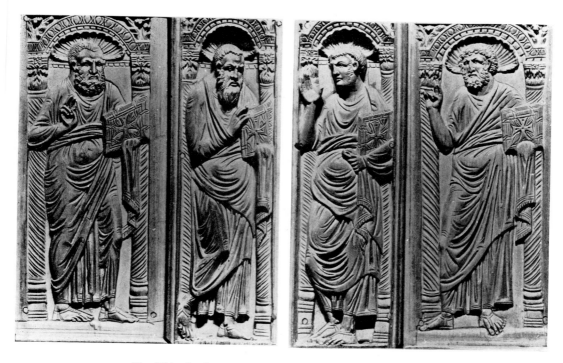

Fig. 204 a, b. *Ravenna*, Throne of Maximianus. Evangelists.

from Georgia; but this attempt does not carry conviction. It is much more likely that it was earlier, Byzantine models, rather than contemporary ones which furnished Nicholas with those classical motifs and, moreover, with the entire classical surface treatment of his golden figures. It was convincingly pointed out by Professor Kitzinger that the damp fold style with its richly folded drapery clinging to organically moving bodies was not, after all, a monopoly of Hellenistic or of middle Byzantine art, but was carried over from pagan into early Christian and early Byzantine sculpture; and that there exists an indisputable relationship between the best surviving work of the time of Justinian, about the middle of the sixth century, and the figure types and the style of Nicholas. The hirsute faces of the Cologne prophets and those of the ivory Cathedra of Bishop Maximianus in Ravenna (Figs. 204 a, b) have a definnite likeness, and the draperies in Nicholas' latest and most classicist work, the Chasse of Tournai (Fig. 205), show a number of unusual features which connect them with Justinianic art: I refer to those garments which are gathered up about the middle of the body and form a hanging garland of folds across the hips, resembling a tucked up pinafore, or the pointed design around the knees, or, generally speaking, the rendering of the folds with plastic ridges running parallel to incised grooves.

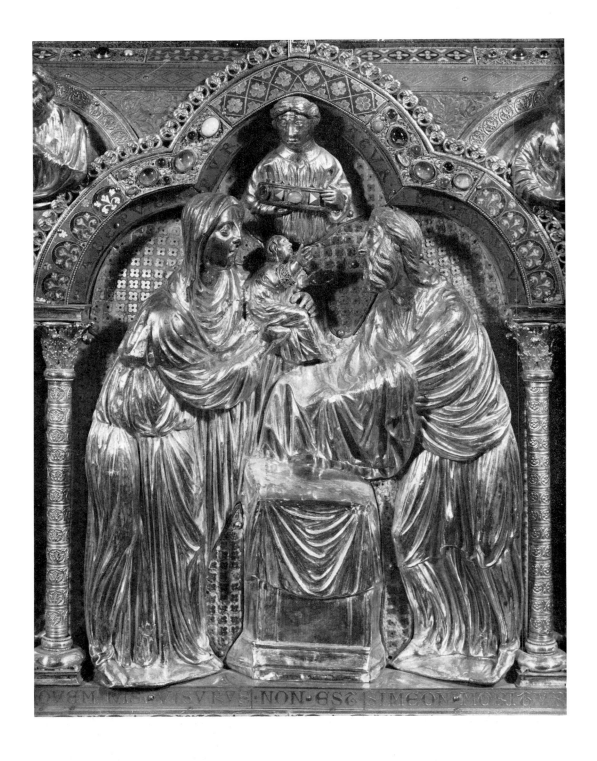

Fig. 205. *Tournai*, Cathedral, Chasse by Nicholas of Verdun. Presentation of Christ.

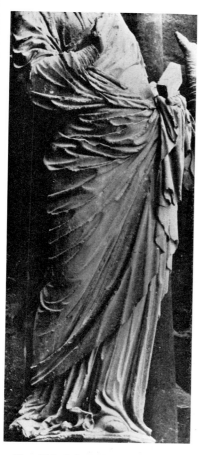

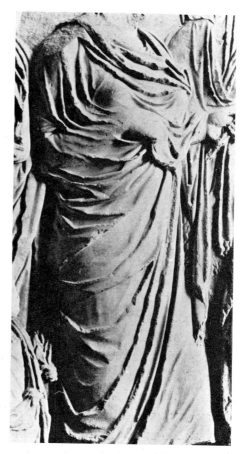

Fig. 206. *Reims*, Cathedral, West Porch. Virgin from Visitation, Detail.

Fig. 207. *Paris*, Louvre, Detail from a fragment of the Ara Pacis in Rome.

It was a highly selective attitude indeed, that enabled Nicholas to use models from the middle of the twelfth century, enrich them in the spirit of the late Comnenian style and finally turn to early Byzantine reliefs for a reinterpretation of the damp fold style. And even this was not the end of his quest: in studying and analyzing Byzantine classicism, contemporary or of the sixth century, he became more and more aware of the classical, the Hellenistic background of that art, that is, of the Greek and Roman ancestry of Byzantium. Whether he ever saw classical Greek sculpture, as has been suggested, remains extremely doubtful; but he certainly had ample opportunity to study Roman works and to reinterpret them in the Greek spirit which he had succeeded in distilling from early Byzantine art.

In doing so Nicholas paved the way for the great masters of northern France. Thus, the Master of the Visitation of Reims (Fig. 206) was able to reproduce the surface treatment of Roman sculpture (Fig. 207) and at the same time to reinterpret the figure in terms of Greek organic movement.[116] Compared with the Roman figure of the first century, his Virgin is imbued with a new grace and a new kinetic energy, curving and turning, lively and spontaneous in her movement in spite of the quiet stance. The drapery has a new *brio*; it is activated in such a way that the Roman figure seems lifeless and academic by comparison, so that a naive viewer might take the Reims figure for the original and the Roman relief for an imitation. One need not, perhaps, go so far as M. Frolow who claimed that the characteristic Gothic stance with one of the hips protruding so that the figure describes an S-curve, was directly derived from Comnenian art;[117] but there is no doubt that something like this curve appears in Byzantium as early as the third quarter of the twelfth century and even earlier, and that, in fact, Byzantine models may have suggested to Western artists this possibility of enlivening the stolid attitudes of Roman figures. It took, of course, the genius of northern France to follow up these hints and to develop them into a new, consistent language of forms. A parallel case is offered by the development of the Gothic systems of architecture and architectural sculpture, which may also owe something to incentives derived from east Christian forms. The problem is, however, not only a thorny one (which can hardly be solved with the material known to us at present), but also one in which the path to solution is barred by strong taboos. It must, therefore, suffice to hint at its existence by pointing to the use of near-Gothic articulations of pillars, vaults and walls in Armenia and in central Greece, all these examples preceding the corresponding Western forms by more than a century.[118] In addition, there are new, almost frightening vistas opened up by the discovery of Byzantine stained glass of the early twelfth century during the work of the Byzantine Institute of America in the Church of the Pantocrator in Constantinople.[119] It is not altogether impossible that the use of stained glass in Byzantium was the result of a reverse movement, an influence which reached Constantinople from the West. Such currents did without doubt exist, at least from the middle of the twelfth century onwards, especially, under Manuel Comnenus who not only was married to a German princess (Berta von Sulzbach) but also introduced into Byzantium Western ideas of feudalism and knighthood; it was during his reign and by his promotion that tournaments were held in Constantinople and French romances translated into Greek.[120] The existence of the Crusader states in Syria and Palestine and their cultural life—such as it was—may also have contributed toward making Byzantium aware of Western art, although the findings of Professor Buchthal do not seem to support such an assumption. Thus it would hardly be justifiable, for instance, to see in the development of the dynamic style of

188

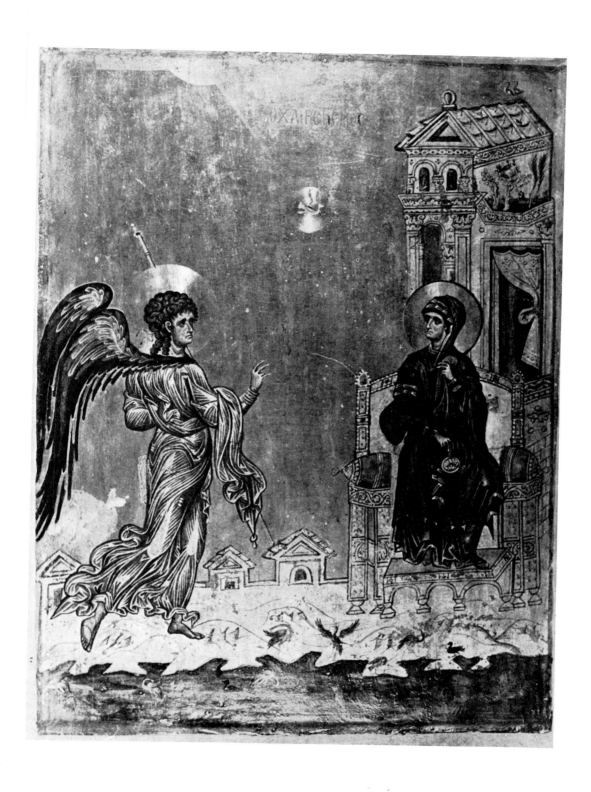

Fig. 208. *Sinai*, Monastery of St. Catherine, Icon. Annunciation.

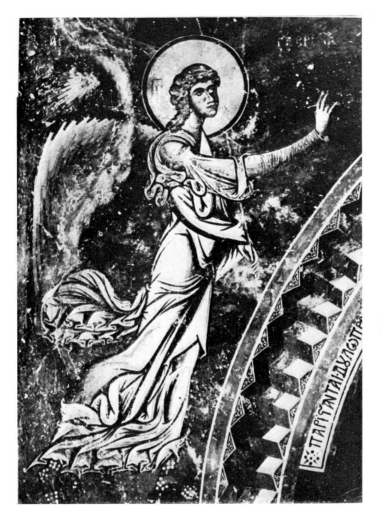

Fig. 209. *Kubinovo*, Yugoslavia, Wall Painting. Angel from Annunciation.

Byzantine art in the second half of the twelfth century, the result of Western influence, nor even the effect of a disturbance produced by late Romanesque mannerism. It does, however, seem legitimate to regard the astounding similarities which exist between the dynamic style of late Comnenian art in Byzantium and the agitated mannerism of Western late Romanesque, not only in motif and form, but in the very spirit, as the first phase of a parallel movement in the two arts, that is something more than, and different from, the effect of one-sided influence.[121] The contact between the two great branches of Christian art had been so intimate in the eleventh and twelfth centuries, the cultural *rapprochement* between the two halves of Europe had been so close in the second half of the twelfth, and the disappearance of the boundaries between East and West owing to the establishment of the Crusader states and the Latin Empire of Constantinople had so great a unifying effect, that there

190

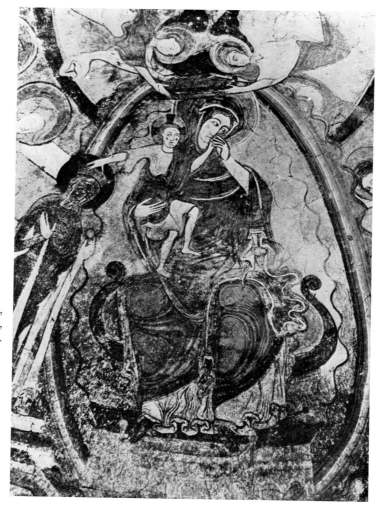

Fig. 210. *Montmorillon*, France, Crypt of Sainte-Cathérine, Wall Painting. The Virgin.

emerged a unison, so to speak, and a parallel rhythm in the Western and the Byzantine evolutions of form. In addition, the two evolutions now began to move in the same direction, namely, toward imparting solidity, weight and bulk to the figures and toward placing these figures in a spatial ambient which became increasingly "inhabitable."

The first phase common to East and West seems, then, to have been the agitated style of the late twelfth century. It dominated the art of Byzantium (Fig. 208) from Constantinople to Cyprus, from Macedonia (Fig. 209) to Sicily and Western art from England to Spain and from France (Fig. 210) to the Veneto (Fig. 153). The common denominator is the extreme, almost hysterical movement of figures, shapes and lines, an agitated mannerism that also expresses itself in the sharpened and often excited expression of the faces. The favorite means of this art, which has a true *fin-de-siècle* touch (a kind of twelfth

191

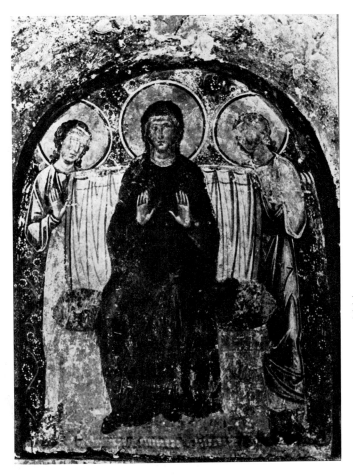

Fig. 211. *Bačkovo*, Bulgaria, Wall Painting. The Virgin and Angels.

century Art Nouveau), is the swiftly drawn, racy line; it appears in bundles and in repetitious configurations of an almost ornamental character. Never freezing into ornament but always moving, it not only delineates the bodies, but slashes them, cuts them up. Light and shade, in strong contrasts, also take linear form or accompany the linear pattern, producing in figures and compositions the effect of a complicated relief. The most active period of this style lasted from the seventies to the early nineties.[122] Toward the end, the playful and the lyrical seem gradually to replace the turbulent and the excited and the overall aspect becomes more and more precious: one feels that the end of the development is in sight and that the pendulum will soon swing back toward the other extreme.

As a matter of fact, a new style made its appearance in Byzantium toward the end of the century (Fig. 211). It is characterized by a new stillness, a new feeling for the totality of form and figure. There is, at first and necessarily,

192

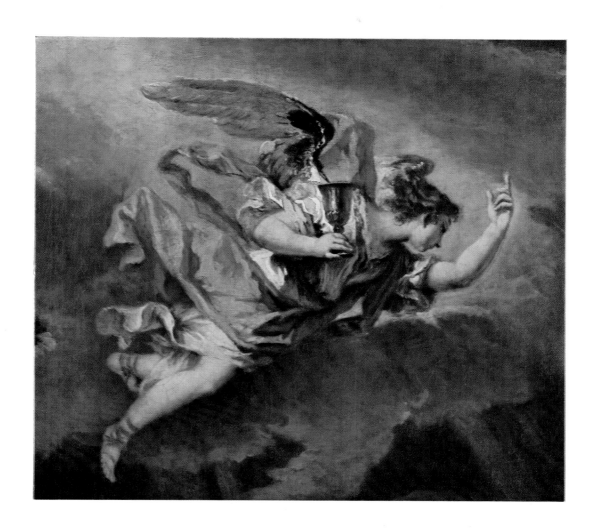

VIII   *Vienna*, Kunsthist. Museum, Sebastiano Ricci. Agony in the Garden, Detail.

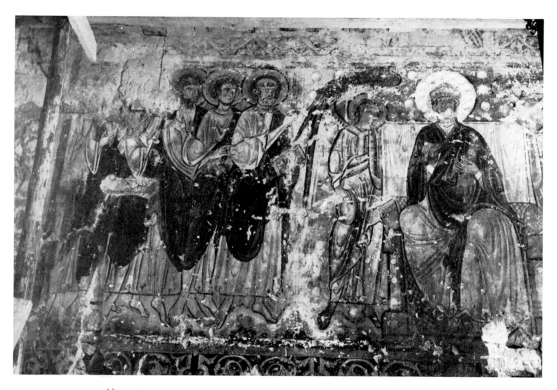

Fig. 212. *Lavaudieu*, France, former Chapter House, Wall Painting. The Virgin, Angel and Apostles.

a reversion to flatness; the beholder is struck by an absence of tension and of sophisticated modeling. The great gain, however, is a genuine monumentality, an inherent greatness which is not dependent on gigantic size. A Virgin with Angels in Bačkovo, in western Bulgaria, shows the new style in its first purity. It is quite characteristic that this fresco is usually (but erroneously) dated about 1080, for it has something of the classical air of the late eleventh century. It is, however, certainly a work of about 1200. The corresponding phase in the West announces itself in the classicism of Sigena (Figs. 151, 179) in Spain and is most impressively represented by the great wall painting in the chapter house of Lavaudieu in south-central France (Fig. 212). This neoclassical style was as widely disseminated as its forerunner: in the East, the frescoes of Studenica, of 1209 (Fig. 246), or contemporary Sinai icons (Fig. 191), in the West, Nicholas of Verdun's late Tournai Chasse (Fig. 209), the Westminster and the Ingeborg Psalters (Fig. 47) bear witness to the domination of this lucid classicism over all the arts.[123] From then onward the Western equivalents of the Byzantine styles are to be found not so much in the realm of painting as in that of sculpture.

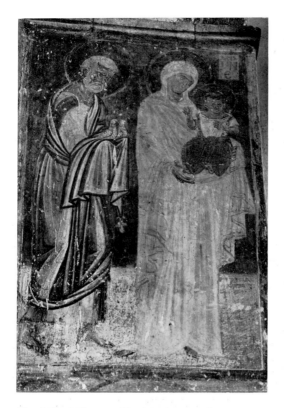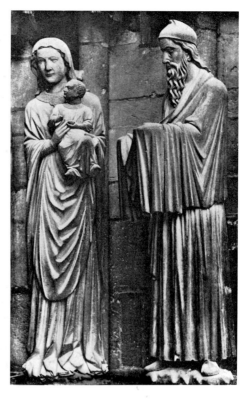

Fig. 213. *Mileševo*, Yugoslavia, Wall Painting. Joseph and Mary from the Presentation.

Fig. 214. *Amiens*, Cathedral, Porch. The Virgin and Simeon from Presentation.

The trend toward increasing volume found, in the West, its natural sphere in monumental sculpture, while it manifested itself in Byzantium in painting only; the attempts of the Frankish dominators of Constantinople and Greece to transplant to their Byzantine territories monumental sculpture, at least for their own sepulchers, had very poor results. Thus, the style of Mileševo, in Serbia (Fig. 213), of approximately 1230, with its plastic firmness and its terse scheme of vertical lines has its counterpart in the sculpture of Amiens cathedral (Fig. 214);[124] and the voluminous and organic figures of the Apostles and Prophets of Sopočani (Fig. 215), of the 1260's and 1270's, are most closely paralleled by the so-called donors of Naumburg cathedral (Fig. 216) of the same date. Plastically and spiritually, these figures, the Greek and the Franco-German, reach out into space and envelop space. The discovery and the conquest of space, even beyond the reach of the sculptural, was finally the great task of the later thirteenth century.[125] The bulk and the heaviness of figures, architectural and landscape elements went on increasing until they reached

194

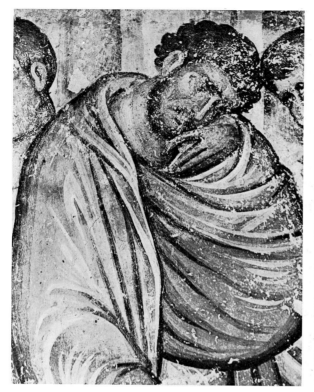 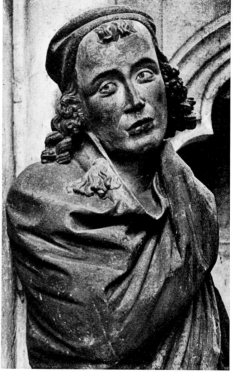

Fig. 215. *Sopočani*, Yugoslavia, Wall Painting. Apostle from Death of the Virgin.

Fig. 216. *Naumburg*, Cathedral, Sculpture.

a peak of cubic massiveness around 1300. The frescoes of the Peribleptos church in Ohrid (Fig. 256), which characterize this phase in the East, might be compared to the over-heavy French sculpture of the period; but better parallels are to be found again in painting (Fig. 257), in Giotto's frescoes of the Arena Chapel for instance, with their block-like figures.[126] The parallelism extends even into the fourteenth century, when East and West explored the possibilities of dynamic space.[127] After that, Byzantium dropped out of the race, its energies sapped by the Turkish menace that was moving ever nearer the metropolis itself. In the course of the later fourteenth century, Byzantine art, for so long the teacher and the pacemaker of European art, became a provincial phenomenon. It withered soon after it had assisted the birth of Gothic.[128]

There were two exceptions from the unison, as it were, of development which established itself between Byzantium and the West between about 1180 and 1320, namely, Italy and Germany. Italian art, especially painting, was throughout the greater part of the thirteenth century still so much under the guiding

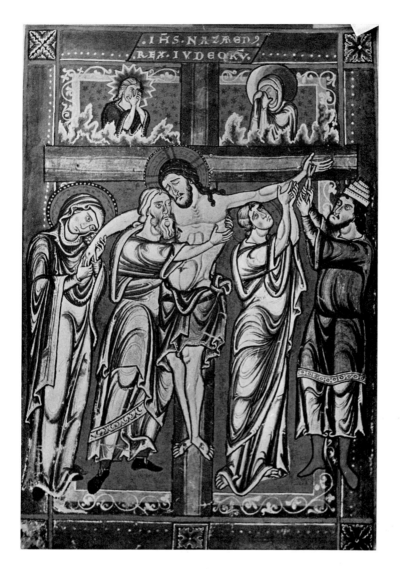

Fig. 217. *Brandenburg,*
Cathedral, Gospel Book.
Descent from the Cross.

influence of Byzantine painting that there can hardly be a question of true parallelism, with the exception of the very last decades of the Duecento. It took Italian artists a good deal longer to free themselves from Byzantine influence than it took French or English artists. That their prolonged apprenticeship was not in vain but produced the most far-reaching results, will be shown in the next chapter. In Germany, on the other hand, it was not, as in Italy, an overpowering Byzantine influence which kept central European painting from developing in the direction of Gothic; it was, on the contrary, the rejection of Gothic, a kind of protest against the new Western style, which made German painters adhere to Byzantine models and caused them to develop a number of "escapist" styles, some of which they evolved to almost

196

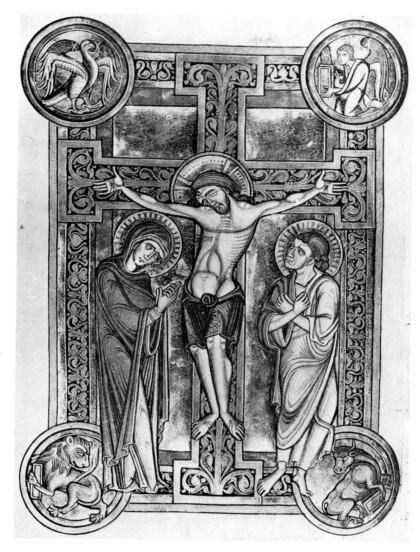

Fig. 218. *New York,* Pierpont Morgan Library, Missal of Abbot Berthold, Crucifixion.

heroic heights of absurdity. It began with a prolonged adherence to the agitated linearism of the late twelfth century, in some schools right down to the 1240's. The swinging rhythm of massed form-designing lines in the Brandenburg Gospels (Fig. 217) and the almost grotesque playfulness of detail contrast oddly with the developed plasticity of the bodies and the sobriety of the compositions. One has the impression that the artist was something of an eccentric, much like the Master of the Berthold Missal, active between 1220 and 1230 in the Bavarian abbey of Weingarten (Fig. 218), whose expressive art, tragic and humorous, looks almost like a parody of its Byzantine models. Some of the Berthold Master's types give the impression that the painter wanted to out-Byzantine Byzantium.[129]

197

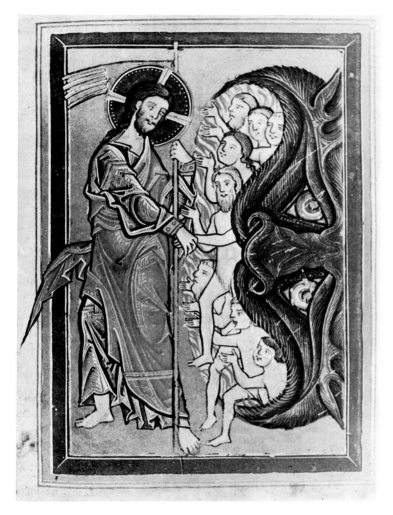

Fig. 219. *Stuttgart*, Landesbibliothek. Psalter of Hermann von Thüringen.
Harrowing of Hell.

A good many other Byzantinizing styles were developed in German painting
during the first half of the thirteenth century, but the absolute peak, both
in originality and in madness, was reached with the so-called zigzag style
which turned up (if we neglect some preparatory stages) in the second decade
in Saxony (Fig. 219) and lasted, in the valleys of the Austrian Alps, down to
the very end of the thirteenth century, living out its life in an otherwise fully
Gothicized environment (Fig. 220).[130] The wall paintings of Göss, in Styria,
for instance, decorate a chapel built in a fully developed Gothic style. It is
not easy, at first glance, to see the Byzantine parentage of this zigzag style,
into the making of which went, of course, a good many other elements as
well, beginning with Carolingian and Anglo-Saxon memories. And the preva-

198

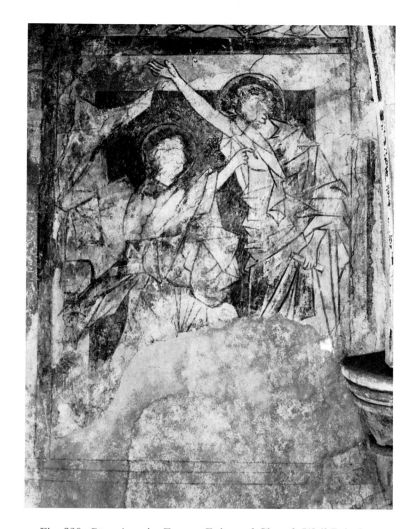

Fig. 220. *Göss*, Austria, Former Episcopal Chapel, Wall Painting.

lent Nordic character of the style can by no means be denied. But a great deal of the material of the style was of Byzantine origin. Not only were iconographic and compositional schemes and facial types borrowed from Byzantine prototypes, but the modeling too, with hard, glittering lights arranged in comb-like shapes, is derived from Byzantine models in the so-called cloisonné style which had inspired Monte Cassino painting four generations earlier. The models of the German works were not primarily eleventh century miniatures, however, but Byzantine paintings of the late twelfth or the early thirteenth centuries. Modeling practices of the kind found in the Psalter of Landgrave Hermann of Thuringia (Fig. 219), for instance, turn up in Byzantine art soon after the middle of the twelfth century (for instance, in

199

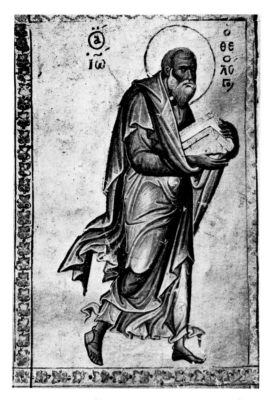

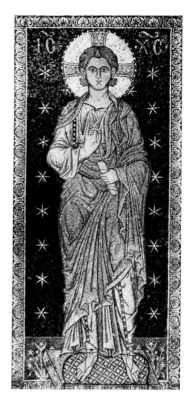

Fig. 221. *Rome*, Bibl. Vat., Cod. gr. 1156, 756
St. John.

Fig. 222. *Venice*, San Marco,
Mosaic. Christ Emmanuel.

the Palatine chapel of Palermo, ca. 1160) (Fig. 135), to become (with others)
the favorite devices of the early thirteenth century not only in mosaic but
also in fresco, panel and miniature painting. From these almost contemporary
models the saxon painters also derived their highly *recherché* color schemes,
with bluish lights on brown and pink lights on blue. What is not found in
contemporary Byzantine art, however, at least not in the art of the central
regions, is the most conspicuous peculiarity of these German works, namely,
the zigzag seams and the broken, splintery folds, those surface effects which
gave the style its name. Nevertheless, there is a Byzantine element in this
linear mannerism too. Quite apart from the general trend toward overcom-
plicated linear configurations, as it was developed in late Comnenian painting,
there existed certain tendencies in earlier Byzantine art which, together with
others, might have played a part in the development of the zigzag style. The
Greek Gospel Book No. 756 in the Vatican Library (Fig. 221) portrays the
Evangelists, especially St. John, in ample garments, whose flying ends and
seams show a great amount of zigzagging which, in the hands of imitators
trained in the violent linear mannerism of the late twelfth century, might

200

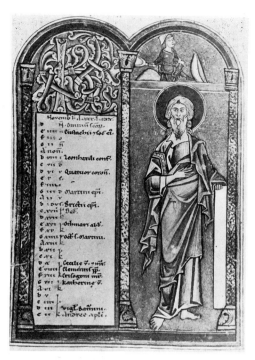

Fig. 223. *Stuttgart*, Landesbibliothek,
Psalter of Hermann von Thüringen.
Calendar Page.

easily have been exaggerated into something approaching the early zigzag
style. It is not impossible that Venice played a certain part in this since some
Venetian mosaics—the prophets and especially the youthful figure of Christ
in the aisle of the western cross arm of San Marco (Fig. 222)—show astonishing
affinities with German works of the early thirteenth century. The lightening
zigzag of the seams is most conspicuous, of course, but also to be noted are the
extremely refined color schemes, the elaborate patterns set in a highly skilled
technique with the use of precious material—mother of pearl, etc.—the "beauti-
fied" shapes of faces, hands and feet, and, most important of all, the monumental grandeur which these figures show in spite of all the preciousness of
detail and execution. It is this monumentality which was, perhaps, the greatest
gift that Byzantine painting of the early thirteenth century bestowed on
Western art in general and German art in particular. In the Psalter of Hermann (Fig. 223) and its parallels and derivatives, the effect of monumentality
is greatest in the figures of apostles, prophets and saints that adorn the calendar in tall panels filling the right half of the page. The contrast between
the main figure and the tiny figures representing the labors of the months on
top, make the large figure appear even larger.

It is not suggested here that the Saxon miniatures were copied from the
Venetian mosaics; it is even possible that the mosaics are a little later than
the psalter and that they are the product of a movement which was in part

201

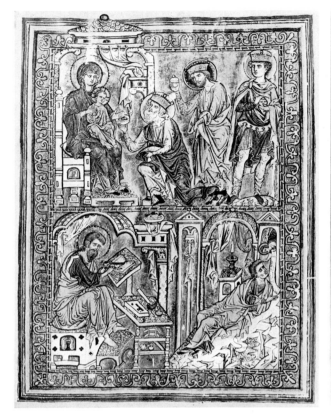

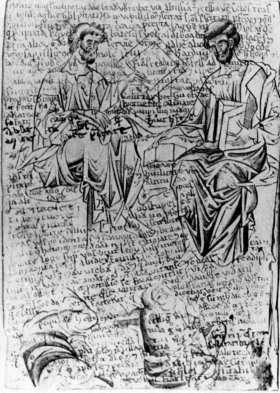

Fig. 224. *Goslar*, Germany, City Hall, Gospel Book. Adoration of the Magi and Evangelist.

Fig. 225. *Wolfenbüttel*, Germany, Herzog August Bibliothek, Pattern Book. Evangelists.

an echo of the Northern current. But the models of both must have been Byzantine works, mosaics, miniatures, icons, silk paintings such as St. Justus in Trieste, or frescoes as we still have them in Yugoslavia, in Žiča, Studenica or, a little later, in Mileševo. However, Byzantine models not only helped, along with others, to trigger the movement of the German zigzag style; they also contributed to its further development. The style of one of the most important—and artistically most impressive—groups of Saxon works of the 1230's, must be regarded as the result of renewed Byzantine influences. This is, of course, the style which found its earliest and, perhaps, highest realization in the Goslar Gospel Book (Fig. 224). The story of this current and its connection with the model book of Wolfenbüttel (Fig. 225) and its Byzantine prototypes has been told in the first chapter.[131] It is one of the most interesting instances demonstrating how an entire movement was sparked by the close study of a very few Byzantine models, a movement which was not confined to miniature painting but extended also to wall painting, panel painting and even relief

202

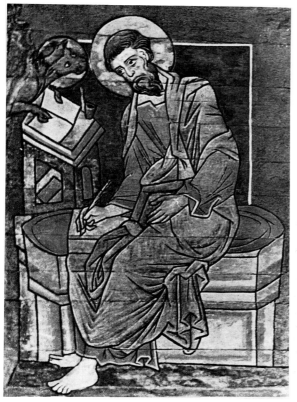

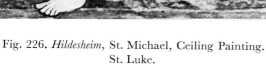

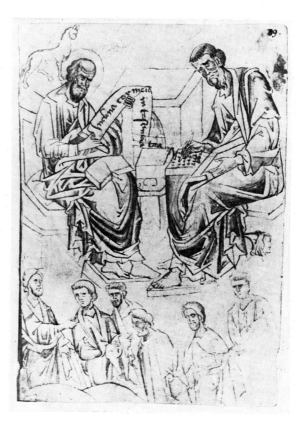

Fig. 226. *Hildesheim*, St. Michael, Ceiling Painting. St. Luke.

Fig. 227. *Wolfenbüttel*, Germany, Herzog August Bibliothek, Pattern Book. Evangelists.

sculpture. The painted ceiling of Saint Michael's in Hildesheim is as much connected with this movement (Figs. 226, 227)—even with its key document, the Wolfenbüttel model book, with which it shares the figures of the evangelists—as are the reliefs of Hamersleben (Fig. 228), which follow the same model. The frescoes of Brunswick cathedral are also very close in style to the Hildesheim ceiling; they originated a few years later, towards the middle of the century. It is a tribute to the force inherent in the Byzantine models which inaugurated this style, that their Greek, classical spirit succeeded in making itself felt in spite of the mannerist leanings of the German artists who employed them. However, even this force could not, in the long run, stand up to the pressure of the environment: the Saxon Renaissance—if we may call it by this name—was soon swamped again in the turmoil of the unmitigated zigzag style which dominated the third quarter of the century in the entire German speaking world. This world did not contribute much to the birth of Gothic. When Gothic finally came, with a powerful onrush, in the last third

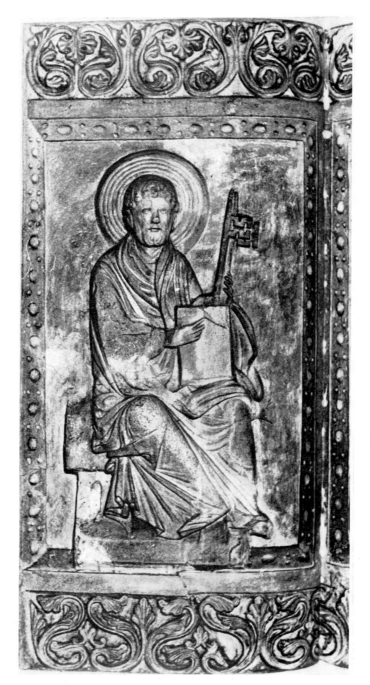

Fig. 228. *Hamersleben*, Germany,
Relief. St. Peter.

of the century, the last vestiges of Byzantine influence in the North were
swept away. Guided through centuries by models from Byzantium, Northern
art had finally found its own way: first, its way back to classical antiquity,
then, with the help of antique art, forward towards its own new style, the
first all-embracing style of Western Europe, the Gothic.

204

6

The Dawn of European Painting

In the title of this chapter it is suggested that Byzantium had something to do with the genesis of modern painting. This far-reaching statement is not new: a similar title, "The Birth of Western Painting," was chosen in 1930 by two young authors for a book in which a similar claim was upheld and in which Robert Byron and David Talbot Rice, the first a writer, the second then a budding Byzantine scholar, attempted to convey their enthusiasm for the art of Byzantium and set forth their belief that—to put it crudely—Western painting would not exist but for the art of Byzantium and its transfer to the West by early and late Byzantine painters, including Greco. By now, one of the two authors is dead—he fell a victim to the war— and the other has become a very well known Professor of the History of Byzantine Art; I think it is safe to say that neither of them would now uphold their youthful doctrines without qualification.[132]

Nevertheless, the claim that Byzantium had something to do with the genesis of modern painting holds good even today. If Byzantium had done nothing more than to preserve and to transmit to the West the antique technique and form of panel painting, the claim would be justifiable. For this was without doubt the medium in which modern painting (and by this I mean Western painting from Masaccio to Cézanne) emerged and developed. Had it not been for the transformation of Hellenistic panel painting into Byzantine icon painting and the transfer of this art form to the West, the chief vehicle of Western pictorial development would not have existed or would have come into existence a good deal later. The quattrocento, in any case, would have had to be postponed.

From the time of Charlemagne, Byzantine panel paintings were brought to the West, if not in a powerful stream, at least in a steady trickle. Greek ambassadors who negotiated marriage contracts had in their entourage painters ready to portray prospective brides. They were not always successful, as can

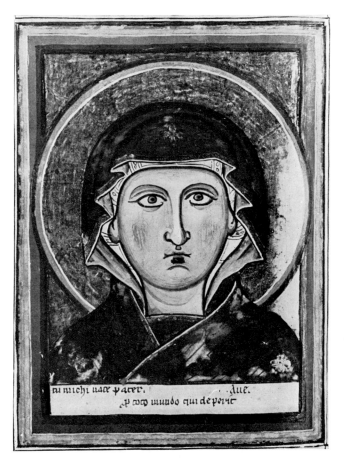

Fig. 229. *Donaueschingen*, Germany, Library, Psalter. The Virgin.

be gleaned from Ekkehard of Saint Gall; he tells the priceless story of the German princess, Hadwig, who, because she did not want to be married off to Byzantium, kept pulling faces at the Greek painter trying to portray her. He had to desist and the marriage proposal was off.[133] However, most of the panel paintings which Western patrons or artists ever saw were icons. We know little about the dates of the arrival of certain identifiable Greek icons in the West. The Virgin of Spoleto turns up, as a gift of Barbarossa, in 1185 and the Sainte-Face de Laon, a Bulgaro-Byzantine icon of the late twelfth century, came to France as a present of Pope Urban IV but had been in Rome before. Byzantine icons must have been among the loot which Crusaders brought back from Constantinople after the taking and the sack of the city in 1204—although relics and especially precious reliquaries must have held greater attraction for the pious robbers.[134] Traces of the existence of such icons in the North and the West occur in manuscript illuminations, as in an early thirteenth century psalter at Donaueschingen (Fig. 229), where the oddly lifeless image of the Virgin is certainly a copy after a Byzantine icon, or in the

206

numerous progeny of Byzantine diptychs in early Netherlandish, French and German painting, which have been studied by Professor Pächt. However, the North and the West did not offer, in the thirteenth century, great opportunities for panel painting: the accent there was on illumination, stained glass and sculpture. In some cases, German painters got hold of the wrong models—as the painter of the Regensburg Madonna who copied a model from the western Balkans instead of a properly Byzantine one.[135] Thus it was not in Germany, France or England, but in Italy that panel painting found a most fertile soil; it was there that it inaugurated an evolution which, from lowly beginnings in the early thirteenth century, reached a very high peak at its close.[136]

It is difficult to decide what was more important for the growth of this new art: the existence, in Italy, of imported models or the presence and activity of Byzantine artists in person. Both must have played their part. What is astonishing is the length of time it took for Italian painters to learn the lessons taught by Byzantine paintings and by Greek painters. Professor Longhi's very hard "Giudizio sul Duecento,"[137] is certainly valid for the first half of the century; and even later, Italian painters, including the greatest, still regarded themselves as disciples of Byzantine masters. The schooling was most intensive in the early thirteenth century, following the *impresa* of Constantinople, which apparently caused a diaspora of Greek painters, and again after 1260, when the metropolis had been reconquered by the Greeks, inspiring a new vigorous development which soon radiated to Italy. That such a vigorous development could take place in Constantinople immediately after the Greek reconquest of the city, was due to the fact that Byzantine painters had not stopped working in 1204 but had carried on, perhaps in Constantinople itself, but, in any case, certainly in Nicaea, Thessalonica and other secondary centers. The period of the Latin Empire does not, as we know now, constitute a void, a gap in the evolution, but a period of most intensive artistic life.[138]

Nevertheless, it is true that the radiation of Byzantine art was stronger in the first and the seventh decade than in the time between. The effect of the first wave was felt most strongly in Venice—some of the paradigmatic works are to be found in San Marco, among them the great mosaic of the Agony in the Garden and the panels of the side walls—and that of the second in Tuscany. Vasari says in his life of Cimabue that shortly after the middle of the century "some Greek painters were summoned to Florence by the government of the city for no other purpose than the revival of painting in their midst, since that art was not so much debased as altogether lost."[139] In spite of everything that has been said to discredit this piece of information proffered by Vasari (and the formulation follows, in fact, a well known

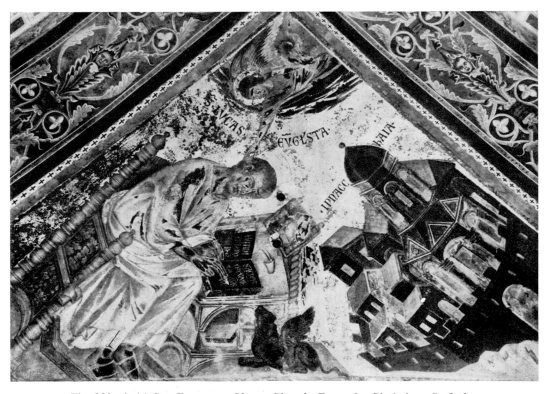

Fig. 230. *Assisi*, San Francesco, Upper Church, Fresco by Cimbabue. St. Luke.

topos), the account is substantially correct, even if the personal apprenticeship of Cimabue with these Greek masters should prove to be an invention by the "father of lies." That Cimabue actually used Greek models is, however, beyond doubt. To quote one instance only: his St. Luke on the vault of the upper church of San Francesco in Assisi is more than inspired by the St. Luke in the Gospel Book in Paris, Gr. 54, a Byzantine work of the third quarter of the century—it is almost a copy (Figs. 230, 231). The process of apprenticeship of the Italian masters to their Greek teachers may have been a painful one; the resentment lived on to the time of Vasari. As a matter of fact, what went on in Italian painting during the thirteenth century was more than a process—it was a revolution. An entirely new art was in the making, with new contents and new functional aims, with a new technique using new formats—a revolution was set off by those overpowering waves of Byzantine influence. Of course, the Byzantine models were, from the very beginning, not only subjected to a thorough transformation, but also adapted to serve the specifically Italian requirements for altar panels[140] and a new kind of devotional image.

Byzantium had known no such thing as an altar panel. Down to the present day the altars of Greek churches are bare, not surmounted by anything. If

208

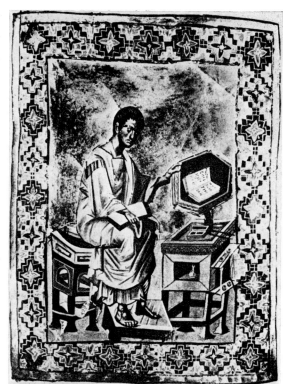

Fig. 231. *Paris*, Bibl. Nat., Cod. gr. 54, St. Luke.

they had any kind of decoration, it was an antependium, almost always of metal, which was affixed to the front of the altar and disappeared, in the eyes of the believers, when it was obscured behind the closed iconostasis. Nevertheless, the antependium, which does not seem to have played an important part at all in Byzantine art, became one of the roots from which the Western altar panel grew. Removed from the front of the altar and placed on top—a change which was made in the West at the end of the twelfth or the beginning of the thirteenth century—the antependium became a retable or reredos, without, at first, changing its shape very much. It is not too much to claim that the Pala d'Oro of San Marco (Fig. 19),[141] which was promoted from an antependium to a retable at the beginning of the thirteenth century, became by this simple translocation the most important single influence in a process leading by way of the polyptych of the fourteenth century, to the Sacra Conversazione of the fifteenth century and to the glorification piece of the Baroque. This process might have taken a very different course had not the parent form set the problem of finding an ever more homogeneous scheme for representing a series of full figures not connected by any action or event.

209

Another source of the altar panel has been seen in the transfer of monumental apse and cupola mosaics or frescoes to small niches surmounting or surrounding altars; this may have inaugurated that line of development which led to the representation of monumental figures and compositions on large, homogeneous panels. A parallel development seems to have taken its departure from the placing of icons on or above altars. Of course, such icons had to have a very definite connection with the dedication of the altar, again a specifically Western feature: Byzantine altars were hardly ever dedicated to special patron saints. In addition, such icons had to be of a certain size. If these conditions were fulfilled, almost any representation could be made to serve as an "altar panel," and the early periods abound in curious makeshift solutions. One of these can again be studied in San Marco. The back cover of the Pala d'Oro, an important work of 1345 by Paolo Veneziano, with scenes from the story of the city-patron's relics, depicts the rediscovery in 1094 of those relics believed lost during the building of the church. On the wall above the altar shown in the background of the scene appears the figure of a saint which might be taken for a mosaic or a painted panel. In reality, this figure, which is still preserved (although demoted from its place as an altar panel), is a stone relief representing St. Leonard, the patron saint of the altar near which the miraculous apparition of the relics was believed to have taken place (Fig. 232). The relief panel that belonged to the corresponding altar in the left transept is also preserved and helps to prove, together with the painted wooden relief of St. Donatus in Murano, that single figures in relief—inspired by Byzantine relief icons in marble—were used as altar panels in thirteenth century Venice. It is quite possible that genuine Byzantine relief icons (and not only Western imitations as the three Venetian examples cited) were also used for this purpose.[142]

Of course, most or all Byzantine painted icons were disqualified as altar panels by their small size and scale. To be used for this purpose, an icon had to be large enough to be seen from an appreciable distance. It was for this reason that Italian painters of the thirteenth century had to employ such vast formats, not for the first time, after all, for their Roman predecessors of the seventh and eighth centuries seem to have had similar problems.[143]

A special problem was posed if an altar panel was meant to tell the story of the patron saint in addition to portraying his figure. It has been believed until recently that the classical solution of this problem was found by Franciscan painters in Tuscany and Umbria, namely, an arrangement representing the saint as a large central figure, flanked by scenes from his legend in small rectangular pictures surrounding the main image. Owing to new finds,

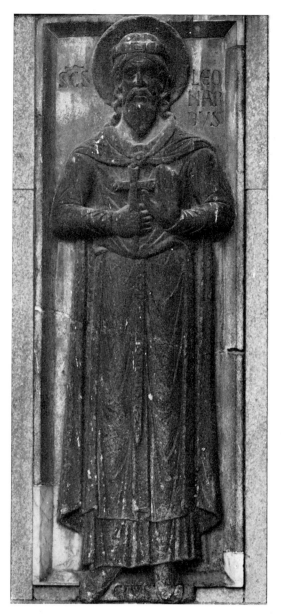

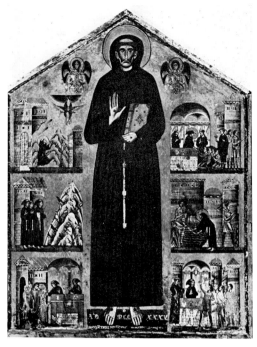

Fig. 233. *Pescia*, Italy, San Francesco, Panel Painting. St. Francis and Scenes from his Life.

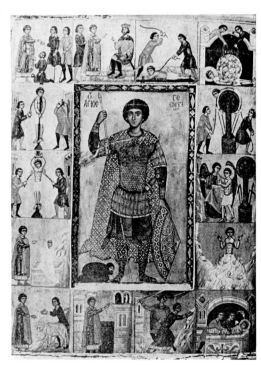

Fig. 232. *Venice*, San Marco, Relief. St. Leonard.

Fig. 234. *Sinai*, Monastery of St. Catherine, Icon. St. George and Scenes from his Life.

however, the Franciscan painters must be deprived of the honor of this invention: the exact scheme is already found in Byzantine icons from Mount Sinai, which date from the eleventh and twelfth centuries and may have had even earlier predecessors (Figs. 233, 234).[144] Furthermore, two other specialized forms of panel painting which accquired great importance in the West are also Byzantine imports: the diptych and the triptych. The Sinai collection of Byzantine icons contains a good many examples of such early date that the existence of a continuous tradition of these forms from antiquity is a virtual certainty.[145]

However, the impact of Byzantine panel painting can be felt not only in matters of format and composition but also in modeling technique, style and, especially, in the humane qualities, in the more direct appeal of the image, in a new empathy which, combined with the effects of a classical renaissance, prepared the soil for the great new art of the West. The humanizing influence of Byzantine painting on Italian Duecento art manifests itself most impressively, perhaps, in the change which various facial types underwent in the last third of the century. The face of Coppo's Virgin in the Servi church of Orvieto

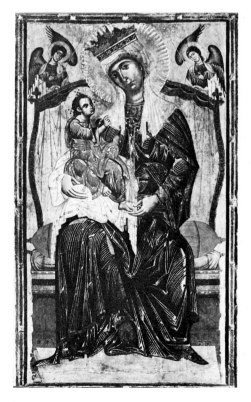

Fig. 235. *Orvieto*, Church of the Servi, Panel Painting. The Virgin.

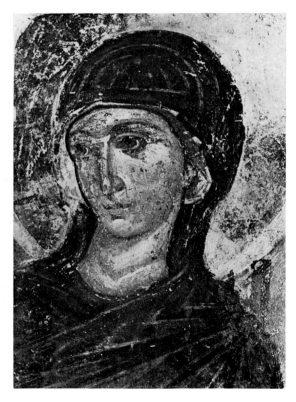

Fig. 236. *Mileševo*, Yugoslavia, Wall Painting. Virgin from Annunciation.

212

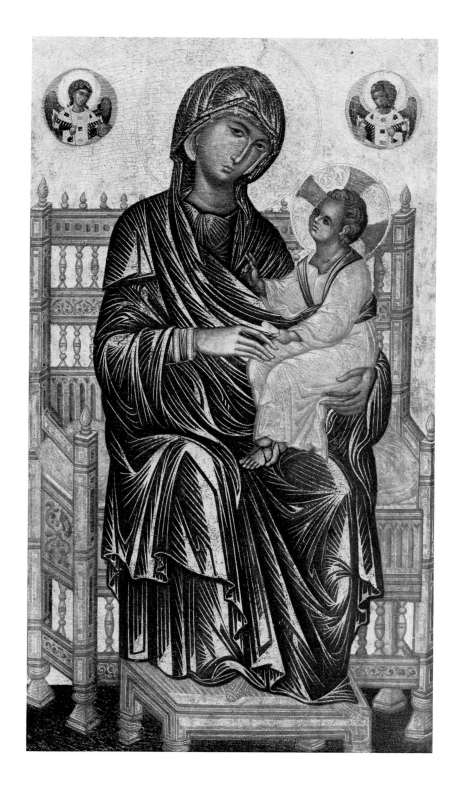

Fig. 237. *Washington*, D.C., National Gallery of Art, Icon. Enthroned Madonna and Child.

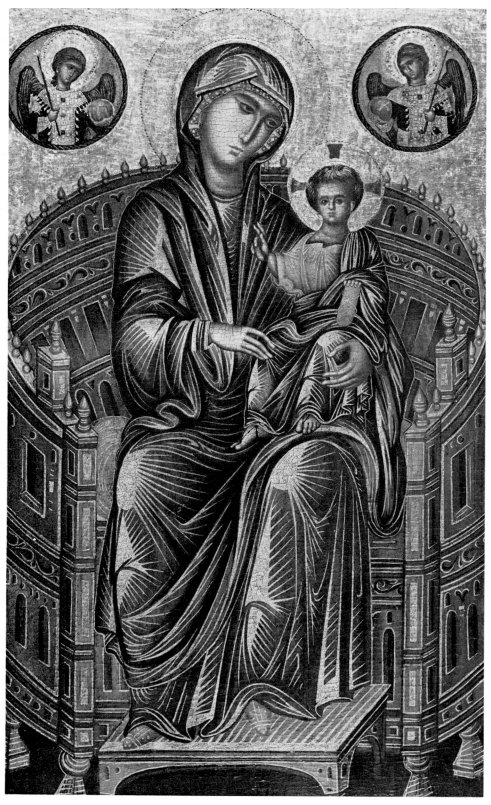

Fig. 238. *Washington*, D.C., National Gallery of Art, Icon. Enthroned Madonna and Child.

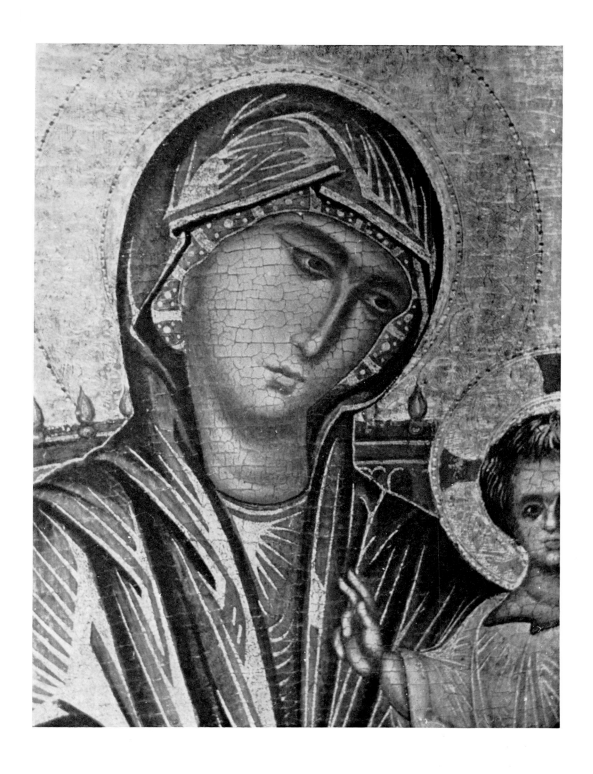

Fig. 239. *Washington*, D.C., National Gallery of Art, Icon. Enthroned Madonna and Child. Detail.

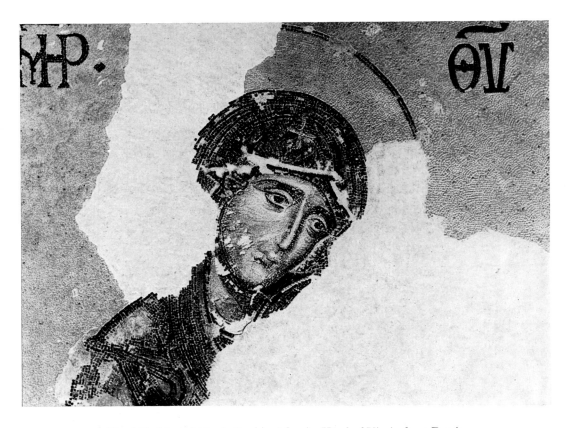

Fig. 240. *Istanbul*, Hagia Sophia, Mosaic. Head of Virgin from Deesis.

is undoubtedly one of the loveliest and most appealing faces painted in Tuscany in the 1270's (Fig. 235). Its very structure, with the vigorously sculptured nose—including the triangular bridge and the rounded tip—the modeling of the eyes, and so forth, is unthinkable without a close study of Byzantine models.[146] But, compared with a Byzantine face that is even a generation earlier, that of the Virgin of the Annunciation in Mileševo, of the 1230's (Fig. 236), the head of the Coppo Madonna looks archaic, hard, medieval, notwithstanding the fact that Coppo was perhaps the greater artist of the two. The contrast becomes even stronger, if Coppo's panel is compared with a Constantinopolitan icon that is only about a decade and not, as is Mileševo, more than a generation older. This icon is one of a pair which turned up in Calahorra in Spain and are now at the National Gallery in Washington (Figs. 237, 238).[147] They are controversial works: a good many authors thought and still think them Italian panels of the late Duecento, while Bernard Berenson correctly recognized them as Constantinopolitan but dated them in the twelfth century because he believed that there was no artistic

216

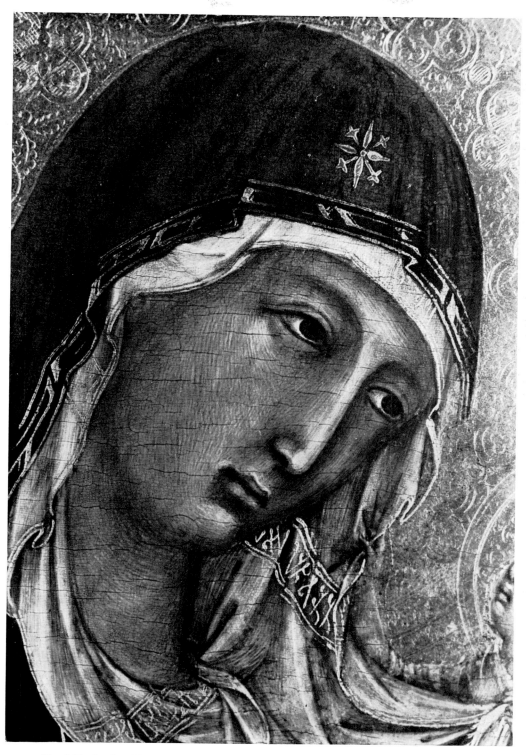

Fig. 241. *London*, National Gallery, Triptychon by Ducciodi Buoninsegna, No. 566.
The Virgin, Detail.

activity in Constantinople in the thirteenth century. However, to prove both their thirteenth century date and their Constantinopolitan origin, it ought to suffice to compare the head of one of the Washington Madonnas (Fig. 239) with the mosaic head of the Virgin from a large Deesis of the thirteenth century in the south gallery of Hagia Sophia in Constantinople, a work whose Greek origin will hardly be doubted (Fig. 240). Not only the general cast of the two heads, their lyrical expression, and their soft modeling, but also minute details such as the drawing of the eyes with their oval pupils, the projection of the mouth and the blueish tone of the shadows are so similar that the two Washington panels must have originated in the closest proximity to the mosaic, perhaps even in the very workshop of the master who made the drawing for the mosaic.[148] It took Italian painters another twenty years until they succeeded in matching the soft modeling and the dreamy charm of the Constantinople Madonnas: it required, in fact, the two greatest Italian painters, Cimabue and Duccio, to match and, being very great painters, to surpass models of this kind, thus establishing in Italian painting a type of thougthful, lyrical beauty which was still alive at the time of Raphael (Fig. 241).

Similar parallel sequences of Byzantine prototypes and Italian approximations might be demonstrated for most of the facial types which were evolved in the thirteenth century and which furnished the most eagerly exploited models for later art. It should, however, be sufficient to point to one more. It is only in the work of Cavallini (Fig. 242) that we meet the Byzantine type of wise old man, a true father image, which was resurrected from the inexhaustible store of antique prototypes by the great Byzantine renaissance movement of the early Palaeologan period and found its most classical formulation, hardly ever to be surpassed in grandeur and dignity, in Greek frescoes of the third quarter of the thirteenth century, for instance, in Sopočani Fig. (253). The serene beauty and dignity which is expressed in these heads of the Madonna and saints was perhaps the greatest and most lasting contribution which Byzantine art made to the Italian repertory of types, but it was not the only one. It has always been felt (and almost as often said) that the profound difference in feeling between the two Crosses of the Pisa Museum, Nos. 15 and 20 (Fig. 243, 244), is due to the influence of Byzantine models; this is, no doubt, true. The Western, triumphant type of Christ on the Cross was replaced by the dead Christ whose face and body show all the signs of suffering (Fig. 245).[149] As a matter of fact, the second Crucifix represents a type, the Byzantine models of which must be dated in the second decade of the thirteenth century or even around 1220, the first decade being characterized by

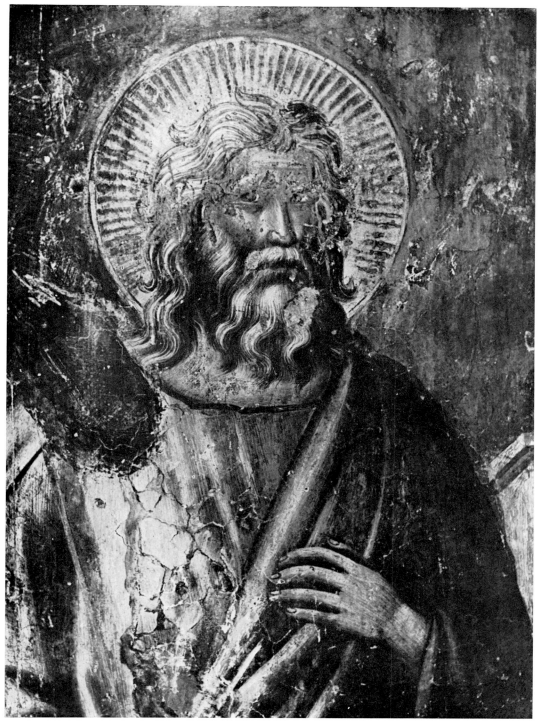

Fig. 242. *Rome*. Santa Cecilia in Trastevere, Wall Painting by Cavallini.
Last Judgment, Head of St. Andrew.

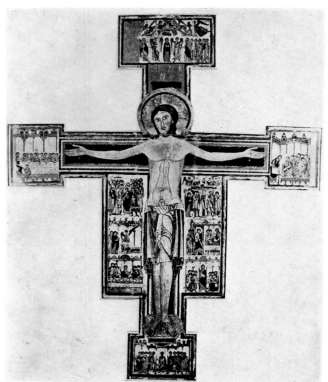

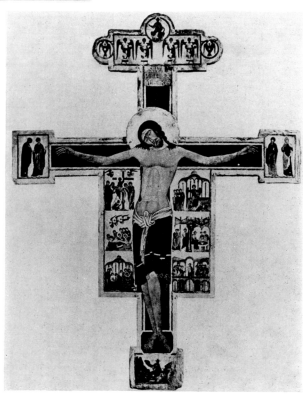

Fig. 243. *Pisa*, Museo
Nazionale, Crucifixion,
No. 15.

Fig. 244. *Pisa*, Museo
Nazionale, Crucifixion,
No. 20.

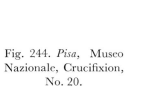

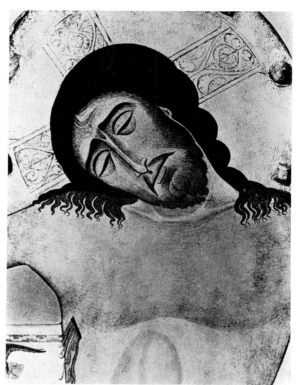

Fig. 245. *Pisa*, Museo
Nazionale, Crucifixion,
No. 20, Detail.

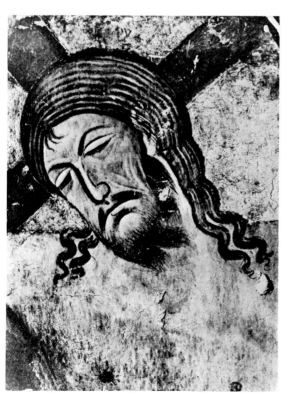

Fig. 246. *Studenica*, Yugoslavia,
Monastery Church, Wall Painting.
Head of Christ from Crucifixion.

221

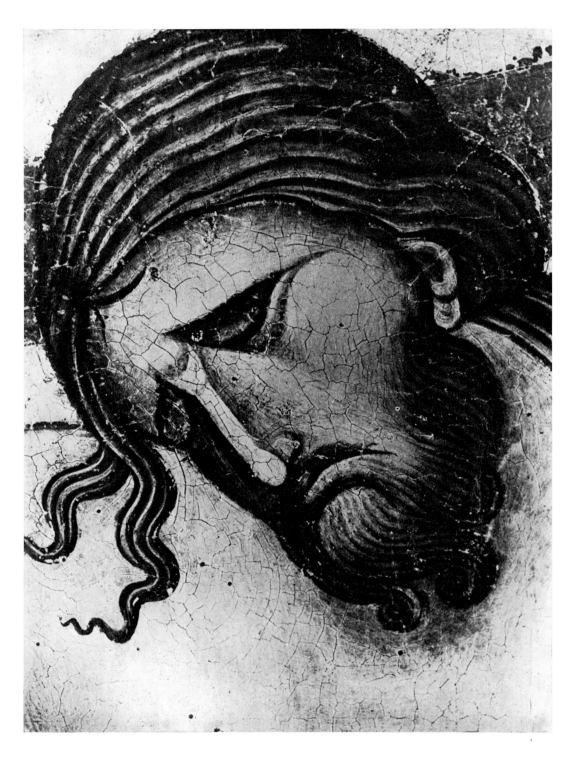

Fig. 247. *Bologna*, San Domenico, Crucifixion by Giunta Pisano, Detail.

222

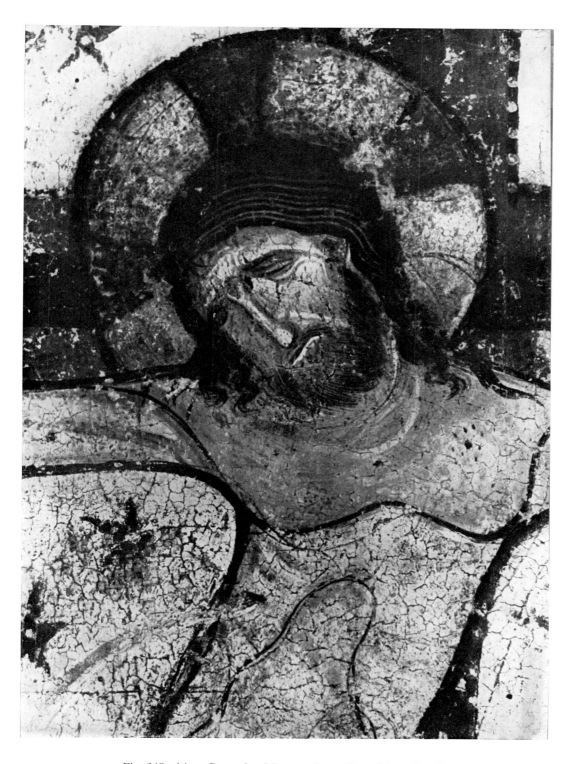

Fig. 248. *Athens*, Byzantine Museum, Icon. Crucifixion, Detail.

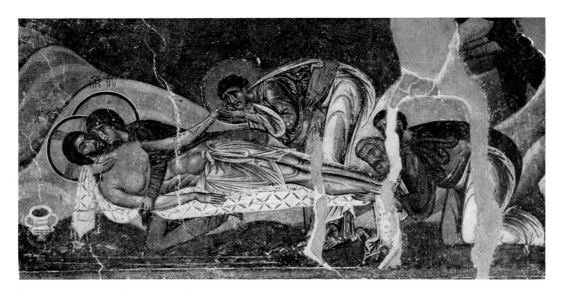

Fig. 249. *Nerezi*, Yugoslavia, Wall Painting. Lamentation of Christ.

the serene beauty of the first classical phase as it is represented by the crucified Christ of Studenica (Fig. 246). As the century progressed, the marks of suffering become more evident. A mid-thirteenth century head of Christ from a panel in the Byzantine Museum of Athens may represent the high-water mark of this development. It, too, was copied in the West: the contorted features of Christ in Giunta's (Fig. 247) or Coppo's or even Cimabue's Crucifixes are derived from almost contemporary Byzantine prototypes (Fig. 248).

One of the great themes of lyrical expressionism in Byzantine art was the Threnos, the Lamentation of Christ preceding his burial, an iconographic theme whose fascinating history from its probable origin in the Bewailing of Actaeon in Hellenistic times to its full development in the twelfth century, has been studied by Kurt Weitzmann.[150] The fully developed composition consists of the Virgin embracing the dead body of her son and receiving it in her lap, St. John caressing Christ's hand, Nicodemus and Joseph of Arimathia stooping down to hold Christ's feet, a group of holy women approaching from the sides, and weeping angels winging the air (Fig. 249): One of the most impressive examples, of the 1160's, is in Nerezi. Compositions like this, full of pathos and drama, were avidly imitated by Italian painters, among them Coppo (or one of his assistants) who, in the San Gimignano Cross (Fig. 250) repeated the main features but drew the figures nearer together. It did not matter to him that as a result most of the figures lost their function—John does not fondle Christ's hand, and the two old men do not hold his

224

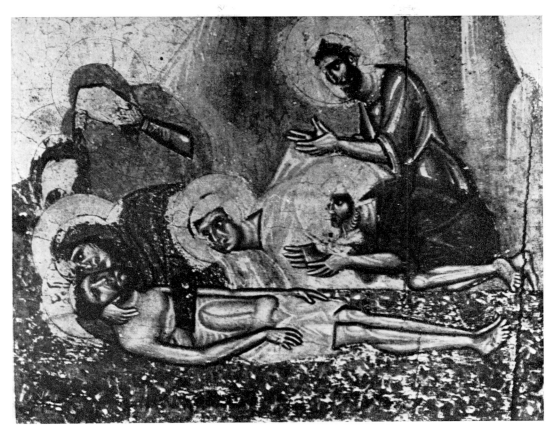

Fig. 250. *San Gimignano*, Italy, Museo Civico, Panel Painting. Lamentation of Christ, from Crucifixion.

feet—the main thing for Coppo was the concentration of expressive motifs. It was Giotto (Fig. 251) who, while changing, regrouping and augmenting the cast, restored their proper actions. Christ's hands are now caressed by two of the holy women and his feet are held by another. It is evident that Giotto had seen Byzantine thirteenth century formulations of the theme and was not dependent on his Italian predecessors.

It should not detract from Giotto's unique greatness if it is assumed that his obligation to Byzantium went further than iconographic schemes and that the solution of some of his problems was adumbrated by Greek painters. It ought to be kept in mind that the revolution of Italian art was preceded by a revolution in Byzantine painting which reached its critical point in the third quarter of the thirteenth century. A single monument, such as the royal church of Sopočani,[151] houses figures which seem worlds apart but are not separated in time by more than one or two decades at the most. Some of the figures of patriarchs or prophets are works in an obsolete, provincial style in which

225

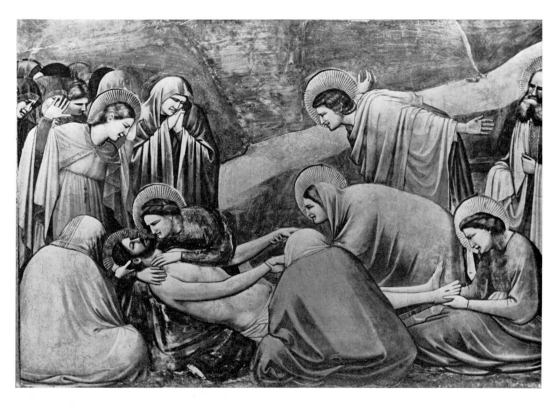

Fig. 251. *Padua*, Cappella dell'Arena, Wall Painting by Giotto. Lamentation of Christ.

the linear effects of late Comnenian art still play an important part (Fig. 252), while others show the sovereign mastery of an artist who knew how to give his figures full plastic volume and great statuesque dignity (Fig. 253). There are intermediary stages which show the revolutionary effect of this artist on his collaborators. We have good reason to assume that something like this art was transferred to Italy by Greek painters of the kind mentioned by Vasari— fresco painters whose work is now lost, some of it, perhaps, hidden behind the acres of loquacious Trecento paintings. It is only in out-of-the way places, where time stood still (until a few years ago), that a few remnants of Greek frescoes of the thirteenth century are found, for instance in Santa Maria in Tuscania (at the foot of the hill on which San Pietro stands). The apse decoration of the church (Fig. 254) is the work of a very poor artist but it may give us an inkling of the appearance of the frescoes noted by Vasari, which must have been the models from which Tuscan and Roman painters learned how to shape figures in the round. In addition, we have works of Italian pupils of Greek masters, disciples who almost became Greeks in their faithful adherence to Byzantine standards of modeling and design. In any case, this is one of

226

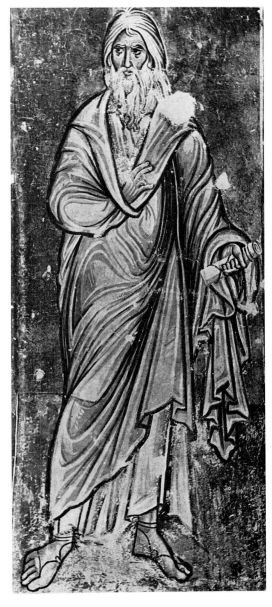 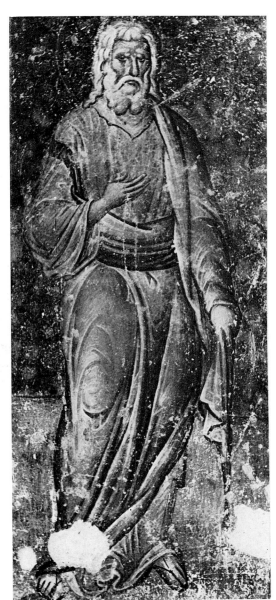

Fig. 252. *Sopočani*, Yugoslavia, Wall Painting. Prophet.

Fig. 253. *Sopočani*, Yugoslavia, Wall Painting. Apostle.

the sources from which Torriti, the Isaac Master (whoever he was) and, finally, Cavallini drew their inspiration. The mighty figure of Abraham in the Sacrifice of Isaac in the Upper Church of Assisi (Fig. 255) would fit very well with the frescoes of Sopočani, where it might have been designed in the 1260's or 1270's by one of the less precocious assistants of the chief master. And would it be going too far to suggest that Giotto himself may have been

227

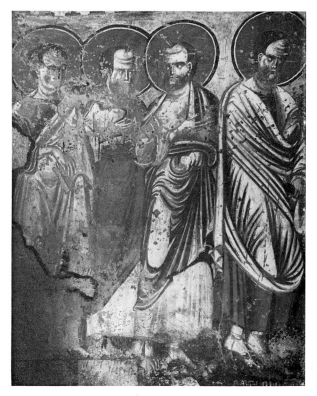
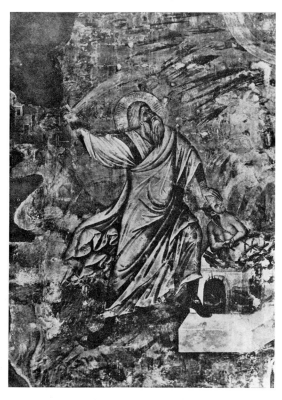

Fig. 254. *Tuscania*, Italy, Santa Maria Maggiore, Wall Painting.

Fig. 255. *Assisi*, San Francesco, Upper Church, Wall Painting. Sacrifice of Abraham.

assisted in his attempts to give his figures that extreme solidity, plastic weight and presence by studying works of Greek painters, perhaps akin to, but better than, those two overproductive artisans, Michael and Eutychios, whose first work, the decoration of St. Mary Peribleptos in Ohrid, is dated 1295 (Fig. 256)?[153] Is the predilection for squatting and crouching figures in the works of these Greeks and of Giotto a pure coincidence?

The mastery of plastic volume was followed, in Italy, by the conquest of pictorial space.[154] Here too, Byzantine painting had something to offer, but only, I believe, to a very limited extent. Byzantine art never attempted the direct representation of interior space. We never find even those box shaped rooms which were so frequent in late antique illumination and which were also the most important single motif in the evolution of pictorial space in the later Duecento. In Byzantine art interiors are indicated by a special grouping of architectural motifs taken from the exterior aspects of buildings, and by curtains or hangings draped or stretched over or between these individual architectural elements. The elements, however, have substance, a certain

228

material and spatial quality. Most of them are massive blocks pierced by windows or doors, while some are shallow niches, and others sprawling structures supported by columns or pillars; they all show that their designers were passionately though helplessly obsessed by the problem of enclosed space in its relation and contrast to open space.

This is the structure of the "architectural landscape" of Byzantine painting in the thirteenth century in its latest, almost cubist aspect, exemplified by the Koimesis fresco of the Peribleptos church of Ohrid (1295); and this or rather the preceding phase provided the material which was used by Italian Duecento painting up to about 1280, when the problem of making such plastic structures inhabitable, of rendering unified interior and exterior spaces, began to be seriously tackled by the greatest artists of the period. But, to a large extent, even these artists used the Byzantine vocabulary of plastically differentiated architectural blocks, arranged within a vaguely three-dimensional ambient. Thus far, Byzantium was able to help the Italian painters in their quest for

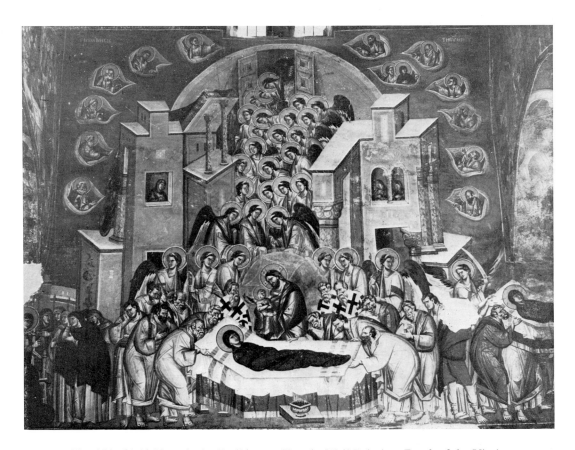

Fig. 256. *Ohrid*, Yugoslavia, Peribleptos Church, Wall Painting. Death of the Virgin.

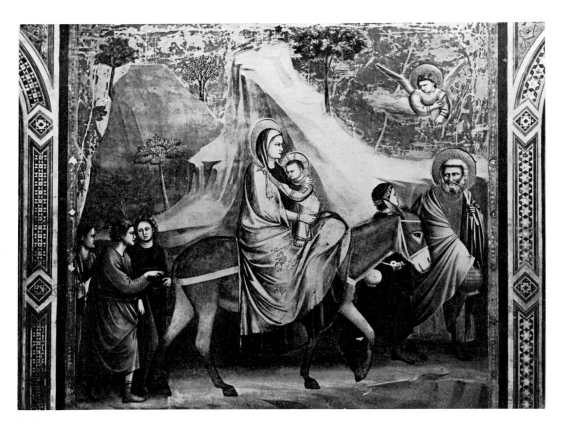

Fig. 257. *Padua*, Cappella dell'Arena, Wall Painting by Giotto. Flight into Egypt.

spatial representation, but no further. What happened in this sphere also happened in many others: the Byzantine models were superseded by models from classical antiquity. However, as in other cases, Byzantium had pointed the way—even without being able to follow it herself.

Perhaps the most important contribution made by Byzantium toward the new art concerned the representation of landscape—landscape not only as scenery but as an orchestral accompaniment to the melody of figure composition.[155] This also concerns, of course, architectural landscape, but it is much clearer in the field of landscape proper, groupings of ground, hills, rocks and vegetation. Our admiration for the wisdom and strength of Giotto's use of landscape (Fig. 257) should not blind us to the fact that the motifs and their functional uses are prefigured in Byzantine painting. Hills and rocks frame and accentuate the silhouettes of figures and groups; they also indicate direction and speed of their movements and provide the key for the prevailing moods, not only in Giottos frescoes of the Scrovegni Chapel but also in the mosaics of Monreale (Fig. 258) more than a century earlier; and this very

230

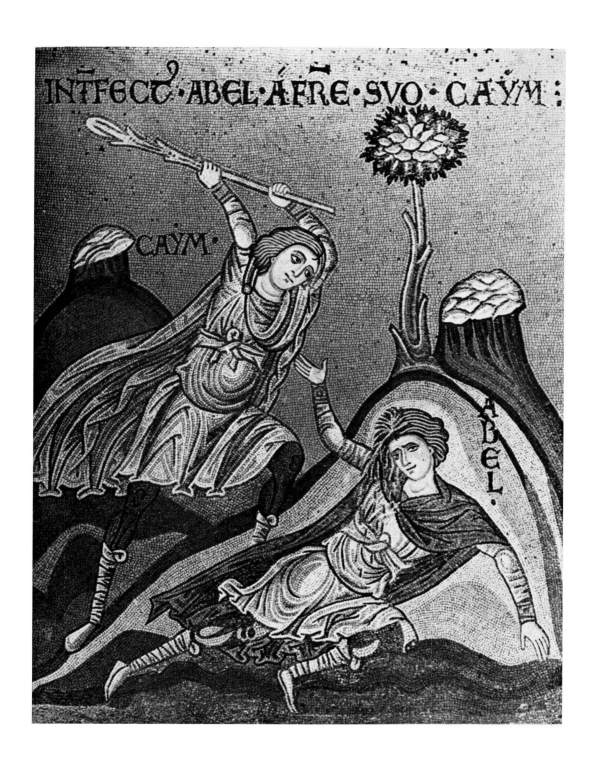

Fig. 258. *Monreale*, Cathedral, Mosaic. Slaying of Abel.

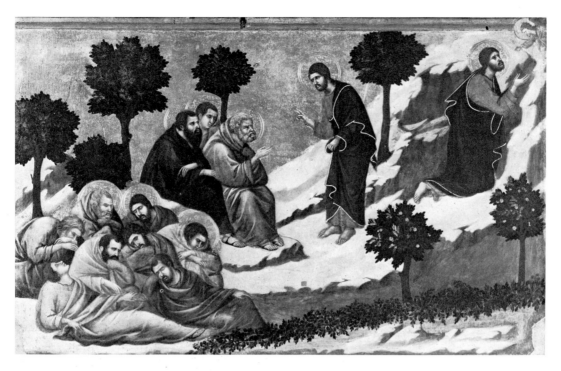

Fig. 259. *Siena*, Opera del Duomo, Maestà by Duccio, Detail. Agony in the Garden.

expressive use of "landscape-commentary" on the action of the figures was further elaborated in Byzantine thirteenth century painting. It was also in the art of this period that the function of landscape was raised from that of a backdrop to that of a stage with various layers of depth, so as to make it possible for a scene to be depicted not only as an action in relief but as an event in space. Duccio (Fig. 259), for one, was deeply indebted to the new scheme—a late example of which, though still preceding the Maestà by a decade, appears in the Peribleptos church of Ohrid (Fig. 260). Duccio also made use of the terraced landscape which was, perhaps, one of the most important parts of the classical heritage preserved or resurrected in Byzantine art and developed by it into most complicated configurations of crags, rocks, shelves and ravines in the fourteenth century. All this provided the material for European landscape art, as far as Italy is concerned, well into the fifteenth century. In this field (in contrast to the representation of the human figure) there was no possibility of a more direct recourse to classical antiquity: here, Byzantium remained the model until it was superseded by nature.

While all this happened in Tuscany, another process was going on in Venice, a process which—it goes almost without saying—concerned not plastic and spatial values but qualities of light and color. Venice was, of course, pre-

232

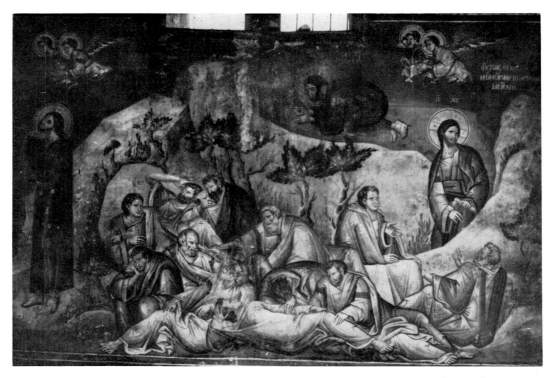

Fig. 260. *Ohrid*, Yugoslavia, Peribleptos Church, Wall Painting. Agony in the Garden.

destined to become the great mediator between Byzantium and the West with respect to those purely pictorial means, color and highlights which (to use Ernst Kitzinger's phrase) "produce an illusion of three-dimensional shapes and, at the same time, suffuse these shapes with light and suggest their envelopment in real space." Byzantium, of course, owed this technique of illusionism, which had such a strong appeal for the West, to the heritage of Hellenism, to survivals and revivals of the great pictorial art of late antiquity, but it transformed this heritage by making it a vehicle of its new spiritual values.[156]

One of the most conspicuous elements in this transformation was the use of a golden ground that envelops the figures in an otherworldly light (Pl. V). This was certainly a decisive step away from the illusionistic naturalism of late antique painting and a decisive step towards the conceptual attitude of medieval art. And, as if the magic of the golden ground were not strong enough to make the figures appear as beings of a higher order, the gold invades their contours, illuminating them with a golden light that shines through them. What would appear as highlights in Hellenistic painting is here stylized into a golden web of almost ornamental design. These golden highlights seem to have appeared first in early Christian mosaics, but their use soon became one

233

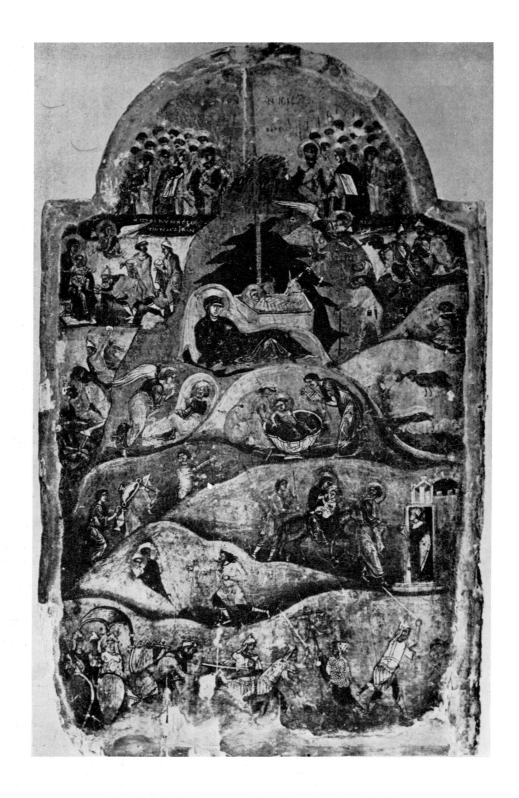

Fig. 261. *Sinai*, Monastery of St. Catherine, Icon. Nativity.

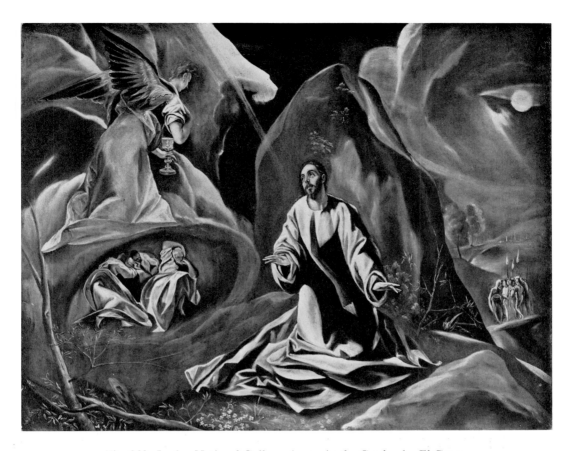

Fig. 262. *London*, National Gallery. Agony in the Garden by El Greco.

of the favorite technical devices of a certain festive and sacred "mode" in Byzantine painting, that is, in miniatures, panels, mosaics and frescos. In the art of enamel gold even provides the support, and the figures seem to be caught in a net of gold. Now, it can hardly be upheld that the use of gold in itself, as ground and as *chrysographia* (or golden lineament), constituted an especially "modern" element in Western or, for that matter, in Byzantine painting. On the contrary, it was avidly seized upon by Western artists intent on evading contemporary issues by heaping up decorative effects—in the fifteenth century as much as in the twentieth. Gold was used if one wanted to produce archaic effects, as Crivelli did in Venice or even that most modern of Venetian painters, Giovanni Bellini, in some of his stately and consciously archaizing Madonna panels, which owe more than their golden highlights— namely, also their compositional schemes—to Byzantine models. There are, however, exptions. The late Theodor Hetzer pointed out that yellow as a distinctive color played a very important part in the work of Titian and that

235

the "dark golden mysteries of San Marco" had a great influence on his color scheme, where all colors find their final justification in the all-pervading gold. With Tintoretto, the influence of the color atmosphere of San Marco is even more explicit. As in many mosaics in the church (for some of which the painter himself made cartoons), in some of Tintorettos paintings blue is the most distinctive color, contrasted against a foil of golden tones. It may also be due to the painter's intimate knowledge of the mosaics that he often placed dark figures against a luminous ground—again with predominantly yellow tones— as complete silhouettes, without their long contours being cut across by other lines or forms; and some of his regressive treatment of space may stem from the same source.[157]

It was, however, in another, less obvious manner that the use of gold as a background in Byzantine painting had a lasting influence on Venetian art and through Venetian art on that of the rest of European. If they wanted to avoid the effect of dark silhouettes on a shiny ground, Byzantine painters had to strengthen the contrasts between light and dark within their figures and make these contrasts as abrupt as possible. Only in this way could color differentiations be made visible at all against the golden background. Lights, in these contexts, had, of course, to be very light indeed to be seen and to be appreciated as highlights. Thus, they were laid on in gold or in white, giving a sparkling effect to the whole. Professor Gombrich has pointed out (in a lecture held in 1964, in the Royal Society of Arts in London) that the distinction between *lumen* and *splendor*, between light and highlight, which was explicitly made by Pliny, was lost in medieval art, where there was no light, only highlights; but he might have added that the art of the highlight was developed in Byzantium to a higher pitch than in the art of any other place or period. Highlights in Byzantine art are not a kind of seasoning, as it were, for they belong to the very substance of painting, bringing out texture and structure—and, at the same time, making the figures insubstantial.[158]

Some of the greatest Venetian painters of the sixteenth century found in this Byzantine highlight technique the surest means of producing that ambivalent atmosphere which was already the essence of Hellenistic illusionism, as Professor Kitzinger has shown, in which reality is enhanced and, at the same time, transfigured into something magic and mysterious. Jacopo Bassano's glittering night pieces (Pl. VII), Tintoretto's fairy landscapes and even those poems of light of the aged Titian and the visions of Greco are the mature results of this meeting of Venetian sensibility and Hellenistic tradition preserved in Byzantine painting. How far Florence was from understanding the possibilities of the Byzantine highlight technique becomes almost comically clear

236

from Alberti's philippic, in the second book of his *Della Pittura*, against the excessive use of white by painters. He says that he wished white pigments were as expensive to buy as the most precious jewels, for then painters would use them sparingly.[159]

To the Hellenistic tradition which had survived in Byzantium belonged also a special way of handling color itself, particularly medium and dark tones. (Pls. II, VI). Color in illusionism is not something absolute, not something unchangeable. Blue is not just blue in varying degrees of saturation; it turns brown or purple in the shadows, and, as a result, the specifically blue parts of the blue are made to appear bluer than if the whole expanse of, say, a drapery had been uniformly blue. It is one of the miracles of Byzantine conservatism that something of the subtle relativism of Hellenistic color treatment was preserved and embodied in an art which strove for the rendering of the absolute. Every new wave of Byzantine influence brought to Italy another aspect of this art of the complementary saturation of colors. In the frescoes of Sant'Angelo in Formis, as pointed out in a previous chapter, this coloristic *savoir faire*, which is more than a technique, is one of the most important results of Byzantine teaching; a later, more mannerist, phase is seen in the *changeant* colors of thirteenth century painting, in Byzantium (Ohrid) as well as in the West, where even Giotto succumbed to its influence. That the *changeant* color treatment had a great success in Venice from the thirteenth century on, goes without saying.

The related Byzantine practice in which color is used very sparingly in the half-shades, between the white of the highlights and a neutral tone which is usually the uniform brownish color of the ground became even more important for Western painting. This gives to the shaded parts a special transparency and to the entire painting a peculiar homogeneity, since all color is referred to, and seems to emanate from, the neutral ground. An icon of the Twelve Apostles in Moscow, of about 1300 (Pl. V), is a very fine example of this practice, which is, of course, another part of the Hellenistic heritage and which, needless to say, is at the root of much of Titian's, Tintoretto's and even Rembrandt's use of the toned ground as the matrix of color. It was still used with all the rest of Veneto-Byzantine tricks of color treatment in eighteenth century painting (Pl. VIII), both Italian and south German or Austrian, and died a lingering death in the academies of the nineteenth century.

All these practices were, of course, also known to that painter who united in his art the Byzantine and the Venetian heritage. I know that it is now highly unpopular to speak at all of the former, and I feel that I ought to apologize for doing so at all. But to speak about Byzantine art and the West and shirk the issue of El Greco, would hardly be permissible.[160] The inundation of the market and, consequently, the galleries with spurious "early Grecos" had led to a wholesale repudiation of the "Byzantine Greco" by some serious scholars, a situation which has hardly been improved by well-intentioned attempts at vindication. I shall not proffer any opinion on these so-called early Grecos, not even on the problem whether the Master Domenikos of the Modena Triptych is or is not identical with El Greco, but I should like in passing, to point to some features in El Greco's art which, I still think, are best understood in connection with his Byzantine ancestry. Whether these features are to be explained as the results of the early training which he must have had in Candia—the real art of Crete has long been obscured by bad Western imitations and is only now being properly studied[161]—or as atavisms, is another question. It looks, in any case, as if those features in the art of El Greco which appear as most Byzantine came out more strongly in his later than in his earlier works.

One of these features is the tendency to articulate and subdivide compositions in lobes, with every unit being framed by a domed contour and possessing its own scale and color. This arrangement which is in principle that of composite Byzantine schemes, especially of landscape compositions (Fig. 261), appears in Greco's oeuvre not only in landscapes like that of the London *Agony in the Garden* (Fig. 262) (or any of the better versions) but also in compositions such as the *Allegory of the Holy League* in the Escorial. It is legitimate I think, to see in the relationship between the earthly and the heavenly halves of the *Burial of Count Orgaz* a parallel to Byzantine fourteenth- or fifteenth-century representations of the Koimesis, the Death of the Virgin. It seems that El Greco's ideas of space in general are best understood in conjunction with Byzantine principles of spatial dynamics—be it the vertical rush of his *Resurrection* (Fig. 263), where the guardians seem to be falling out of the picture just as the Apostles are in the *Transfiguration* of the Paris manuscript of John Kantakuzenos, of about 1375 (Fig. 264); or the circular movement of the Chicago *Last Supper* which has a parallel in late Byzantine representations of the same theme. I leave aside more obvious parallels such as the attitudes of half-length figures and the iconic character of portraits, but I should like, in concluding to point to El Greco's treatment of highlights and his skillful way of holding extremes of color together by the neutral tones of the ground, his great colorism, in short, which can only, I think, be understood as a late flowering of that Hellenistic art of light that was transmitted to the West by the painting of Byzantium. It does not make much difference whether El Greco learned the elements of this art in Candia or in Venice; in any case,

238

the fact that he was himself a Greek must have made it easier for him to appropriate them. Thus, if it is wrong to make El Greco a Byzantine painter who was marooned in Toledo, it is surely right to see him as an apprentice of Hellenistic art. Thus, even in the sixteenth and seventeenth centuries, the Byzantine variety of Hellenism was able to give something to Europe—at a time when the need of Western art for guidance had long ceased to exist. Generally speaking, Western art came of age at the beginning of the thirteenth century in the Gothic Northwest and toward the end of the century in Italy. Later waves of Byzantine influence had, as a rule, a rather retarding effect—as in the gorgeously archaizing mosaics of the mid-fourteenth century in the Baptistery of San Marco.[162]

The apprenticeship of Western art lasted, then, for about seven hundred years, from the early seventh to the late thirteenth century. I have attempted to sketch the main lines of this development, hoping that I have not grossly overstated my case. I may have presented, it is true, a one-sided picture insofar as I have not considered those developments which were not tinged by Byzantine influence. On the other hand, I have also excluded (or alluded to only in passing) other phenomena which seem to me to belong to the realm of oddities—such as much of German painting, however Byzantinizing, or much of Italian Duecento work. I have tried to concentrate on those currents and values which seem essential.

Now, what did the influence of Byzantium on European art amount to? I can only point to a few things. To begin with, it served to turn Western art away from exhausting itself in the creation of sophisticated surface eflects: it helped to make Western art an instrument for shaping and propagating ideas in monumental form and helped it, as well, to instill into human figures and their actions a kind of dignity and a feeling of life; it transmitted and revived age-old standards of harmony in form and color; and it gave the medieval West a first taste of humanism—not the superficial humanism of the intellect, but a deeper humanism of the spirit. And, finally, it transmitted an expert knowledge of the painterly use of color and its effects.

This was possible only because Byzantine art was the living continuation of Greek art and so was able to lead Western artists back to the classical sources. Thus, the process which I have attempted to sketch is really part of a much larger all-embracing process—that of the survival, the transmission, and the revival of Hellenism. Of course, Byzantium was able to play its part in this process only because of the ability of Western artists actually to *see* the *Greek* behind the *Byzantine*. How all-important this was can, perhaps, be realized, if, for a moment, we try to imagine artists who were as deeply influenced by

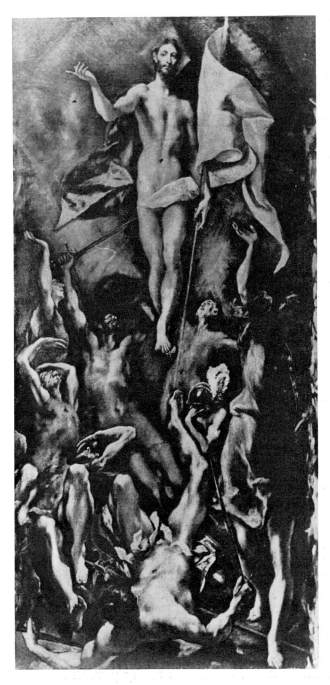

Fig. 263. *Madrid*, Prado.
Resurrection of Christ by
El Greco.

Byzantine art but had no possibility of refering back to the classical sources of Byzantium. Such artists did, in fact, exist: namely, the icon painters of Russia. They too were disciples of Byzantium but they never became students of antiquity. Thus, their way did not lead to a renaissance or a new humanism. It lost itself in the decorative mazes of folk art.

240

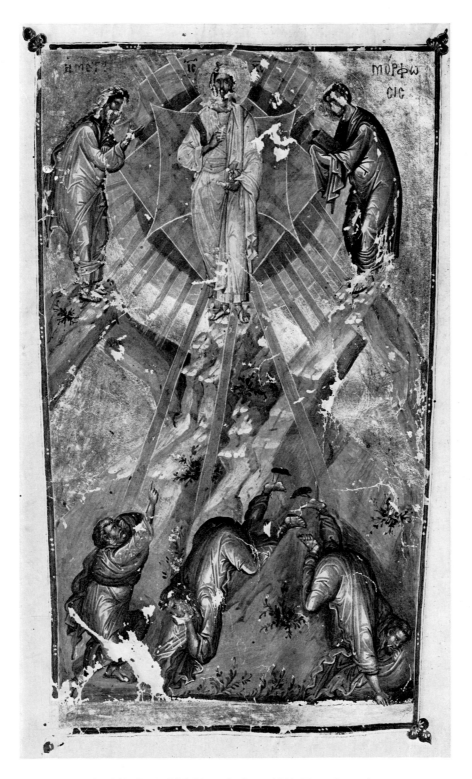

Fig. 264. *Paris*, Bibl. Nat., Cod. gr. 1242, Transfiguration.

241

Notes

Chapter I

1. E. Kitzinger, "The Byzantine Contribution"; G. Cames, *Byzance*; R. Dölling, "Byzantinische Elemente"; W. Koehler, "Byzantine Art"; D. Talbot Rice, "Britain"; S. Runciman, "Byzantine Art"; G. Vitzthum, "Zur byzantinischen Frage"; W. F. Volbach, "Byzanz und sein Einfluß"; W. Weidlé, "Les caractères"; K. Weitzmann, "Various Aspects."

2. For the most recent treatment of the style of Cappadocian painting see M. Restle, *Die byzantinische Wandmalerei*; for Ayvali Kilise in particular, N. and M. Thierry, "Ayvali Kilise." On the presumed relationship between Cappadocian and Western wall painting G. de Jerphanion, *Les églises*, Text vol. II, 2, pp. 455 ff.

3. The most important of the numerous recent publications on wall paintings in Yugoslavia are: R. Hamann-MacLean. *Die Monumentalmalerei*; G. Millet-A. Frolow, *La peinture*, vols. I–III; S. Radojčić, *Staro srpsko slikarstvo*, all with numerous illustrations and ample bibliographies.

4. On Romanesque wall painting see O. Demus, *Romanische Wandmalerei*, with bibliography.

5. L. Abatangelo, *Chiese-cripte*; B. Cappelli, Aspetti; G. Kalbi, "Olevano," I, II; A. Medea, "La pittura."

6. O. Demus, *Romanische Wandmalerei*, pp. 202 ff., with bibliography.

7. W. Frodl. "Die romanischen Wandgemälde"; E. Weiss, "Der Freskenzyklus"; O. Demus, *Romanische Wandmalerei*, p. 208.

8. O. Demus, "Die Rolle"; O. Demus, "Vorbildqualität." On Byzantine art in general see: J. Beckwith, *The Art*; O. M. Dalton, *Byzantine Art*; Ch. Delvoye, *L'art byzantin*; O. Demus, *Byzantine Mosaic Decoration*; Ch. Diehl, *Manuel*; A. Grabar, *La peinture byzantine*; A. Grabar, *Byzanz*; I. Hutter, *Frühchristliche, byzantinische Kunst*; V. N. Lazarev, *Storia*; D. Talbot Rice-M. Hirmer, *Kunst aus Byzanz*; D. Talbot Rice, *Byzantine Painting*; O. Wulff, *Altchristliche und byzantinische Kunst.*

9. D. V. Ainalov, *The Hellenistic Origins*; E. Kitzinger, "The Hellenistic Heritage"; E. Panofsky, *Renaissance*; K. Weitzmann, "The Classical"; K. Weitzmann, *Geistige Grundlagen*; K. Weitzmann, "The Survival."

10. O. Demus, "Two Palaeologan Mosaic Icons"; K. Weitzmann, "The Survival."

11. E. Berger, *Beiträge*; G. Cames, *Byzance*, pp. 290 ff.; G. Loumyer, *Les traditions.*

12. K. Wessel, *Die byzantinische Emailkunst*, with bibliography.

13. F. Mercier, *Les primitifs*, pp. 43 ff., 64 ff.; C. P. Duprat, "Enquête."

14. H. Karlinger, *Die hochromanische Wandmalerei*; G. Swarzenski, *Die Regensburger Buch-malerei*.

15. O. Demus, *Byzantine Mosaic Decoration*.

16. J. Deér, *The Dynastic Porphyry Tombs*; Ch. Delvoye, "Les ateliers"; O. Demus, "Das älteste venezianische Gesellschaftsbild"; J. Ebersolt, *Les arts somptuaires*; A. Grabar, *L'empereur*; E. Kitzinger, "On the Portrait"; O. Treitinger, *Die oströmische Kaiser- und Reichsidee*.

17. B. Dudan, *Il dominio*; J. Ebersolt, *Orient et Occident*, vols. I, II; D. Geanakoplos, *Byzantine East*; R. Grousset, *L'Empire*; W. Heyd, *Histoire*; P. Lamma, *Comneni*; J. Longnon, *L'empire*; W. Miller, *Essays*; S. Runciman, *A History*, G. Schreiber, "Christlicher Orient"; G. Soyter, "Die byzantinischen Einflüsse"; Sp. Vryonis, *Byzantium*.

18. C. Angelillis, *Le porte*; M. Cagiano de Azevedo, "La porta"; H. Leisinger, *Romanische Bronzen*; P. Toesca, *Storia*, pp. 1105 ff.

19. J. J. Tikkanen, "Die Genesismosaiken"; S. Tsuji, "La chaire"; K. Weitzmann, "Observations."

20. A. L. Frothingham, "Byzantine Artists"; E. Muentz, "Les artistes."

21. On Castelseprio see note 38. I do not believe in the assumption of Professor G. Panazza, "La chiesa," that one of the painters of San Salvatore in Brescia was a pupil or a follower of the chief master of Castelseprio.

22. I. J. Arne, "Ryskbysantinska malningar"; B. G. Söderberg, *Svenska Kyrkomalningar*.

23. A. Acocella, *La decorazione*; H. Bloch, "Monte Cassino"; G. Giovannoni, *L'Abbazia*; H. R. Hahnloser, "Magistra"; G. Ladner, "Die italienische Malerei," pp. 38 ff.; O. Morisani, *Bisanzio*; E. Scaccia Scarafoni, "Note"; J. Wettstein, *Sant'Angelo*.

24. P. Baldass, "Disegni"; M. Inguanez-M. Avery, *Miniature*; G. Ladner, "Die italienische Malerei," pp. 38 ff.; J. Wettstein, *Sant'Angelo*, pp. 99 ff.

25. G. Matthiae, *Mosaici*; G. Matthiae, *Pittura*; W. Oakeshott, *The Mosaics*.

26. See Note 85; E. Kitzinger, "The Byzantine Contribution"; E. Kitzinger, "Norman Sicily."

27. See Note 84; O. Demus, *Die Mosaiken*; E. Kitzinger, "The Byzantine Contribution."

28. K. Weitzmann, "Constantinopolitan Book-Illumination"; K. Weitzmann, "Zur byzantinischen Quelle."

29. H. Buchthal, *Miniature Painting*; K. Weitzmann, "Thirteenth Century Crusader Icons."

30. R. Longhi, "Apertura"; R. Longhi, "Postilla."

31. G. Cames, *Byzance*, pp. 247 ff.; R. W. Scheller, *A Survey*.

32. G. Cames, *Byzance*, pp. 270 f.; O. Demus, *The Mosaics*, pp. 276, 445 f.; O. Homburger, "Das Freiburger Einzelblatt"; E. Kitzinger, *The Mosaics*, pp. 84 f.; R. W. Scheller, *A Survey*; K. Weitzmann, "Icon Painting," pp. 78 f., figs. 62–65.

33. G. Cames, *Byzance*, pp. 284 ff.; J. Sommer, *Das Deckenbild*, pp. 79 ff.; K. Weitzmann, "Constantinopolitan Book-Illumination"; K. Weitzmann, "Zur byzantinischen Quelle."

34. O. Demus, *The Mosaics*, pp. 285, 446 ff.; E. Kitzinger, "Norman Sicily," pp. 130f. N. Mayers, *Studien*, pp. 34 ff., pointed to the parallel between the *Hortus* and the Protaton; J. Walter, *Herrade*.

35. For the suggested dependence of the *Descent from the Cross* in the Ingeborg Psalter on Byzantine Ivories of the Romanos Group (e.g., the plaque in Hannover) see F. Deuchler, *Der Ingeborgpsalter*, pp. 54f.; W. Grape drew my attention to the much closer parallel on Mount Athos; see M. Chatzidakis, "Eikones," pl. 83.

Chapter II

36. A. Grabar, *L'iconoclasme*.

37. See note 25; in addition E. Kitzinger, *Römische Malerei*; P. J. Nordhagen, "Nuove constatazioni"; For Santa Maria Antiqua see W. de Grüneisen, Sainte-Maria Antique; P. J. Nordhagen, "The earliest decorations"; P. Romanelli-P. J. Nordhagen, *Sta. Maria Antiqua*; E. Tea, *La basilica*; J. Wilpert, *Die römischen Mosaiken*, vols. II, IV. On the point of view of C. R. Morey see M. Avery, "The Alexandrian Style"; C. R. Morey, *Early Christian Art*.

38. G. P. Bognetti, *Castelseprio*; G. P. Bognetti et al., *Santa Maria de Castelseprio*; K. Weitzmann *The Fresco Cycle*. The difficult problems connected with the dating of this fresco cycle, debated by Messrs. Bognetti, Cecchelli, Grabar, Schapiro, Tselos and Weitzmann, have lately been restated by H. Belting, "Probleme," pp. 119ff. and E. Kitzinger, "Byzantine Art," pp. 8ff.; see also V. N. Lazarev, "L'arte"; D. Tselos, "A Greco-Italian School."

39. On the relationship between the Cappadocian frescoes of Ayvali Kilise and the mosaics of Hagia Sophia at Thessalonika, see N. and M. Thierry, "Ayvali Kilise," pp. 145 ff. Similar abstract tendencies as in monumental painting are visible in manuscripts such as the marginal psalters or those of the so-called gold figure group; see K. Weitzmann, *Die byzantinische Buchmalerei*. On the role of the Oriental hinterlands see G. de Francovich, "L'arte siriaca"; G. de Francovich, "L'Egitto."

40. Although there is as yet no comprehensive treatment of the question of Byzantine and east Christian influence on pre-Carolingian art, it becomes increasingly clear that the most important influences came, in the early period, not from Byzantium itself, but from Armenian, Coptic and Syrian art.
   For good illustrations see the recent publication by J. Hubert et al., *L'Europe*; For the Byzantine and east Christian elements in Insular art see S. Casson, "Byzantium"; F. Henry, *Early Christian Irish Art*; W. Holmquist, "Einflüsse"; J. Hubert, et al., *L'Europe*; T. D. Kendrick et al., *Codex Lindisfarnensis*; F. Masai, *Essai*; C. Nordenfalk, "Eastern style Elements"; J. Raftery, "Irische Beziehungen"; D. Talbot Rice, "Britain"; F. Saxl, "The Ruthwell Cross." On pre-Carolingian art of the Continent see P. Goubert, "Byzance"; P. I. Müller, "Beiträge"; A. Thiery, "L'oriente."

41. A. Boeckler, "Malerei"; W. Braunfels, ed., *Karl der Große*; J. Hubert et al., *L'Empire*; H. Fichtenau, *The Carolingian Empire*; *Karl der Große* (Catalogue); W. Ohnsorge, "Das Kaisertum." On the relationship of Carolingian art to Byzantium, see J. Beckwith, "Byzantine Influence."

42. F. F. Leitschuh, *Geschichte*, pp. 9ff.; H. Schade, "Die Libri Carolini."

43. H. Schlunk-M. Berenguer, *La pintura*.

44. P. Bloch, "Das Apsismosaik"; A. Khatchatrian, "Notes"; M. Viellard-Troiekouroff, "À propos de Germigny-des-Prés."

45. H. Schnitzler, "Das Kuppelmosaik"; H. Schrade, "Zum Kuppelmosaik."

46. H. Belting, "Probleme." The standard work on Carolingian book illumination is still W. Koehler, *Die karolingischen Miniaturen*. On the Godescalc Gospels see *ibid.*, II, pp. 22 ff. The most important problems have been restated by F. Mütherich, "Die Buchmalerei." For the iconographic and stylistic sources of the so-called Ada Group see A. Boeckler, "Die Evangelistenbilder"; A. Boeckler, "Formgeschichtliche Studien"; H. Buchthal, "A Byzantine Miniature"; E. Rosenbaum, "The Evangelist Portraits."

47. A. Boeckler, "Die Evangelistenbilder"; E. Kitzinger, Review of W. Koehler, *Karolingische Miniaturen*, vol. III; M. Schapiro, Review of K. Weitzmann, *The Fresco Cycle*.

48. W. Koehler, *Die Karolingischen Miniaturen*, vol. III, 1, pp. 22 ff.; C. Nordenfalk, Review of W. Koehler.

49. A. Grabar-C. Nordenfalk, *Das frühe Mittelalter*, pp. 144 ff.

50. K. Weitzmann-I. Ševčenko, "The Moses Cross." On the Utrecht Psalter and the provenance of its style, G. M. Benson, "New Light"; E. De Wald, *The Illustrations*; J. H. A. Engelbregt, *The Utrecht Psalter*; D. T. Tselos, "The Greek Element"; D. T. Tselos, "A Greco-Italian School"; F. Wormald, *The Utrecht Psalter*.

51. F. W. Deichmann, "Gründung"; R. Krautheimer, *Early Christian and Byzantine Architecture*, pp. 169 f.; K. Wessel, "San Vitale."

52. G. Bandmann, "Die Vorbilder"; H. Fichtenau, "Byzanz"; L. Hugot, "Die Pfalz"; E. Lehmann, "Die Architektur"; H. Schnitzler, *Der Dom*; W. Schöne, "Die künstlerische und liturgische Gestalt"; L. Schürenberg, "Mittelalterlicher Kirchenbau"; M. Vieillard-Troiekouroff, "L'architecture."

53. For the question Aachen-Ravenna see H. Belting, "Probleme"; also H. Hoffmann, "Die Aachener Theoderich Statue"; K. Holter, "Der Buchschmuck"; H. Schrade, "Zum Kuppelmosaik"; D. H. Wright, "The Codex."

54. On Carolingian ivories in general see the standard work by A. Goldschmidt, *Die Elfenbeinskulpturen*; in addition, W. Volbach, *Elfenbeinarbeiten*; J. Beckwith, "Byzantine Influence"; J. Beckwith, "The Werden Casket"; H. Fillitz, "Die Elfenbeinreliefs"; On the Andrews Diptych see J. Beckwith, *The Andrews Diptych*; On the Monza Diptych see *Karl der Große* (Catalogue), No. 505.

55. On the Lorsch ivories see *Karl der Große* (Catalogue), Nos. 521, 522, with bibliography; M. H. Longhurst-C. R. Morey, "Covers"; H. Schnitzler, "Die Komposition."

56. J. Beckwith, "Byzantine Influence."

57. J. Ebersolt, *Orient et Occident*, vol. I, pp. 56 ff.

Chapter III

58. On Ottonian art in general, H. Jantzen, *Ottonische Kunst*; F. Mütherich, "Ottonian Art." On the byzantine elements in Ottonian art, in general, W. Messerer, "Zur byzantinischen Frage."

59. A. Boeckler, *Das goldene Evangelienbuch*; Ph. Schweinfurth, "Das goldene Evangelienbuch."

60. F. Dölger, *Byzanz*; F. Dölger, "Die Ottonenkaiser"; W. Ohnsorge, *Abendland*; W. Ohnsorge, *Konstantinopel*.

61. A. Goldschmidt-K. Weitzmann, *Die byzantinischen Elfenbeinskulpturen*, vol. II, No. 85; P. E. Schramm, *Kaiser*; P. E. Schramm-F. Mütherich, *Denkmale*, No. 73.

62. The cupola fresco of Wieselburg is as yet unpublished. On the history of the site H. Ladenbauer-Orel, "Das ottonische Castellum."

63. H. Sedlmayr in V. Milojčić, "Bericht."

64. L. H. Grondijs, *L'iconographie*, and the review by E. Lucchesi-Palli; the dead Christ already occurs in Hosios Lukas, in the first half of the 11th century; on ivories even earlier. The Cologne crucifixes of the late tenth century testify to an early influence of Byzantine prototypes.

65. A. Boeckler, "Bildvorlagen"; A. Boeckler, "Die Reichenauer Buchmalerei"; A. Boeckler, "Ikonographische Studien"; H. Buchthal, "Byzantium and Reichenau"; G. Cames, *Byzance*; C. R. Dodwell-E. H. Turner, *Reichenau*; K. Künstle, *Die Kunst*.

66. H. Buchthal, "Byzantium and Reichenau"; H. Buchthal, *The Miniatures*, pp. 56 ff.; K. Weitzmann, *Illustrations*.

67. K. Weitzmann, "Byzantine Miniature"; K. Weitzmann, "The Narrative."

68. E. Arslan, *La pittura*; U. Chierici, "Il Maestro"; G. de Francovich, "Arte Carolingia"; R. Salvini, "La pittura"; P. Toesca, *La pittura*.

69. G. Swarzenski, *Die Regensburger Buchmalerei*.

70. P. Bloch-H. Schnitzler, *Die ottonische Kölner Malerschule*; A. Boeckler, "Kölner ottonische Buchmalerei"; K. Ehl, *Die ottonische Kölner Buchmalerei*.

71. O. Demus, *Romanische Wandmalerei*, pp. 20, 31, 135 ff., pl. XXXVIII.

72. O. Demus, *Romanische Wandmalerei*, pp. 18 ff., 30 ff. 140 ff.; P. Deschamps-M. Thibout, *La peinture murale*, pp. 71 ff.

73. E. Bertaux, *L'art*; J. Wettstein, *Sant'Angelo*. On the Exultet rolls, M. Avery, *The Exultet Rolls*.

74. See Note 23 and R. Causa, *Sant'Angelo*; N. Cilento, "Sant'Angelo"; O. Demus, *Romanische Wandmalerei*, pp. 114 ff.; E. Dobbert, "Zur byzantinischen Frage"; F. X. Kraus, "Die Wandgemälde"; G. Ladner, "Die italienische Malerei," pp. 76 ff.; O. Morisani, *Gli affreschi*; O. Morisani, "La pittura"; J. Wettstein, *Sant'Angelo*.

75. E. B. Garrison, *Studies*; F. Hermanin, *L'arte*; G. Ladner, "Die italienische Malerei"; R. van Marle, *La peinture*; G. Matthiae, *Pittura*; J. Wilpert, *Die Mosaiken*. On later (Baroque) copies of medieval Roman paintings, S. Waetzoldt, *Die Kopien*.

76. L. Coletti, "Arte Benedittina"; G. de Francovich, "Problemi," pp. 475 ff.; E. B. Garrison, *Studies*, vol. II, pp. 27 ff.; vol. III, pp. 195 ff.; A. Pantoni, "Opinioni."

77. E. B. Garrison, *Studies*, vol. II, pp. 21 ff., 79 ff., 121 ff., 171 ff.; vol. III, pp. 5 ff., 17 ff., (Scriptorium of Santa Cecilia); 100 ff., 184 ff.

78. O. Demus, *Romanische Wandmalerei*, p. 122; G. Matthiae, *Pittura*, vol. II, pp. 30 ff.; C. A. Isermeyer, "Die mittelalterlichen Malereien."

79. *L'art roman* (Catalogue); *Byzance et la France médiévale* (Catalogue); J. Porcher, "Les ivoires."

80. O. Demus, *Romanische Wandmalerei*, pp. 34 f., 45 ff., 82 ff., 136 f.; C. P. Duprat, "Enquête," III, pp. 188 ff.; J. Evans, *Cluniac Art*; A. Grabar, "L'étude," pp. 171 ff.; W. Koehler, "Byzantine Art"; F. Mercier, *Les primitifs*; M. Schapiro, *The Parma Ildefonsus*.

81. R. Hamann-MacLean-H. Hallensleben, *Die Monumentalmalerei*, pp. 15 ff., pls. 1–28.

Chapter IV

82. On Byzantine colonial art in Italy see E. Kitzinger, "The Byzantine Contribution," with bibliography.

83. V. Lazarev, *Old Russian Murals*; V. Lazarev, *Mozaiki*; V. Lazarev, *Mikhailovskie Mozaiki*.

84. O. Demus, *Die Mosaiken*; O. Demus, *The Church*; O. Demus, "Das älteste venezianische Gesellschaftsbild"; O. Demus, "Bisanzio e la pittura."

85. O. Demus, *The Mosaics*; F. Di Pietro, *La Cappella*; E. Kitzinger, "On the Portrait"; E. Kitzinger, *The Mosaics*; E. Kitzinger, "Norman Sicily."

86. E. Diez-O. Demus, *Byzantine Mosaics*.

87. A. M. Damigella, "Problemi, II"; The date proposed for the apostles by Signora Damigella seems much too late. O. Demus, "Das Problem."

88. O. Demus, *The Church*, pp. 90 ff., with bibliography.

89. O. Demus, *Romanische Wandmalerei*, p. 112, pls. 9, 10; P. L. Zovatto, *Il Battistero*.

90. On the Lambach frescoes see O. Demus, *Romanische Wandmalerei*, pp. 202 ff., with bibliography, and pls. XCIII–XCVI, 225–230; the leading work on Salzburg miniature painting is still G. Swarzenski, *Die Salzburger Malerei*. On Custos Bertold, P. Buberl. "Über einige Werke." On Byzantine elements in Civate, A. Grabar, "Influences."

91. P. Buberl, "Die romanischen Wandmalereien"; G. Cames, *Byzance*, pp. 198 ff.; O. Demus, *Romanische Wandmalerei*, p. 206, with bibliography.

92. O. Demus, *Romanische Wandmalerei*, p. 127, with bibliography.

93. O. Demus, *Romanische Wandmalerei*, pp. 131 f., with bibliography; N. Rasmo, *Hocheppan*.

94. The problem of Veneto-Byzantine influence on Bohemian painting has not yet been studied. For general information see A. Matêjček-J. Pešina, *La peinture*.

95. E. Kitzinger, "The Byzantine Contribution."

96. O. Demus, "Regensburg"; O. Demus, *Romanische Wandmalerei*, pp. 94, 188 f., with bibliography.

97. O. Demus, *Romanische Wandmalerei*, p. 92; F. Lambert, *Byzantinische und westliche Einflüsse*; G. Tröscher, *Sächsische Monumentalmalerei*, pp. 38 ff.

98. F. Crooy, *Les émaux*, with wrong date; O. Demus, "Die sizilischen Mosaiken," p. 134; E. Kitzinger, "Norman Sicily," p. 132.

99. O. Demus, *Romanische Wandmalerei*, pp. 186f.; W. Jung, *Die ehemalige Prämonstratenserstiftskirche*.

100. O. Demus, *The Mosaics*, pp. 453f.; O. Demus, *Romanische Wandmalerei*, pp. 53, 118.

101. On San Silvestro, Tivoli, see O. Demus, *Romanische Wandmalerei*, pp. 57f., 124ff.; on Anagni, *ibid.*, pp. 124ff., with bibliography.

102. H. Buchthal, "The Beginnings"; H. Buchthal, "Some Sicilian Miniatures"; H. Buchthal, "Early Fourteenth Century Illuminations"; H. Buchthal, "A School"; A. Daneu Lattanzi, *Lineamenti*.

103. E. Kitzinger, "The Byzantine Contribution"; W. Oakeshott, *The Artists*.

104. O. Pächt, "A Cycle"; O. Demus, *Romanische Wandmalerei*, pp. 81, 84, 166ff., 173f., with bibliography.

105. See note 29.

Chapter V

106. W. Koehler, "Byzantine Art." About the role of Byzantine art in the genesis of the Gothic figure style see also E. Kitzinger, "The Byzantine Contribution"; E. Kitzinger, "Norman Sicily"; W. Oakeshott, *Classical Inspiration*; W. F. Volbach, "Byzanz"; F. Worringer, *Griechentum*.

107. W. Voege, *Die Anfänge*.

108. See in general, M. Aubert, *La sculpture*; R. Hamann-MacLean, "Antikenstudium"; R. Rey, *La sculpture*, On Saint-Gilles see R. Hamann, *Die Abteikirche*.

109. S. Collon-Gevaert, *Histoire*, pp. 136ff.

110. For this and the following see W. Oakeshott, *Classical Inspiration*; F. Saxl-R. Wittkower, *British Art*.

111. On the dynamic style of late Comnenian art see O. Demus, *The Mosaics*, p. 418ff.; E. Kitzinger, "The Byzantine Contribution"; E. Kitzinger, *The Mosaics*, pp. 69ff.; K. Weitzmann, "Eine spätkomnenische Verkündigungsikone."

112. On the phases of the Byzantine development from 1200 to 1300 see O. Demus, "Die Entstehung."

113. There is as yet no comprehensive study on Byzantine sculpture of the Comnenian and Palaeologan periods. Particular aspects have been studied by S. Bettini, *La scultura*; L. Bréhier, "Études"; L. Bréhier, "Nouvelles recherches"; L. Bréhier, *La sculpture*; L. Bréhier, "La sculpture iconographique"; L. Bréhier, "Les voussures"; O. Demus, *The Church*, pp. 109ff. R. Lange, *Die byzantinische Reliefikone*; K. Wessel, "Byzantinische Plastik."

114. On the relationship between Byzantine ivory reliefs and Romanesque sculpture see A. Goldschmidt, Die "Stilentwicklung"; W. Sauerländer, "Die kunstgeschichtliche Stellung."

115. O. Demus, "Nicola di Verdun," with bibliography; E. Kitzinger, "The Byzantine Contribution," pp. 39ff.; F. Röhrig, *Der Verduner Altar*; [H. Schnitzler-J. Hoster]. *Der Meister*.

116. W. Oakeshott, *Classical Inspiration*. H. Reinhardt, *La cathédrale*.

117. A. Frolow, "L'origine."

118. J. Baltrusaitis, "La croisée"; J. Baltrusaitis, "Le problème."

119. A. H. S. Megaw, "Notes."

120. P. Lamma, *Comneni*.

121. The idea of the parallel development in Byzantium and the West, first expressed, 10 years ago, in my contribution to the forthcoming vol. 4 (studies) of the work on the Kariye Djami (ed. by P. Underwood), was independently developed also by Professor E. Kitzinger; see" The Byzantine Contribution," p. 43.

123. O. Demus, "Die Entstehung," pp. 25f.; E. Kitzinger, "The Byzantine Contribution," pp. 40f. The dating of Bačkovo is controversial: most authors date all the frescoes in the eleventh century; V. Lazarev, *Storia*, p. 222, believes that they originated in the second half of the twelfth century.

124. On the stylistic phase of ca. 1230 see O. Demus, "Die Entstehung," pp. 27f.; On the chief monument of this phase, the frescoes of Mileševo, see S. Radojčić, *Mileševa*.

125. On the stylistic phase of ca. 1260 see O. Demus, "Die Entstehung," p. 29f. On the chief monument of this phase, the frescoes of Sopoćani, see V. J. Djurić, *Sopoćani*.

126. On the "cubistic" phase of ca. 1290 see O. Demus, "Die Entstehung," p. 30. On the chief monument, the frescoes of the Peribleptos church in Ohrid (Sv. Kliment), see P. Miljković-Pepek, *L'oeuvre*, pp. 43ff., with bibliography.

127. On the representation of space in late Byzantine painting see T. Velmans, "Le rôle."

128. The most recent book on late Byzantine painting is D. Talbot Rice, *Byzantine Painting*.

129. G. Cames, *Byzance*, pp. 198ff.; H. Swarzenski, *Die lateinischen illuminierten Handschriften*; H. Swarzenski, *The Berthold Missal*.

130. P. Clemen, *Die romanische Monumentalmalerei*; O. Demus, "Der sächsische Zackenstil"; O. Demus, *Romanische Wandmalerei*, pp. 98ff.; O. Gillen, *Das Goslarer Evangeliar*; A. Goldschmidt, *Das Evangeliar*; A. Haseloff, *Eine thüringisch-sächsische Malerschule*; G. Swarzenski, "Aus dem Kunstkreis." On the Byzantine element in Saxon art in general see F. Lambert, *Byzantinische und westliche Einflüsse*.

131. See note 33; on the reliefs of Hamersleben see E. Fründt, *Sakrale Plastik*, fig. 37; for the frescoes of Brunswick see O. Demus, *Romanische Wandmalerei*, pp. 193ff., with bibliography.

Chapter VI

132. R. Byron-D. Talbot Rice, *The Birth*. For the general problem of Byzantine influence on Italian painting see E. Kitzinger, "The Byzantine Contribution"; G. Millet, "L'art des Balkans"; K. M. Setton, "The Byzantine Background"; J. H. Stubblebine, "Byzantine Influence"; W. F. Volbach, "Byzanz." A paradigmatic case has been treated by J. Hueck, "Ein Madonnenbild."

133. The story of Hadwig and the painter in Ekkehard (IV), *Casus Sci Galli*, *Mon.Germ.Hist.*, *Scriptores*, II, pp. 122ff. For Byzantine artists in the West see above, Chapter I.

134. On the booty of the Fourth Crusade see J. Ebersolt, *Orient*, II; P. E. D. Riant, *Des dépouilles*; P. E. D. Riant, *Exuviae*. On special questions, see C. Bertelli, "Storia"; C. Bertelli, "The Image"; A. Grabar, *La Sainte Face*; S. G. Mercati, "Sulla Santissima Icone"; O. Pächt, "The Avignon Diptych."

135. Chr. Salm, "Neue Forschungen."

136. F. Bologna, *La pittura*; E. B. Garrison, *Italian Romanesque Panel Painting*; E. B. Garrison, *Studies*; H. Hager, *Die Anfänge*; R. Oertel, *Die Frühzeit*; *Pittura Italiana* (Catalogue).

137. R. Longhi, *Giudizio*.

138. O. Demus, "Die Entstehung"; D. Talbot Rice, *Byzantine Painting*, pp. 39 ff.

139. G. Vasari, *Le vite*, K. Frey, ed., p. 389.

140. H. Hager, *Die Anfänge*.

141. J. Pomorisać-de Luigi, *Les émaux byzantines*; see W. F. Volbach et al., *La Pala d'Oro*, and the review by O. Demus, "Zur Pala d'Oro"; K. Wessel, *Die byzantinische Emailkunst*, pp. 133 ff.

142. O. Demus, "Zwei marmorne Altarikonen."

143. P. Cellini, *La Madonna*; P. Cellini, "Una Madonna"; C. Bertelli, "L'imagine"; C. Bertelli, *La Madonna di Santa Maria in Trastevere*; C. Bertelli, "La Madonna del Panteon"; E. Kitzinger, "The Cult"; E. Kitzinger, "On some Icons."

144. G. and M. Sotiriou, *Icônes*, Pls. 54, 165–170, etc.

145. On the reconstruction of one of these triptychs in the Sinai collection K. Weitzmann, "The Mandylion." The earliest icons reproduced in G. and M. Sotiriou's book on the Sinai icons are fragments of triptychs. For diptychs see also O. Pächt, "The Avignon Diptych," and W. Kermer, *Studien*.

146. C. Brandi, "Il Restauro"; G. Coor-Achenbach, "A Visual Basis"; G. Coor, "Coppo."

147. The two panels were believed Roman by R. van Marle, *La peinture*, pp. 227 f., and Siculo-Byzantine by V. Lazarev; recognized as Byzantine but dated in the twelfth century by B. Berenson, "Two Twelfth Century Paintings." In 1958 I claimed tham as Constantino-politan works of the third quarter of the thirteenth century (O. Demus, "Zwei Konstantinopler Marienikonen"). Lately they have again been thought Italo-Byzantine and dated at the end of the thirteenth century by Professor J. Stubblebine, "Two Byzantine Madonnas."

148. Th. Whittemore, *The Mosaics*, 4; V. Lazarev, *Storia*, p. 198, still adheres to the earlier twelfth century dating. For a date in the third quarter of the thirteenth entury see O. Demus, "Zwei Konstantinopler Marienikonen," and "Die Entstehung," pp. 16, 69 f.

149. E. Carli, *Pittura*; G. de Francovich, "L'origine."

150. K. Weitzmann, "The Origin."

151. V. J. Djurić, *Sopočani*; A. Grabar-T. Velmans, "Gli affreschi."

152. B. Kleinschmidt, *Die Basilika*; F. J. Mather, *The Isaac Master*; G. Matthiae, *Pittura*, vol. II; M. Meiss, *Giotto*; P. Toesca, *Gli affreschi*.

153. H. Hallensleben, *Die Malerschule*; R. Hamann-MacLean-H. Hallensleben, *Die Monumentalmalerei*; P. Miljković-Pepek, *L'oeuvre*.

154. M. S. Bunim, *Space*; E. Panofsky, "Die Perspektive"; T. Velmans, "Le rôle"; J. White, *The Birth*.

155. O. Demus, *The Mosaics*, pp. 335 ff.; E. Kitzinger, *The Mosaics*, pp. 86 f.

156. E. Kitzinger, The Hellenistic Heritage"; W. Schöne, *Über das Licht*.

157. Th. Hetzer, *Tizian*.

158. E. H. Gombrich, "Light"; W. Schöne, *Über das Licht*.

159. L. B. Alberti, *Kleinere Kunsttheoretische Schriften*, p. 139.

160. E. Arslan, "Cronistoria"; R. Byron-D. Talbot Rice, *The Birth*; M. Chatzidakis, *Theotocopoulos*; S. Cirac, "L'Hellénisme"; M. Florisoone, "La mystique"; P. Kelemen, *El Greco revisited*; R. Pallucchini, "Il Greco"; F. Rutter, "The Early Life"; H. E. Wethey, *El Greco*; J. F. Willumsen, *La jeunesse*.

161. M. Chatzidakis, *Icônes*; M. Chatzidakis, *La peinture*; A. Embiricos, *L'école*; Th. Gouma Peterson, "Crete"; G. Millet, *Monuments*; A. Xyngopoulos, *Schediasma*.

162. S. Bettini, *La pittura*; D. Frey, "Giotto"; V. N. Lazarev, "Maestro Paolo"; P. Likhačev, *Istoričeskoie značenie*; R. Tozzi, "I mosaici."

Bibliography

L. Abatangelo, *Chiese-cripte e affreschi italo-bizantini di Massafra*. 2 vols. Taranto, 1966.

N. Acocella, *La decorazione pittorica di Montecassino dalle didascalie di Alfano I*. Salerno, 1966.

D. V. Ainalov, *The Hellenistic Origins of Byzantine Art*. New Brunswick, 1961.

L. B. Alberti, *Kleinere Kunsttheoretische Schriften* ed. H. Janitschek, Vienna 1877.

M. Alpatoff, "Les fresques de Sainte-Sophie de Nicée," *Echos d'Orient*, 25, 1926, pp. 42 ff.

C. Angelillis, *Le porte di bronzo bizantine nelle chiese d'Italia*. Arezzo, 1924.

I. J. Arne, "Ryskbysantinska malningar en Gotlandskyrka," *Fornvännen*, 1912.

E. Arslan, "Cronistoria del Greco Madonnero," *Commentari*, 15, 1964, pp. 213 ff.

E. Arslan, *La pittura e la scultura Veronese dal secolo VIII al secolo XIII*. Milan, 1943.

L' art roman à Saint-Martial de Limoges. Catalogue d'Exposition. Limoges, 1950.

M. Aubert, *La sculpture française au Moyen-Age*. Paris, 1946.

M. Avery, *The Exultet Rolls of South Italy*. Princeton, 1936.

M. Avery, "The Alexandrian Style at Santa Maria Antiqua, Rome." *Art Bulletin*, 7, 1925, pp. 132 ff.

P. Baldass, "Disegni della scuola cassinese del tempo di Desiderio," *Bolletino d'Arte*, 28, 1952, pp. 102 ff.

J. Baltrusaitis, "La croisée d'ogives dans l'architecture transcaucasienne," *Recherche*, 1, 1939, p. 73 ff.

J. Baltrusaitis, *Le problème de l'ogive et l'Arménie*. Paris, 1936.

G. Bandmann, "Die Vorbilder der Aachener Pfalzkapelle," *Karl der Große*, W. Braunfels, ed., vol. III, Düsseldorf, 1965, pp. 424 ff.

J. Beckwith, *The Andrews Diptych*. London, 1958.

J. Beckwith, *The Art of Constantinople*. London, 1961.

J. Beckwith, "Byzantine influence on Art at the Court of Charlemagne," in *Karl der Große*, W. Braunfels, ed., Vol. III, Düsseldorf, 1965, pp. 288 ff.

J. Beckwith, "The Werden Casket Reconsidered," *Art Bulletin*, 40, 1958, pp. 1 ff.

H. Belting, "Probleme der Kunstgeschichte Italiens im Frühmittelalter," *Frühmittelalterliche Studien*, 1, 1967, pp. 95 ff.

G. M. Benson, "New Light on the Utrecht Psalter," *Art Bulletin*, 13, 1931, pp. 13 ff.

B. Berenson, "Two Twelfth Century Paintings from Constantinople," in *Studies in Mediaeval Painting*, New Haven, 1930, pp. 1 ff.

E. Berger, *Beiträge zur Entwicklungsgeschichte der Maltechnik*. 4 vols. Munich, 1897.

E. Bertaux, *L'art dans l'Italie Méridionale*. Paris, 1904.

C. Bertelli, "The Image of Pity in Santa Croce in Gerusalemme," in *Essays in the History of Art presented to R. Wittkower*, London, 1967.

C. Bertelli, "L'imagine del Monasterium Tempuli," *Annales Fratrum Predicatorum*, 1961, pp. 88 ff.

C. Bertelli, "La Madonna del Pantheon," *Bollettino d'Arte*, IV/46, 1961, pp. 24 ff.

C. Bertelli, *La Madonna di Santa Maria in Trastevere*. Rome, 1961.

C. Bertelli, "Storia e vicende dell'immagine Edessena," *Paragone*, 217, 1968, pp. 5 ff.

O. Bertolini, *Roma di fronte a Bisanzio e ai Longobardi*. Bologna, 1941.

S. Bettini, *La pittura di icone cretese-veneziana e i Madonneri*. Padua, 1933.

S. Bettini, *La scultura bizantina*. Florence, 1944.

H. Bloch, "Monte Cassino, Byzantium and the West in the Earlier Middle Ages," *Dumbarton Oaks Papers*, 3, 1946, pp. 163 ff.

P. Bloch, "Das Apsismosaik von Germigny-des-Prés. Karl der Große und der Alte Bund," in *Karl der Große*, W. Braunfels, ed., vol. III, Düsseldorf, 1965, pp. 234–261.

P. Bloch and H. Schnitzler, *Die ottonische Kölner Malerschule*. Vol. I, Düsseldorf, 1967.

A. Boeckler, "Bildvorlagen der Reichenau," *Zeitschrift für Kunstgeschichte*, 12, 1949, pp. 7 ff.

A. Boeckler, "Kölner ottonische Buchmalerei," in *Beiträge zur Kunst des Mittelalters*, Berlin, 1950, pp. 144 ff.

A. Boeckler, "Die Reichenauer Buchmalerei," in *Die Kultur der Abtei Reichenau*, Munich 1925, pp. 956 ff.

A. Boeckler, *Das goldene Evangelienbuch Heinrichs III.* Berlin, 1933.

A. Boeckler, "Die Evangelistenbilder der Ada-Gruppe," *Münchner Jahrbuch der Bildenden Kunst*, 3rd ser., 3/4, 1952/53, pp. 121 f.

A. Boeckler, "Formgeschichtliche Studien zur Adagruppe," *Bayerische Akademie der Wissenschaften, Abhandlungen*, N.S. 42, 1946.

A. Boeckler, "Ikonographische Studien zu den Wunderszenen in der ottonischen Malerei der Reichenau," *Abhandlungen der Bayerischen Akademie der Wissenschaften*, N.S. 52, 1961.

A. Boeckler, "Malerei und Plastik im ostfränkischen Reich," in *I problemi della civiltà carolingia. Settimane di Studio sull'alto medioevo*, Spoleto, I, 1954, pp. 161 ff.

G. P. Bognetti, *Castelseprio. Archéologie, art et histoire*. Venice, 1960.

G. P. Bognetti, G. Chierici and A. de Capitani d'Arzago, *Santa Maria di Castelseprio*. Milan, 1948.

F. Bologna, *La pittura italiana delle origini*. Florence, 1962.

C. Brandi, "Il Restauro della Madonna di Coppo di Marcovaldo nella Chiesa dei Servi di Siena," *Bollettino d'Arte*, 35, 1950, pp. 160 ff.

W. Braunfels, ed., *Karl der Große*. 3 vols, Düsseldorf, 1965.

L. Bréhier, "Études sur l'histoire de la sculpture byzantine," *Missions scientifiques*, 3, Paris, 1912.

L. Bréhier, "Nouvelles recherches sur l'histoire de la sculpture byzantine," *Nouvelles archives des missions scientifiques*, 9, Paris, 1916.

L. Bréhier, "La sculpture iconographique dans les églises byzantines," *Bulletin de l'Académie Roumaine, Sect. Hist.*, 11, 1924.

L. Bréhier, *La sculpture et les arts mineurs byzantins*. Paris, 1936.

L. Bréhier, "Les voussures à personnages sculptés du Musée d'Athenes," *Mélanges Schlumberger*, Paris, 1924, pp. 425 ff.

P. Buberl, "Die romanischen Wandmalereien im Kloster Nonnberg in Salzburg und ihre Beziehungen zur Salzburger Buchmalerei und zur byzantinischen Kunst," *Jahrbuch der k.k. Zentralkommission*, 3, 1909, pp. 25 ff.

P. Buberl, "Über einige Werke der Salzburger Buchmalerei des XI. Jahrhunderts," *Kunstgeschichtliches Jahrbuch der k.k. Zentral-Kommission*, 1907, pp. 29 ff.

254

H. Buchthal, "Byzantium and Reichenau,' in *Byzantine Art and European Art*, Athens 1966, pp. 43 ff.

H. Buchthal, "A Byzantine Miniature of the Fourth Evangelist and its Relatives," *Dumbarton Oaks Papers*, 15, 1961, pp. 129 ff.

H. Buchthal, "The Beginnings of Manuscript Illumination in Norman Sicily," in *Studies in Italian Mediaeval History Presented to Miss E. M. Jamison (Papers of the British School at Rome*, 24, 1956).

H. Buchthal, "Early Fourteenth-Century Illuminations from Palermo," *Dumbarton Oaks Papers*, 20, 1966, pp. 130 ff.

H. Buchthal, *Miniature Painting in the Latin Kingdom of Jerusalem*. Oxford, 1957.

H. Buchthal, *The Miniatures of the Paris Psalter*. London, 1938, pp. 56 ff.

H. Buchthal, "Some Sicilian Miniatures of the thirteenth century," in *Festschrift H. Schnitzler*, Düsseldorf, 1965, pp. 185 ff.

H. Buchthal, "A School of Miniature Painting in Norman Sicily," in *Late Classical and Mediaeval Studies in Honor of A. M. Friend, Jr.*, Princeton, 1955, pp. 312 ff.

M. S. Bunim, *Space in Medieval Painting*. New York, 1940.

R. Byron and D. Talbot Rice, *The Birth of Western Painting*. London, 1930.

Byzance et la France médiévale. (Catalogue d'Exposition). Paris, 1958.

M. Cagiano de Azevedo, "La porta bronzea della Basilica desideriana di Montecassino," *Felix Ravenna*, 44, 1967, pp. 69 ff.

M. Cagiano de Azevedo, "La Porta di Desiderio a Montecassino," *XIV. Corso di Cultura sull'arte Ravennate e Bizantina*, Ravenna, 1967, pp. 81 f.

G. Cames, *Byzance et la peinture romane de Germanie*. Paris, 1966.

E. Carli, *Pittura medievale Pisana*. Milan, 1958.

S. Casson, "Byzantium and Anglo-Saxon Sculpture," *Burlington Magazine*, 61, 1932, pp. 265 ff.

R. Causa, *Sant'Angelo in Formis*. Milan, 1963.

P. Cellini, "Una Madonna molto antica," *Proporzioni*, 3, 1950, pp. 1 ff.

P. Cellini, *La Madonna di San Luca in Sta. Maria Maggiore*. Rome, 1943.

M. Chatzidakis, "Eikones epistyliou apo to Hagion Oros," *Deltion tes Christianikes Archaiologikes Hetairias* 4/4, 1964/65, pp. 377 ff.

M. Chatzidakis, *Icônes grecques de Venise*. Venice 1962.

M. Chatzidakis, *La peinture crétoise et la gravure sur cuivre italienne* (in Greek). Heraklion, 1947.

M. Chatzidakis, *Theotocopoulos and Cretan Painting* (in Greek). Heraklion, 1950.

U. Chierici, "Il 'Maestro dell'Apocalisse di Novara'." *Paragone*, 201, 1966, pp. 13 ff.

N. Cilento, "Sant'Angelo in Formis nel suo significato storico," *Studi medievali*, 3/4, Spoleto, 1963, pp. 799 ff.

S. Cirac, "L'hellénisme de Domenico Theotokopouli Crétois," *Kretika Chronika*, 2, 1961/62, pp. 213 ff.

P. Clemen, *Die romanische Monumentalmalerei in den Rheinlanden*. Düsseldorf, 1916.

L. Coletti, "Arte Benedettina," in *Enciclopedia Cattolica*, II, 1949, Cols. 1225 ff.

S. Collon-Gevaert, *Histoire des arts du métal en Belgique*. Brussels 1951.

G. Coor, "Coppo di Marcovaldo. His Art in Relation to the Art of his Time." *Marsyas*, 5, 1950, pp. 1 ff.

G. Coor-Achenbach, "A Visual Basis for the Documents Relating to Coppo di Marcovaldo," *Art Bulletin*, 28, 1946, pp. 233 ff.

F. Crooy, *Les émaux carolingiens de la châsse de Saint Marc à Huy-sur-Meuse*. Paris-Brussels 1948.

O. M. Dalton, *Byzantine Art and Archaeology*. (London 1911); reprint, New York, 1961.

A. M. Damigella, "Problemi della Cattedrale di Torcello. II, I mosaici dell'abside maggiore," *Commentari*, 18, 1967, pp. 273 ff.

Daneu Lattanzi see Lattanzi

J. Deér, *The Dynastic Porphyry Tombs of the Norman Period in Sicily* (Dumbarton Oaks Studies, 5), Cambridge, Mass., 1959.

F. W. Deichmann, "Gründung und Datierung von San Vitale zu Ravenna," in *Arte del primo millenio*, Turin, 1952, pp. 111 ff.

Ch. Delvoye, *L'art byzantin*. Paris, 1967.

Ch. Delvoye, "Les ateliers d'arts somptuaires à Constantinople," *XII Corso di cultura sull'arte ravennate e bizantina*, Ravenna, 1965, pp. 171 ff.

O. Demus, "Zwei marmorne Altarikonen aus San Marco," *Jahrbuch der österr. byzantinischen Gesellschaft*, 4, 1955, pp. 99 ff.

O. Demus, "Bisanzio e la pittura a mosaico del Duecento a Venezia," in *Venezia e l'oriente fra tardo medioevo e rinascimento*, A. Pertusi ed., Florence, 1966, pp. 125 ff.

O. Demus, "Bisanzio e la scultura del Duecento a Venezia," in *Venezia e l'oriente fra tardo medioevo e rinascimento*, A. Pertusi ed., Florence, 1966, pp. 141 ff.

O. Demus, *The Church of San Marco in Venice*. Washington, D.C., 1960.

O. Demus, "Die Entstehung des Paläologenstils in der Malerei," *Berichte zum XI. Intern. Byzantinistenkongreß*, IV/2, Munich, 1958.

O. Demus, "Das älteste venezianische Gesellschaftsbild," *Jahrbuch der österr. byzantinischen Gesellschaft*, 1, 1951, pp. 89 ff.

O. Demus, "Zwei Konstantinopler Marienikonen des 13. Jahrhunderts," *Jahrbuch der österr. byzant. Gesellschaft*, 7, 1958, pp. 87 ff.

O. Demus, *Byzantine Mosaic Decoration*. London, 1948.

O. Demus, *The Mosaics of Norman Sicily*. London, 1950.

O. Demus, "Two Palaeologan Mosaic Icons in the Dumbarton Oaks Collection," *Dumbarton Oaks Papers*, 14, 1960, pp. 87 ff.

O. Demus, *Die Mosaiken von San Marco in Venedig*. Baden-Vienna 1935.

O. Demus, "Die sizilischen Mosaiken, Venedig und der Norden," *Atti dell'VIII Congresso di Studi Biziantini*, Rome, 1953, pp. 131 ff.

O. Demus, "Nicola da Verdun," in *Enciclopedia Universale dell'Arte*, IX, pp. 917 ff.

O. Demus, "Zur Pala d'Oro," *Jahrbuch der österr.byzantinischen Gesellschaft*, 16, 1967, pp. 263 ff.

O. Demus, "Das Problem der ältesten Mosaiken von San Marco," *Atti del XVIII Congresso Internazionale di Storia dell'Arte*, Venice, 1956, p. 151.

O. Demus, "Regensburg, Sizilien und Venedig". *Jahrbuch der österr.byzantinischen Gesellschaft*, 2, 1952, pp. 94 ff.

O. Demus, "Die Rolle der byzantinischen Kunst in Europa," *Jahrbuch der österr.byzantinischen Gesellschaft*, 14, 1965, pp. 139 ff.

O. Demus, "Vorbildqualität und Lehrfunktion der byzantinischen Kunst," in *Stil und Überlieferung in der Kunst des Abendlandes. Akten des 21. Internat. Kongresses für Kunstgeschichte in Bonn, 1964*, vol. I, Berlin, 1967, pp. 92 ff.

O. Demus, *Romanische Wandmalerei*. Photos M. Hirmer. Munich, 1968.

O. Demus, "Der 'sächsische' Zackenstil und Venedig," in *Kunst des Mittelalters in Sachsen. Festschrift W. Schubert*, Weimar, 1967, pp. 307 ff.

P. Deschamps and M. Thibout, *La peinture murale en France. Le haut moyen âge et l'époque romane*. Paris, 1951.

F. Deuchler, *Der Ingeborgpsalter*. Berlin, 1967.

E. De Wald, *The Illustrations of the Utrecht Psalter*. Princeton, 1933.

Ch. Diehl, *Manuel de l'art byzantin*. 2nd ed., Paris, 1926.

E. Diez and O. Demus, *Byzantine Mosaics in Greece. Hosios Lucas and Daphni*. Cambridge, Mass., 1931.

F. Di Pietro, *La Cappella Palatina di Palermo. I mosaici*. Milan, 1954.

V. J. Djurić, *Sopočani*. Belgrade, 1963.

E. Dobbert, "Zur byzantinischen Frage; die Wandgemälde in Sant'Angelo in Formis," *Jahrbuch der kgl. Preuß. Kunstsammlungen*, 15, 1894, pp. 60 ff., 125 ff., 211 ff.

C. R. Dodwell and D. H. Turner, *Reichenau reconsidered. A reassessment of the Place of Reichenau in Ottonian Art* (Warburg Institute Surveys, II) London, 1966.

F. Dölger, *Byzanz und die europäische Staatenwelt*. Ettal, 1953.

F. Dölger, "Die Ottonenkaiser und Byzanz," in *Karolingische und ottonische Kunst*, Wiesbaden, 1957, pp. 49 ff.

R. Dölling, "Byzantinische Elemente in der Kunst des 16. Jahrhunderts," in *Byzant. Arbeit der D.D.R.*, Berlin, 1957.

B. Dudan, *Il dominio Veneziano di Levante*. Bologna, 1938.

C. P. Duprat, "Enquête sur la peinture murale en France à l'époque romane," *Bulletin Monumental*, I, vol. 101, 1943, pp. 165 ff.; II, vol. 102, 1944, pp. 5 ff.; III, pp. 161 ff.

J. Ebersolt, *Orient et Occident: Recherches sur les influences byzantines et orientales en France avant les Croisades*. Paris-Brussels, 1928.

J. Ebersolt, *Orient et Occident: Recherches sur les influences byzantines et orientales en France pendant les Croisades*. Paris-Brussels, 1929.

J. Ebersolt, *Les arts somptuaires de Byzance*. Paris, 1923.

K. Ehl, *Die ottonische Kölner Buchmalerei*. Bonn-Leipzig, 1922.

A. Embiricos, *L'école crétoise. Derniere phase de la peinture byzantine*. Paris, 1967.

J. H. A. Engelbregt, O. F. M., *The Utrecht Psalter, A Century of Critical Investigation* (Orbis Artium, Utrechtse Kunsthistorische Studien, VIII), Utrecht, 1965.

J. Evans, *Cluniac Art of the Romanesque Period*. Cambridge, 1950.

H. Fichtenau, "Byzanz und die Pfalz zu Aachen," *Mitteilungen des Instituts für österr. Geschichtsforschung*, 59, 1951, pp. 1 ff.

H. Fichtenau, *The Carolingian Empire*, P. Munz, trans. Oxford, 1963.

H. Fillitz, "Die Elfenbeinreliefs zur Zeit Karls des Großen," *Aachener Kunstblätter*, 32, 1966, pp. 14 ff.

G. Fiocco, "Tradizioni orientali nella pietà Veneziana," in *Venezia e l'oriente fra tardo medioevo e rinascimento*, A. Pertusi, ed., Florence 1966, p. 117.

M. Florisoone, "La mystique plastique du Greco et les antécédents de son style," *Gazette des Beaux-Arts*, 49, 1957, pp. 19 ff.

G. de Francovich, "Arte Carolingia ed Ottoniana in Lombardia," *Römisches Jahrbuch für Kunstgeschichte*, 6, 1942/44, pp. 115 ff.

G. de Francovich, "L'arte siriaca e il suo influsso sulla pittura medievale nell'Oriente e nell'Occidente," *Commentari*, 1, 1951, pp. 3 ff.

G. de Francovich, "L'Egitto, la Siria e Costantinopoli: Problemi de Metodo," *Rivista dell'Istituto Nazionale di Archeologia e Storia dell'Arte*, 11/12, 1963, pp. 83 ff.

G. de Francovich, "L'origine e la diffusione del Crocefisso gotico doloroso," *Kunstgeschichtliches Jahrbuch der Bibliotheca Hertziana*, 2, 1938, pp. 155 ff.

G. de Francovich, "Problemi della pittura e della scultura preromanica," *Settimane di studio del centro Italiano sull'Alto Medioevo*, 2, Spoleto, 1955, pp. 355 ff.

D. Frey, "Giotto und die maniera greca," *Wallraf-Richartz-Jahrbuch*, 14, 1952, pp. 73 ff.

W. Frodl, "Die romanischen Wandgemälde in Pürgg, nach der Entrestaurierung," *Österr. Zeitschrift für Kunst und Denkmalpflege*, 2, 1948, pp. 147 ff.

A. Frolow, "L'origine des personnages hanchés dans l'art gothique," *Revue archéologique*, 1965, 1, pp. 65 ff.

A. L. Frothingham, "Byzantine Artists in Italy from the sixth to the fifteenth century," *American Journal of Archaeology*, 9, 1894, pp. 32 ff.

E. Fründt, *Sakrale Plastik—Mittelalterliche Bildwerke*. Hanau, 1966.

E. B. Garrison, *Italian Romanesque Panel Painting. An Illustrated Index*. Florence, 1949.

E. B. Garrison, *Studies in Mediaeval Italian Painting*. 4 vols., 1953–1961.

D. Geanakoplos, *Byzantine East and Latin West*. New York, 1966.

O. Gillen, *Das Goslarer Evangeliar*. Goslar, 1932.

G. Giovannoni, *L'Abbazia di Montecassino*. Florence, 1945.

A. Goldschmidt, *Die Elfenbeinskulpturen aus der Zeit der karolingischen und sächsischen Kaiser*. Vol. I, Berlin, 1914.

A. Goldschmidt, *Das Evangeliar im Rathaus zu Goslar*. Berlin, 1910.

A. Goldschmidt, "Die Stilentwicklung der romanischen Skulptur Sachsens," *Jahrbuch der Kgl. preuß. Kunstsammungen*, 21, 1900, pp. 225 ff.

A. Goldschmidt and K. Weitzmann, *Die byzantinischen Elfenbeinskulpturen des zehnten bis dreizehnten Jahrhunderts*. Berlin, 1934.

E. H. Gombrich, "Light, Form and Texture in fifteenth Century Painting," *Journal of the Royal Society of Arts*, 1964, pp. 826 ff.

P. Goubert, "Byzance et l'Espagne wisigothique," *Revue des études byzantines*, 2, 1944, pp. 5 ff.

A. Grabar, *Byzanz. Die byzantinische Kunst des Mittelalters*. Baden-Baden, 1964.

A. Grabar, *L'empereur dans l'art byzantin*. Paris, 1936.

A. Grabar, "L'étude des fresques romanes," *Cahiers archéologiques*, 1, 1947, pp. 163 ff.

A. Grabar, *La Sainte Face de Laon*. Prague, 1930.

A. Grabar, *L'iconoclasme byzantin*. Paris, 1957.

A. Grabar, "Influences byzantines sur les peintures murales de Civate," in *Arte in Europa, Scritti in onore di E. Arslan*, 1966, pp. 279 ff.

A. Grabar, *La peinture byzantine*, Geneva, 1953.

A. Grabar and C. Nordenfalk, *Die romanische Malerei*. Geneva, 1958.

A. Grabar and C. Nordenfalk, *Das frühe Mittelalter*. Geneva, 1957.

A. Grabar and T. Velmans, "Gli affreschi della Chiesa di Sopočani," *L'arte racconta*, 37, Florence and Geneva, n. d.

L. H. Grondijs, *L'iconographie byzantine du Crucifié mort sur la croix*. 2nd ed., Brussels-Utrecht, 1947.

R. Grousset, *L'Empire du Levant*. Paris, 1946.

W. de Grüneisen, *Sainte-Marie Antique*. Rome, 1911.

L. Hadermann-Misguich, "Forme et esprit de Byzance dans l'oeuvre du Greco," *Revue de l'Université de Bruxelles*. 5, 1964, pp. 5 ff.

H. Hager, *Die Anfänge des italienischen Altarbildes*. Munich 1962.

H. R. Hahnloser, "Magistra Latinitas und Peritia greca," in *Festschrift H. von Einem*, Berlin, 1965, pp. 77 ff.

H. Hallensleben, *Die Malerschule des Königs Milutin*. Gießen, 1963.

R. Hamann, *Die Abteikirche von Sainte-Gilles und ihre künstlerische Nachfolge*. Berlin, 1955.

R. Hamann-MacLean, "Antikenstudium in der Kunst des Mittelalters," *Marburger Jahrbuch für Kunstwissenschaft*, 15, 1949/50, pp. 157 ff.

R. Hamann-MacLean and H. Hallensleben, *Die Monumentalmalerei in Serbien und Makedonien vom elften bis zum vierzehnten Jahrhundert*. Gießen, 1963.

A. Haseloff, *Eine thüringisch-sächsische Malerschule des dreizehnten Jahrhunderts*. Strasbourg, 1897.

F. Henry, *Early Christian Irish Art*. Dublin, 1954.

F. Hermanin, *L'arte in Roma dal secolo VIII al XIV*. Bologna, 1945.

Th. Hetzer, *Tizian. Geschichte seiner Farbe*. Frankfurt, 1935.

W. Heyd, *Histoire du commerce du Levant*, F. Raynaud, trans. 2 vols. Leipzig, 1936.

H. Hoffmann, "Die Aachener Theoderich Statue," in *Das erste Jahrtausend*, Düsseldorf, 1962, pp. 318 ff.

W. Holmquist, "Einflüsse der Koptischen Kunst in Westeuropa," in *Katalog der Ausstellung Koptischer Kunst*, Essen, 1963, pp. 157 ff.

K. Holter, "Der Buchschmuck in Süddeutschland und Oberitalien," in *Karl der Große*, W. Braunfels, H. Schnitzler, eds., III, Düsseldorf, 1965, pp. 74 ff.

O. Homburger, "Das Freiburger Einzelblatt. Der Rest eines Musterbuches der Stauferzeit?" in *Festschrift W. Noack*, Freiburg im Br., 1959, pp. 16 ff.

J. Hubert, J. Porcher and W. F. Volbach, *L'empire Carolingien* (L'Univers des Formes). Paris, 1968.

J. Hubert, J. Porcher and W. F. Volbach, *L'Europe des invasions* (L'Univers des Formes). Paris, 1967.

J. Hueck, "Ein Madonnenbild im Dom von Padua—Rom und Byzanz," *Mitteilungen des Kunsthistorischen Institutes in Florenz*, 13, 1967, pp. 1 ff.

L. Hugot, "Die Pfalz Karls des Großen in Aachen," in *Karl der Große*, W. Braunfels, H. Schnitzler, eds., III, Düsseldorf, 1965, pp. 534 ff.

I. Hutter, *Frühchristliche Kunst, byzantinische Kunst*. Stuttgart, 1968.

M. Inguanez and M. Avery, *Miniature cassinesi del secolo XI illustranti la vita di San Benedetto*. Monte Cassino, 1934.

C. A. Isermeyer, "Die mittelalterlichen Malereien der Kirche S. Pietro in Tuscania," *Kunstgeschichtliches Jahrbuch der Bibliotheca Hertziana*, 2, 1938, pp. 291 ff.

H. Jantzen, *Ottonische Kunst*. Munich, 1947 (new ed. Hamburg, 1959).

G. de Jerphanion, *Les églises de Cappadoce*. 4 vols. Paris, 1925–1942.

W. Jung, *Die ehemalige Prämonstratenserstiftskirche Knechtsteden*. Ratingen, 1956.

G. Kalbi, "Olevano sul Tusciano, La cripta di S. Michele Arcangelo," *Rassegna storica salernitana*, 24/25, 1963/64, pp. 81 ff.

G. Kalbi, "Olevano sul Tusciano, La cripta eremitica (II)," *Napoli nobilissima*, 1964, pp. 22 ff.

Karl der Große (Catalogue of Aachen Exhibition). Aachen, 1965.

H. Karlinger, *Die hochromanische Wandmalerei in Regensburg*. Munich-Berlin-Leipzig, 1920.

P. Kelemen, *El Greco Revisited. Candia, Venice, Toledo*. New York, 1961.

T. D. Kendrick et al., *Codex Lindisfarnensis*. Lausanne, 1956.

W. Kermer, *Studien zum Diptychon in der sakralen Malerei* (Diss. Tübingen). Düsseldorf, 1966.

A. Khatchatrian, "Notes sur l'architecture de l'église de Germigny-des-Prés," *Cahiers archéologiques* 7, 1954, pp. 162 ff.

E. Kitzinger, "Byzantine Art in the Period between Justinian and Iconoclasm," *Berichte zum XI. Internat. Byzantinisten-Kongreß*, Vol. IV, 1. Munich, 1958.

E. Kitzinger, "The Cult of Images in the Age before Iconoclasm," *Dumbarton Oaks Papers*, 8, 1954, pp. 83 ff.

E. Kitzinger, "The Byzantine Contribution to Western Art of the Twelfth and Thirteenth Centuries," *Dumbarton Oaks Papers*, 20, 1966, pp 25 ff., 265 f.

E. Kitzinger, "The Hellenistic Heritage in Byzantine Art," *Dumbarton Oaks Papers*, 17, 1963, pp. 95 ff.

E. Kitzinger, "On some Icons of the Seventh Century," in *Late Classical and Mediaeval Studies in Honor of A. M. Friend, Jr.*, Princeton, 1955, pp. 132 ff.

E. Kitzinger, *Römische Malerei vom Beginn des siebten bis zur Mitte des achten Jahrhunderts* (Diss.). Munich, 1934.

E. Kitzinger, *The Mosaics of Monreale*. Palermo, 1960.

E. Kitzinger, "On the Portrait of Roger II in the Martorana," *Proporzioni*, 1950, pp. 30 ff.

E. Kitzinger, "Norman Sicily as a Source of Byzantine Influence on Western Art in the Twelfth Century," in *Byzantine Art an European Art. Lectures*. Athens, 1966, pp. 121.

E. Kitzinger, "Review of W. Koehler, *Die karolingischen Miniaturen, III/1*," *Art Bulletin*, 44, 1962, pp. 61 ff.

B. Kleinschmidt, *Die Basilika zu San Francesco in Assisi*. 2 vols. Berlin, 1915.

W. Koehler, "Byzantine Art in the West," *Dumbarton Oaks Papers*, 1, 1941, pp. 61 ff.

W. Koehler, *Die karolingischen Miniaturen*. Vol. II, *Die Hofschule Karls des Großen*. Berlin, 1958.

W. Koehler, *Die karolingischen Miniaturen*. Vol. III/1, *Die Gruppe des Wiener Krönungsevangeliars*. Berlin, 1960.

F. X. Kraus, "Die Wandgemälde von Sant' Angelo in Formis," *Jahrbuch der Kgl. Preußischen Kunstsammlungen*, 14, 1893, pp. 3 ff., 84 ff.

K. Künstle, *Die Kunst des Klosters Reichenau im neunten und zehnten Jahrhundert*. Freiburg im Br., 1906.

H. Ladenbauer-Orel, "Das ottonische Castellum Wieselburg an der Erlauf," *Jahrbuch des röm.-german. Zentralmuseums, Mainz, 12*, 1965, pp. 127 ff.

G. Ladner, "Die italienische Malerei im elften Jahrhundert," *Jahrbuch der Kunsthistorischen Sammlungen in Wien*, n. s., 5, 1931, pp. 33 ff.

F. Lambert, *Byzantinische und westliche Einflüsse in ihrer Bedeutung für die sächsische Malerei und Plastik im zwölften Jahrhundert* (Diss.). Berlin, 1926.

P. Lamma, *Comneni e Staufer. Ricerche sui rapporti fra Bisanzio e l'occidente nel secolo XII.* 2 vols. Rome, 1955.

R. Lange, *Die byzantinische Reliefikone*. Recklinghausen, 1964.

A. Daneu Lattanzi, *Lineamenti di Storia della miniatura in Sicilia*. Florence, 1966.

V. N. Lazarev, "L'arte bizantina e particolarmente la pittura in Italia nell'alto medioevo," in *L'oriente Cristiano nella storia della civiltà*, Rome, Accad. dei Lincei, 1964, pp. 661 ff.

V. N. Lazarev, "Maestro Paolo e la pittura veneziana del suo tempo," *Arte Veneta*, 3, 1954, pp. 77 ff.

V. Lazarev, *Mozaiki Sofii Kievskoi*. Moscow, 1960.

V. Lazarev, *Mikhailovskie Mozaiki*. Moscow, 1966.

V. Lazarev, *Old Russian Murals and Mosaics*. London, 1966.

V. Lazarev, "Early Italo-Byzantine Painting in Sicily," *Burlington Magazine*, 60, 1933, pp. 279 ff.

V. N. Lazarev, *Storia della pittura bizantina*. Turin, 1967.

E. Lehmann, Die Architektur zur Zeit Karls des Großen," in *Karl der Große*, W. Braunfels, H. Schnitzler eds., vol. III, Düsseldorf, 1965, pp. 301 ff.

H. Leisinger, *Romanische Bronzen. Kirchentüren im mittelalterlichen Europa*. Zürich, 1956.

F. F. Leitschuh, *Geschichte der karolingischen Malerei*. Berlin, 1894.

P. Likhačev, *Istoričeskoie značenie italo-grečeskoi ikonopisi*. St. Petersburg, 1911.

Lindisfarne Gospels (Facsimile Edition). 2 vols. Bern, 1951.

R. Longhi, "Apertura sui trecentisti Umbri," *Paragone*, 191, 1966, pp. 3 ff.

R. Longhi, "Postilla all'apertura sugli Umbri," *Paragone*, 195, 1966, pp. 3 ff.

R. Longhi, Guidizio sul Duecento, Proporzioni, 2, 1948, pp. 5 ff.

M. H. Longhurst and C. R. Morey, "Covers of the Lorsch Gospels," *Speculum*, 3, 1928, pp. 64 ff.

J. Longnon, *L'empire latin de Constantinople et la principauté de Morée*. Paris, 1949.

G. Loumyer, *Les traditions techniques de la peinture médiévale*. Brussels-Paris, 1920.

E. Lucchesi-Palli, "Review of L. H. Grondijs, *L'iconographie du Crucifié mort sur la croix*," *Zeitschrift f. Kathol. Theologie*, 70, 1948, pp. 369 ff.

R. van Marle, *The Development of the Italian Schools of Painting*. The Hague, 1923 ff.

R. van Marle, *La peinture Romaine au moyen âge*. Strasbourg, 1921.

F. Masai, *Essai sur les origines de la miniature dite irlandaise*. Brussels, 1947.

A. Matějček and J. Pešina, *La peinture gothique tchéque. Peinture sur panneau, 1350–1450*. Prague, 1955.

F. J. Mather, *The Isaac Master*. Princeton, 1932.

G. Matthiae, *Mosaici medioevali delle chiese di Roma*. 2 vols. Rome, 1967.

G. Matthiae, *Pittura Romana del medio evo*. 2 vols. Rome, 1965.

N. Mayers, *Studien zum Hortus Deliciarum der Herrad von Landsberg* (Diss.). Vienna. 1966.

A. Medea, "La pittura bizantina nell'Italia meridionale nel medioevo (V–XIII s.)," in *Atti del Convegno internaz. sul tema "L'oriente Cristiano nella storia della civiltà,"* Rome, Accad. Naz. dei Lincei, 1964, pp. 719 ff.

A. H. S. Megaw, "Notes on Recent Work of the Byzantine Institute in Istanbul," *Dumbarton Oaks Papers*, 17, 1963, pp. 333 ff.

M. Meiss, *Giotto and Assisi*. New York, 1960.

S. G. Mercati, "Sulla Santissima Icone nel duomo di Spoleto," *Spoletium*, 3, 1956, pp. 3 ff.

F. Mercier, *Les primitifs français. La peinture Clunisienne en Bourgogne à l'époque romane*. Paris, 1931.

W. Messerer, "Zur byzantinischen Frage in der ottonischen Kunst," *Byzantinische Zeitschrift*, 52, 1959, pp. 32 ff.

P. Miljković-Pepek, *L'oeuvre des peintres Michel et Eutych* (in Serbian, with French resumé). Skopje, 1967.

W. Miller, *Essays on the Latin Orient*. Cambbridge, 1921.

G. Millet, *Monuments de l'Athos. Les peintures*. Paris, 1927.

G. Millet, "L'art des Balkans et l'Italie au XIIIe siècle," in *Atti del V Congresso Internazionale di Studi Bizantini, 1936*, 2, Rome, 1940, pp. 272 ff.

G. Millet and A. Frolow, *La peinture du moyen âge en Yougoslavie*. 3 vols. Paris, 1954 ff.

C. R. Morey, *Early Christian Art*. 2nd ed., Princeton, 1953.

O. Morisani, *Gli affreschi di S. Angelo in Formis*. Cava dei Tirreni, 1962.

O. Morisani, *Bisanzio e la pittura cassinese*. Palermo, 1955.

O. Morisani, "La pittura cassinese e gli affreschi di Sant'Angelo in Formis," in *Atti VIII Congresso internazionale di studi bizantini*, II, Rome, 1953, pp. 220 ff.

P. I. Müller, "Beiträge zum byz. Einfluß in der früh- und hochmittelalterlichen Kunst Rätiens," *Zeitschrift f. schweiz. Archäologie und Kunstgeschichte*, 24, 1965/66, pp. 137 ff.

E. Muentz, "Les artistes byzantins dans l'Europe latine du Ve au XVIe siècle," *Revue de l'art chrétien*, IV/4, 1893, pp. 181 ff.

F. Mütherich, "Die Buchmalerei am Hofe Karls des Großen," in *Karl der Große*, W. Braunfels, H. Schnitzler, eds., vol. III, Düsseldorf, 1965, pp. 9ff.

F. Mütherich, "Ottonian Art. Changing Aspects," in *Acts of the 20th International Congress of the History of Art*, Princeton, 1963, I, pp. 27ff.

C. Nordenfalk, "Review of W. Koehler, *Die karolingischen Miniaturen, III/1*," *Kunstchronik*, 14, 1961, pp. 243ff.

C. Nordenfalk, "Eastern Style Elements in the Book of Lindisfarne," *Acta Archaeologica*, 13, 1942, pp. 157ff.

C. Nordenfalk, see also A. Grabar and C. Nordenfalk.

P. J. Nordhagen, "Nuove constatazioni sui rapporti artistici fra Roma e Bisanzio sotto il pontificato di Giovanni VII," in *Atti del 3. Congresso internazionale di Studi sull'alto Medioevo*, Spoleto, 1959, pp. 451ff.

P. J. Nordhagen, "The Earliest Decorations in Sta. Maria Antiqua and their Date," *Acta ad archaeologiam et artium historiam pertinentia*, 1, 1962, pp. 53ff.

P. J. Nordhagen, "The mosaics of John VII (705–707 A.D.)," *Acta ad archaeologiam et artium historiam pertinentia*, 2, 1965, pp. 121ff.

W. Oakeshott, *The Artists of the Winchester Bible*. London, 1945.

W. Oakeshott, *Classical Inspiration in Medieval Art*. London, 1959.

W. Oakeshott, *The Mosaics of Rome from the Third to the Fourteenth Centuries*. London, 1967.

R. Oertel, *Die Frühzeit der italienischen Malerei*. 2nd ed., Stuttgart, 1966.

W. Ohnsorge, "Das Kaisertum der Eirene und die Kaiserkrönung Karls des Großen," *Saeculum*, 14/2, 1963, pp. 221ff.

W. Ohnsorge, *Abendland und Byzanz*. Darmstadt, 1958.

W. Ohnsorge, *Konstantinopel und der Okzident*. Darmstadt, 1966.

O. Pächt, "The Avignon Diptych and its Eastern Ancestry," in *De Artibus opuscula XL, Essays in Honor of Erwin Panofsky*, New York, 1961, pp. 402ff.

O. Pächt, "*A Cycle of English Frescoes in Spain*," *Burlington Magazine*, 103, 1961, pp. 166ff.

R. Pallucchini, "Il Greco e Venezia," in *Venezia e l'Oriente fra tardo medioevo e rinascimento*, A. Pertusi, ed, Florence, 1966, pp. 351ff.

R. Pallucchini, *La Pittura Veneziana del Trecento*. Venice-Rome, 1964.

G. Panazza, "La chiesa di San Salvatore in Brescia," in *Atti VIII Congresso di studi sull'arte dell'alto medio evo*, II, 1962, pp. 232ff.

E. Panofsky, "Die Perspektive als symbolische Form," *Vorträge der Bibliothek Warburg*, 1924/25, pp. 258ff.

E. Panofsky, *Renaissance and Renascences*. Stockholm, 1960.

A. Pantoni, "Opinioni, valutazioni critiche e date di fatto sull'arte benedettina in Italia," *Benedictina*, 13, 1959, pp. 111ff.

Th. Gouma Peterson, "Crete, Venice, the 'Madonneri' and a Creto-Venetian Icon in the Allen Art Museum," *Allen Memorial Art Museum Bulletin*, 25/2, 1968, pp. 53ff.

Pittura Italiana del duecento e trecento (Catalogo della Mostra Giottesca di Firenze del 1937). Florence, 1943.

J. Pomorisać-de Luigi, *Les émaux byzantins de la Pala d'Oro de l'église de Saint-Marc à Venise*. 2 vols, Zürich, 1966.

J. Porcher, "Les ivories byzantins et l'enluminure limousine à la fin du 10e siêcle," in *Spätantike und Byzanz*, Baden-Baden, 1951, pp. 189f.

S. Radojčič, *Mileševa*. Belgrade, 1963.

S. Radojčič, *Staro srpsko slikarstvo*. Belgrade, 1966.

J. Raftery, "Irische Beziehungen zum koptischen Ägypten," in *Christentum am Nil*, Kl. Wessel, ed., Recklinghausen, 1964, pp. 260 ff.

N. Rasmo, *Hocheppan*. Bozen, 1967.

H. Reinhardt, *La cathédrale de Reims*. Paris, 1963.

M. Restle, *Die byzantinische Wandmalerei in Kleinasien*. 3 vols., Recklinghausen, 1967.

R. Rey, *La sculpture romane languedocienne*. Toulouse-Paris, 1936.

P. E. D. Riant, *Des dépouilles réligieuses enlevées à Constantinople au XIIIe siècle par les Latins*. Paris, 1875.

P. E. D. Riant, *Exuviae sacrae Constantinopolitanae*. Vols. I, II, Geneva, 1875; Vol. III, Paris, 1904.

D. Talbot Rice, "Britain and the Byzantine World in the Middle Ages," in *Byzantine Art an European Art. Lectures*. Athens, 1966, pp. 21 ff.

D. Talbot Rice, M. Hirmer, Photog., *Kunst aus Byzanz*, Munich, 1959.

D. Talbot Rice, *Byzantine Painting: The Last Phase*. London, 1968.

R. Röhrig, *Der Verduner Altar*. Klosterneuburg 1955.

P. Romanelli and P. J. Nordhagen, *Sta. Maria Antiqua*. Rome, 1964.

E. Rosenbaum, "The Evangelist portraits of the Ada School and their models," *Art Bulletin*, 38, 1956, pp. 81 ff.

S. Runciman, "Byzantine Art and Western Mediaeval Taste," in *Byzantine Art an European Art. Lectures*. Athens, 1966, pp. 1 ff.

S. Runciman, *A History of the Crusades*. 3 vols., Cambridge, 1954.

F. Rutter, "The Early Life of El Greco." The Burlington Magazine, 60, 1932, p. 274 ff.

Chr. Salm (Altgraf zu), "Neue Forschungen über das Gnadenbild in der alten Kapelle in Regensburg," *Münchner Jahrbuch der Bildenden Kunst* 13, 1962, pp. 49 ff.

R. Salvini, "La pittura dal sec. XI al XII," in *Storia di Milano*, III, 1954, pp. 601 ff.

W. Sauerländer, "Die kunstgeschichtliche Stellung der Westportale von Notre-Dame in Paris," *Marburger Jahrbuch für Kunstwissenschaft*, 17, 1959, pp. 1 ff.

F. Saxl, "The Ruthwell Cross," *Journal of the Warburg and Courtauld Institutes*, 6, 1943, pp. 1 ff.

F. Saxl and R. Wittkower, *British Art and the Mediterranean*. Oxford, 1947.

E. Scaccia Scarafoni, "Note su fabbriche ed opere d'arte medioevali a Montecassino," *Bollettino d'Arte*, 30, 1936, pp. 97 ff.

H. Schade, "Die Libri Carolini und ihre Stellung zum Bild," *Zeitschrift für Kathol. Theologie*, 79, 1957, pp. 74 ff.

M. Schapiro, *The Parma Ildefonsus. A Romanesque Illuminated Manuscript from Cluny and Related Works*. New York, 1964.

M. Schapiro, "Review of K. Weitzmann, *The Fresco Cycle of S. Maria di Castelseprio*," *Art Bulletin*, 34, 1952, pp. 147 ff.

R. W. Scheller, *A Survey of Mediaeval Model Books*. Haarlem, 1963.

H. Schlunk and M. Berenguer, *La pintura mural asturiana de los siglos IX y X*. Madrid, 1957.

H. Schnitzler, *Der Dom zu Aachen*. Düsseldorf, 1950.

H. Schnitzler, "Die Komposition der Lorscher Elfenbeintafeln," *Münchner Jahrbuch der bildenden Kunst*, 1, 1950, pp. 26 ff.

H. Schnitzler, "Das Kuppelmosaik der Aachener Pfalzkapelle," *Aachener Kunstblätter*, 29, 1964, pp. 17 ff.

[H. Schnitzler and J. Hoster], *Der Meister des Dreikönigschreins* (Catalogue). Cologne, 1964.

W. Schöne, "Die künstlerische und liturgische Gestalt der Pfalzkapelle Karls des Großen in Aachen," *Zeitschrift für Kunstwissenschaft*, 15, 1961, pp. 97 ff.

W. Schöne, *Über das Licht in der Malerei.* Berlin, 1954.

H. Schrade, "Zum Kuppelmosaik der Pfalzkapelle und zum Theoderich-Denkmal in Aachen," *Aachener Kunstblätter*, 30, 1965, pp. 25 ff.

P. E. Schramm, "Kaiser, Basileus und Papst in der Zeit der Ottonen," *Historische Zeitschrift*, 129, 1924, pp. 447 ff.

P. E. Schramm, *Die deutschen Kaiser und Könige in Bildern ihrer Zeit.* Leipzig-Berlin, 1928.

P. E. Schramm and F. Mütherich, *Denkmale der deutschen Könige und Kaiser.* Munich, 1962.

G. Schreiber, "Christlicher Orient und mittelalterliches Abendland," *Oriens Christianus*, 39, 1955, pp. 66 ff.

L. Schürenberg, "Mittelalterlicher Kirchenbau als Ausdruck geistiger Strömungen," *Wiener Jahrbuch für Kunstgeschichte*, 14, 1950, pp. 24 ff.

Ph. Schweinfurth, "Das goldene Evangelienbuch Heinrichs III und Byzanz," *Zeitschrift für Kunstgeschichte*, 10, 1941, pp. 42 ff.

H. Sedlmayr in: V. Milojcic et al., "Bericht über die Ausgrabungen und Bauuntersuchungen in der Abtei Frauenwörth auf der Fraueninsel im Chiemsee, 1961–1964," *Abhandlungen der Bayr. Akademie der Wissenschaften*, n. s., 65 A, Munich, 1966.

K. M. Setton, "The Byzantine Background to the Italian Renaissance," *Proceedings of the American Philosophical Society*, 100/1, 1956.

B. G. Söderberg, *Svenska Kyrkomalningar fran medeltiden.* Stockholm, 1951.

J. Sommer, *Das Deckenbild der Michaeliskirche zu Hildesheim.* Hildesheim, 1966.

G. et M. Sotiriou, *Icônes du Mont Sinai.* 2 vols., Athens, 1958.

G. Soyter, "Die byzantinischen Einflüsse auf die Kultur des mittelalterlichen Deutschland." *Leipziger Vierteljahrsschrift für Osteuropa*, 5, 1941, p. 153.

J. Stubblebine, "Byzantine Influence in thirteenth-Century Italian Panel Painting," *Dumbarton Oaks Papers*, 20, 1966, pp. 85 ff.

J. Stubblebine, "Two Byzantine Madonnas from Calahorra, Spain," *Art Bulletin*, 48, 1966, pp. 379 ff.

G. Swarzenski, *Die Regensburger Buchmalerei des zehnten und elften Jahrhunderts.* Leipzig, 1901.

G. Swarzenski, "Aus dem Kunstkreis Heinrichs des Löwen," *Städel-Jahrbuch*, 7/8, 1932, pp. 241 ff.

G. Swarzenski, *Die Salzburger Malerei von den ersten Anfängen bis zur Blütezeit des romanischen Stils.* Leipzig, 1913.

H. Swarzenski, *Die lateinischen illuminierten Handschriften des dreizehnten Jahrhunderts in den Ländern an Rhein, Main und Donau.* Berlin, 1936.

H. Swarzenski, *The Berthold Missal and the Scriptorium of Weingarten Abbey.* New York, 1943.

E. Tea, *La basilica di Santa Maria Antiqua.* Milan, 1937.

N. and M. Thierry, "Ayvali Kilise ou pigeonnier de Gülli Dere, église inédite de Cappadoce", *Cahiers archéologiques*, 15, 1965, pp. 97 ff.

A. Thiery, "Note sull'origine della miniatura mozarabica," *Commentari*, 17, 1966, p. 241.

A. Thiery, "L'oriente e le origini delle miniature precaroline," *Commentari*, 18, 1967, pp. 105 ff.

J. J. Tikkanen, "Die Genesismosaiken von San Marco in Venedig und ihr Verhältnis zu den Miniaturen der Cottonbibel," *Acta Societatis Scientiarum Fennicae*, 17, 1889.

P. Toesca, *Gli affreschi del vecchio e del nuovo testamento nella chiesa superiore del Santuario di Assisi* (Artis monumenta photografice edita, IV). Florence, 1948.

P. Toesca, *La pittura e la miniatura nella Lombardia.* Milan, 1912; 2nd ed. Turin, 1966.

R. Tozzi, "I mosaici del Battistero di S. Marco a Venezia e l'arte bizantina," *Bollettino d'Arte*, 26, 1932/33, pp. 418 ff.

O. Treitinger, *Die oströmische Kaiser- und Reichsidee nach ihrer Gestaltung im höfischen Zeremoniell*. Jena, 1938.

G. Tröscher, *Sächsische Monumentalmalerei von den Anfängen bis zum Jahre 1200* (Diss.). Berlin, 1926).

D. T. Tselos, "The Greek Element in the Utrecht Psalter." *Art Bulletin*, 13, 1931, pp. 53 ff.

D. T. Tselos, "A Greco-Italian School of Illuminators and Fresco Painters; Its Relation to the Principal Reims Mss. and to the Greek Frescoes in Rome and Castelseprio," *Art Bulletin*, 38, 1956, pp. 1 ff.

D. T. Tselos, "The Joshua Roll: Original or Copy?" *Art Bulletin*, 32, 1950, pp. 275 ff.

S. Tsuji, "La chaire de Maximien, la Genèse de Cotton et les mosaïques de Saint-Marc à Venise: à propos du cycle de Joseph," in *Synthronon, Bibliothèque des Cahiers archéologiques*, II, Paris, 1968, pp. 43 ff.

T. Velmans, "Le rôle du décor architectural et la représentation de l'espace dans la peinture des Paléologues," *Cahiers archéologiques*, 14, 1964, pp. 183 ff.

M. Vieillard-Troiekouroff, "L'architecture en France du temps de Charlemagne," in *Karl der Große*, W. Braunfels and H. Schnitzler, eds., III, Düsseldorf, 1965, pp. 336 ff.

M. Vieillard-Troiekouroff, "À propos de Germigny-des-Prés," *Cahiers archéologiques*, 13, 1962, pp. 267 ff.

G. Vitzthum, "Zur byzantinischen Frage," *Byzantinische Zeitschrift*, 20, 1911, pp. 353 f.

W. Voege, *Die Anfänge des monumentalen Stils im Mittelalter*. Strasbourg 1894.

W. F. Volbach, "Byzanz und sein Einfluß auf Deutschland und Italien," in *Byzantine Art an European Art. Lectures*, Athens, 1966, pp. 89 ff.

W. F. Volbach, *Elfenbeinarbeiten der Spätantike und des frühen Mittelalters*. Mainz, 1952.

W. F. Volbach, A. Pertusi, B. Bischof, H. R. Hahnloser and G. Fiocco, *La Pala d'Oro*. Florence, 1965.

Sp. Vryonis, Jr., *Byzantium and Europe*. London, 1967.

S. Waetzoldt, *Die Kopien des 17. Jahrhunderts nach Mosaiken und Wandmalereien in Rom*. Vienna, 1964.

J. Walter, *Herrade de Landsberg, Hortus Deliciarum*. Strasbourg-Paris, 1952.

W. Weidlé, "Les caractères distinctifs du style byzantin et le problème de sa différenciation par rapport à l'Occident," *Actes du VIe Congrès International d'Etudes Byzantines*, (1948), II, 1951, pp. 411 ff.

E. Weiss, "Der Freskenzyklus der Johanneskirche in Pürgg," *Wiener Jahrbuch für Kunstgeschichte*, 22, 1968, p. 7 ff.

K. Weitzmann, "Various Aspects of Byzantine Influence on the Latin Countries from the Sixth to the Twelfth Century," *Dumbarton Oaks Papers*, 20, 1966, pp. 3 ff.

K. Weitzmann, "Constantinopolitan Book-Illumination in the Period of the Latin Conquest," *Gazette des Beaux-Arts*, 86, 1944, pp. 194 ff.

K. Weitzmann, *Die byzantinische Buchmalerei des neunten und zehnten Jahrhunderts*. Berlin, 1935.

K. Weitzmann, "Thirteenth Century Crusader Icons on Mount Sinai," *Art Bulletin*, 45, 1963, pp. 196 ff.

K. Weitzmann, "The Classical in Byzantine Art as a Mode of Individual Expression," in *Byzantine Art an European Art. Lectures*, Athens, 1966, pp. 149 ff.

K. Weitzmann, *The Fresco Cycle of S. Maria di Castelseprio*. Princeton, 1951.

K. Weitzmann, *Geistige Grundlagen und Wesen der Makedonischen Renaissance*. Cologne 1963.

K. Weitzmann, *Illustrations in Roll and Codex.* Princeton, 1947.

K. Weitzmann, "The Mandylion and Constantine Porphyrogenetus," *Cahiers archéologiques*, 11, 1960, pp. 163 ff.

K. Weitzmann, "Byzantine Miniature and Icon Painting in the eleventh Century," *13th International Congress of Byzantine Studies, Oxford, 1966. Main Papers*, VI, Oxford, 1966.

K. Weitzmann, "Eine spätkomnenische Verkündigungsikone des Sinai und die zweite byzantinische Welle des zwölften Jahrhunderts," in *Festschrift für H. v. Einem*, Berlin, 1965, pp. 229 ff.

K. Weitzmann and I. Ševčenko, "The Moses Cross at Sinai," *Dumbarton Oaks Papers*, 17, 1963, pp. 385 ff.

K. Weitzmann, "The Narrative and Liturgical Gospel Illustrations," in *New Testament Manuscript Studies*, M.M. Parvis and A. P. Wikgren, eds. Chicago 1950, pp. 151 ff.

K. Weitzmann, "The Origin of the Threnos," in *De Artibus Opuscula XL. Essays in Honor of E. Panofsky*, New York, 1961.

K. Weitzmann, "Icon Painting in the Crusader Kingdom," *Dumbarton Oaks Papers*, 20, 1966, pp. 51 ff.

K. Weitzmann, "Observations on the Cotton Genesis Fragments," in *Late Classical and Mediaeval Studies in Honor of A. M. Friend, Jr.*, Princeton, 1955, pp. 112 ff.

K. Weitzmann, "Zur byzantinischen Quelle des Wolfenbüttler Musterbuches," in *Festschrift Hans R. Hahnloser*, Basel-Stuttgart, 1961, pp. 223 ff.

K. Weitzmann, "The Survival of Mythological Representations in Early Christian and Byzantine Art and their Impact on Christian Iconography," *Dumbarton Oaks Papers*, 14, 1960, pp. 43 ff.

K. Wessel, *Die byzantinische Emailkunst vom fünften bis dreizehnten Jahrhundert.* Recklinghausen, 1967.

K. Wessel, "Byzantinische Plastik der paläologischen Periode," *Byzantion*, 36, 1966, pp. 217 ff.

K. Wessel, "San Vitale in Ravenna, ein Bau Theoderichs des Großen?" *Zeitschrift für Kunstgeschichte*, 22, 1959, pp. 201 ff.

H. E. Wethey, *El Greco and his School.* Princeton, 1962.

J. Wettstein, *Sant'Angelo in Formis et la peinture médiévale en Campanie.* Geneva, 1960.

J. White, *The Birth and Rebirth of Pictorial Space.* London, 1957.

Th. Whittemore, *The Mosaics of Hagia Sophia at Istanbul. Fourth Preliminary Report. The Deesis Panel of the South Gallery.* Boston-Oxford, 1952.

J. F. Willumsen, *La jeunesse du peintre El Greco.* 2 vols., Paris, 1924.

J. Wilpert, *Die römischen Mosaiken und Malereien der kirchlichen Bauten vom vierten bis dreizehnten Jahrhundert.* 4 vols., Freiburg im Br., 1916.

F. Wormald, *The Utrecht Psalter.* Utrecht, 1953.

F. Worringer, *Griechentum und Gotik, Vom Weltreich des Hellenismus.* Munich, 1928.

D. H. Wright, "The Codex Millenarius and its Model," *Münchner Jahrbuch der bildenden Kunst*, 15, 1964, pp. 37 ff.

O. Wulff, *Altchristliche und byzantinische Kunst.* 2 vols., Wildpark-Potsdam, 1924.

A. Xyngopoulos, *Schediasma historias tes threskeutikes Zographikes meta ten halosin.* Athens, 1957.

P. L. Zovatto, *Il Battistero di Concordia.* Venice, 1948.

Index